Terrains of the Heart

Books by Willie Morris

North Toward Home
Yazoo
Good Old Boy
The Last of the Southern Girls
A Southern Album (with Irwin Glusker)
James Jones: A Friendship
Terrains of the Heart and Other Essays on Home
The Courting of Marcus Dupree
Always Stand In Against the Curve

Terrains
of the Heart
and Other Essays on Home

---

by
WILLIE MORRIS

YOKNAPATAWPHA PRESS / Oxford

Published by Yoknapatawpha Press, Inc.
P.O. Box 248
Oxford, Mississippi 38655

Three of the chapters in this volume have appeared in somewhat different form, after publication in magazines, in the following books: *North Toward Home* (Houghton Mifflin, Boston, 1967); *Yazoo*, Harper's Magazine Press (New York, 1971); *James Jones: A Friendship* (Doubleday, Garden City, 1978).

ISBN 0-916242-23-4   L.C.81-50423

First printing: 1981, Second: 1982, Third: 1985, Fourth: 1998

Printed in the United States of America
Book design by Barney McKee

To Ronnie Dugger,

and to Dean and Larry Wells

Contents

Foreword

WHEN THE YOKNAPATAWPHA PRESS asked me to bring together a collection of my essays—or pieces—from various magazines and journals around the theme of "home," I was at first skeptical, and also wary. A collection is always something of an act of conceit on the part of a writer, and putting it all together can be acutely painful, much as one feels on moving out of an honored house where he lived for a long time, which I have done much too often—sorting through the accumulations of the past: letters, manuscripts, photographs, notes to one's self, all the casual mementos of old time dying. As they tell us of the drowning man, all the scenes of his life pass swiftly before him. Does he seek salvation in these scenes, or is he merely expiring in agony?

In going over many of the pieces I had written for the magazines and journals over the years—*The Texas Observer*, *The Washington Star*, *The New York Times*, *Harper's*, *The Atlantic Monthly*, *The New Yorker*, *Commentary*, *The New Republic*, *The Nation*, *Reader's Digest*, *Parade*, *The Texas Quarterly*, *Time*, *Life*, *Newsweek*, *Mississippi Magazine*, and others—I was astonished by how many times I had used the word "home." As I perused these many thousands of words, some of which I myself had forgotten, this chord of homecoming seemed to be one of the very threads of my existence as a Southern-American of the Twentieth Century. My editor at the Yoknapatawpha Press later told me he was not surprised by this at all. So, I suppose, I had to re-discover this truth for myself.

I concluded, first, that I wanted this volume to be published in my native Mississippi, and second, that it not be a huge and imposing book on the theme arrived upon, but rather a manageable one, of which the author himself, perpetrator of so many words on his innocent audiences all over America, could feel reasonably modest and content. In his preface to his *Short Stories: Five Decades*, my friend Irwin Shaw wrote of "the sad process of winnowing out the stories I would leave behind. It was a little like being the commander of a beseiged town who knows he cannot evacuate all his troops and is forced to decide who shall leave and who shall stay to be overrun by the enemy. And the enemy in this case might be oblivion." As an example, I did not touch those dusty bound volumes containing my Wolfean prose from *The Daily Texan* at the University of Texas in the 1950s, and I only barely drew on the distinguished files of *The Texas Observer* when I was working there in Austin with my mentor and comrade Ronnie Dugger. The dozens of other essays on many subjects not relating to the emotion of home in all those national and regional journals remain where I left them, a decision which likely will please and relieve the reader.

One's instinct, of course, is to apply an editor's pencil to some of these old pieces. The young man's prose leaps out, as in my memoir of Oxford University, stalking one now in middle-age like the beastly predator. Others, written under rigorous deadlines, such as my "Vignettes of Washington," often composed in the newsroom of *The Washington Star* when I was "writer-in-residence" and syndicated columnist there in the Bicentennial year, 1976, plead now and then for a retrospective felicity. I have resisted this temptation.

Even with this strenuous culling of all the available pieces, the reader will find inevitable repetitions here, quite a few of them. I neither defend these nor apologize for them. They are there because the writer is who he is. Certain of my fellow beings, I find, appear time and again in these pages: my grandmother Mamie, my son David, my friends Gloria and James Jones, Rose and William Styron, and Dean and Larry Wells, William Faulkner, of course—not to mention all my dogs, particularly "Pete"—and, of course, myself. No sooner might the perceptive reader forgive these reappearances of figures who have helped bind my life together than he will note the frequency of death and graveyards. This, too, could not be avoided, for death and home go together, at least for me.

I perhaps should say something about the craft of the writer, but I shall benignly abstain except for a point or two. Part of the modern calling, as a financial necessity, is to convert when feasible one's magazine work into portions of one's books. Every good writer I know does this, and it is perfectly honorable. "An Old House on a Hill" and "Loving and Hating It" originally appeared in *Harper's* and were later reshaped into small sections of my *North Toward Home* and *Yazoo*. "I Am Not Resigned" was written especially for *The Atlantic Monthly* and became part of my *James Jones: A Friendship*. Their genesis was in the magazines.

Also, there is no way to elude that venerable Southern Sunday afternoon feeling, when the bars are closed and no one wants to see anyone else, and the church bells ring out to the old recognitions, and it is raining and you are alone with your dog, that none of the words really matter anyway, especially if the writer of the words has his predilection for the graveyards. There is no place under the Lord's heaven which elicits such *angst* and forboding than Sunday afternoons in a small town of

Dixie. Gazing down at the dog-eared script, you wonder if the words in the long sweep of it have meant anything at all. Perhaps not. Only then do you somehow reaffirm in yourself, however, much like the bosky yelp of passion from the country cab driver from Virginia in these pages, that you could not live, literally could not exist, without having tried to write down the words, and that you have other words in you yet.

There is another kind of fear, expressed by my old friend and contemporary from North Carolina, Edwin M. Yoder Jr.

When will it become a matter of, if you will, Dixiefying Dixie? This has been a lurking worry all along. In a piece I wrote for Willie Morris in *Harper's* in 1964 about W.J. Cash, I spoke of the "tacit alliance" that reaches down from the rarefied meditations of professors, journalists, and authors to the inchoate consciousness of the leather-jacketed hot-rodder who sports a Confederate flag on the rear bumper." There was, I said, "little doubt that if the South lacked working mythologists to go on holding up a mirror to the mind of the South, this mind would vanish as a study in distinctive self-consciousness."

The continuing exercise in regional self-consciousness, when it is all that stands between the South and its disappearance, was assuredly worth the candle when we could plausibly suppose that a distinctive historical experience was at stake . . . or when the point was to repel facile cant about a national "mainstream" in which the South should, for its sins, immediately immerse itself. But what now?

Always, when one writes, there is the danger of too much. My defense is that I have tried to be honest to my own perceptions in this eclectic personal record, and that the record itself may stand as a mirror to those times, in America and in the South which is part of it, during which these pieces were written.

One last point. I would like for the first essay, "Coming on Back," and the last, "The Ghosts of Ole Miss," to be taken as part of a piece, one flowing from the other, linked together in their supportive thoughts. Consider them bookends, if you will, with all that lies in between to be absorbed more or less chronologically as one man's comings and goings with his vagabond heart across the terrains.

Ole Miss
Sunday
March 1, 1981

Terrains of the Heart

Coming on Back

HOME, AS the old words say, is where the heart is. But where, then, is the heart? In these times, how might the American heart respond? Thomas Wolfe knew his own answer—knew also, in the deep heart's core, that he could not come home again. All Southerners, Truman Capote said, go home sooner or later, even if in a box, and that is how they brought Thomas Wolfe back to Asheville in the Carolina mountains, where today the descendants of the town which reviled him two generations ago deem his tomb with the angel on top more noteworthy than the Biltmore Mansion, and the spirit behind the homeward-looking angel more everlasting, no doubt, than the Biltmores. Many Americans, travelling the land these days in their modules, gazing out ever so often for some neutral place to set down the ship and be still for a while, may not appreciate the impulses behind my own choice not to tarry until someone requisitioned me a box.

My people settled and founded Mississippi—warriors and politicians and editors—and I was born and raised into it, growing up in a town, half delta and half hills, before the television culture and the new Dixie suburbia, absorbing mindlessly the brooding physical beauty of the land, going straight through all of school with the same white boys and girls. We were touched implicitly even without knowing it with the schizophrenia of race and imbued in the deep way in which feeling becomes stronger than thought with the tacit acceptance that Mississippi was different, with a more profound inwardness and impetuosity and a darker past not just than that of New York, or Ohio, or California, but of Arkansas, Tennessee, Alabama, and Louisiana, which were next door. This was a long time before anyone deigned to think that a Southerner could be elected President of the United States with everything that this would imply—not only elected in large measure with Southern votes but, four years later, in 1980, turned out resoundingly with Southern votes as well. As they said of the heavy-hitting but weak-fielding outfielder for the old Chicago Cubs, who once hit a three-run homerun in one inning and contributed three enemy runs with errors in the next, Hack Wilson giveth and Hack Wilson taketh away. It was a long time too before I myself, a native son, could comprehend retrospectively just how isolated we were, how starkly separate from the national impetus.

I went away to college in Texas, and in England, and ran a newspaper in Texas, and sojourned in California, and edited a national magazine in New York City and, having served my time in our cultural capital as many of us must, moved out to the eastern tip of Long Island to a village by the sea.

In *The Moviegoer*, Mississippi's Walker Percy says that most Southerners have a cousin who went off to New York. I was one of the cousins. I dined in The Four Seasons and The Oak Room of The Plaza and the executive suites of the skyscrapers, and mingled with the scions of the Establishment in the Century, and sipped Bordolino with the movie actresses in Elaine's, and performed on the Talk Shows, and stood on the balconies of the apartments on Central Park West and tinkled the ice in my glass and watched the great lights of Manhattan come on. Like the cotton candy at the county fairs of one's youth, it was all so wonderfully sweet, yet dissolved so swiftly. One summer I even put my family in a country house and commuted, two hours and twenty-eight minutes portal-to-portal as they said, with a Mississippian of my generation, a lawyer from Ole Miss who had to wear a bowler hat down to Thomas Dewey's firm on Wall Street. (There is a more detailed description of this experience later on in this book.) Every morning of that oppressive summer of 1965 we rose to meet the earliest train, and every afternoon we dashed from our offices high above Manhattan to Grand Central for the express to Brewster. We rode in the bar car, surrounded by suburbanites playing bridge, faintheartedly looking out at the bedroom towns flickering past, the placeless settlements of the railway lines. By the end of summer we were physically depleted and emotionally bereft. On the last afternoon of that life we met again in the bar car, ordering the extra-long gin and tonics. My comrade's bowler hat had a cigarette hole in it, his tie was askew, his gaze vague and disarranged. A silence fell upon us, old as time. As we emerged from the tunnel at Ninety-Sixth Street, he finally turned and said, "What were two ol' Mississippi boys doin' bein' commuters anyhow?"

I did not know then that we were exiles, almost in the European sense. When we met our fellow Mississippians by chance far away, the exchange of tales about family and places, the talk of mutual friends down there—and we always knew someone in common in Itta Bena or Iuka or Tchula or Alligator or Kosciusko—the stories about football or fishing or some long-vanished preacher were signs of a strange mutuality. I would meet black Mississippians in the North who were more similar to

5

me in background and preferences than the Yankee Wasps I saw every day. I even began calling New York City "The Big Cave."

One twilight I stood at the corner of Lexington and Forty-Ninth waiting for the light to change. Suddenly a woman appeared from the anonymous manswarm and began hitting me about the shoulders and head with her umbrella. "You beast!" she shouted. "You almost let me get hit by that taxicab." "Madame," I wished to say, "I didn't see it either," but the blows continued to descend, and I retreated into the doorway of a Nedick's, watching as my assailant disappeared into the crowd. An amiable junkie who had been drifting about pointed at me and laughed, drawing several spectators. As I stood there, I remembered for little motive at all the long resonant echo of the noon whistle from down by the river in the drowsing summers of home, confessing somehow to myself that I may have taken on more than I had bargained for.

For reasons having to do with not owning the mimeograph machine, a day came that I resigned from my magazine. By chance that noon—it was March of '71, as I recall—I was lunching with my friend and erstwhile competitor Mr. Manning, the editor-in-chief of *The Atlantic Monthly*, for in our lengthy *mano-a-mano* we had gotten together often to compare stories and complain of ownership and feel each other out, like old coaches long around the league. He consoled me in my melancholy. I apologized that lunch would have to be brief, since Bill Bradley of the New York Knicks had invited my ten-year-old son to work out with the Knicks in Madison Square Garden at 1:30 and I had to meet him there. "God, I'd love to go with you," my rival said. "I've got an appointment with Dean Rusk at the Century Club."

Later in the vast deserted arena, I idled on a front row

and watched my son shoot free throws with Frazier, Reed, and DeBuschere. I had just left everything I ever wanted, I was thinking self-pityingly, and I was suffused now with a terrible sorrow and with the most tender waves of memory, just as I had been in front of the Nedick's. As the bouncing basketballs resounded to the arched roof high above, and my son weaved a fast-break with Rusell and Barnett, I thought of my own father just before his death on grey winter Mississippi afternoons years ago, stopping on the way home from work to watch our team practice in our cramped little gymnasium. Immersed in my *deja vu*, alone in my conjurings in that empty palace, I barely heard the solitary footsteps coming my way. Suddenly the editor-in-chief of *The Atlantic Monthly* stood before me. "I cut Dean Rusk short," he said. "Say, which one's Bradley?"

I often dwell on the homecomings I have made—the acutely physical sensations of returning from somewhere else to all those disparate places I have lived. To the town of my childhood—Yazoo—it was the precarious hills looming like a mountain range at the apex of that triangle known as the Mississippi Delta, the lights of the town twinkling down at night in a diaphanous fog. To the city of my college days—Austin—it was the twin eminences of the University Tower and the grand old State Capitol awash in light from very far away. To the citadel of my young adulthood—Oxford University—it was the pallid sunlight catching all in filigree the spires and cupolas of that medieval fortress on its estuary of the Thames. To the metropolis of my ambition—New York—it was the Manhattan skyline which seemed so forbidding, yet was at once so compact and close-at-hand. To the village of my gentlest seclusion—Bridgehampton—it was the Shinnecock Canal opening onto that other world of shingled houses, flat fields and dunes, and the blue Atlantic breakers.

7

It was in the East that I grew to middle-age. I cared for it, but it was not mine. I had lived nearly twenty years there, watching all the while my home ground from afar in its agonies, perceiving it across the distance, returning constantly on visits or assignments. The funerals kept apace, *Abide With Me* reverberating from the pipe-organs of the churches all too much, until one day I awoke to the comprehension that all my people were gone. As if in a dream, where every gesture is attenuated, it grew upon me that a man had best be coming back to where his strongest feelings lay. For there, then, after all of it, was the heart.

Foremost, the remarkable literary tradition of Mississippi derives from the complexity of a society which still, well into the late Twentieth Century, had retained much of its communal origins, and along with that a sense of continuity, of the enduring past and the flow of the generations—an awareness, if you will, of human history. If modern industrialism and the national urge to homogeneity came to Mississippi later and with greater destructiveness than to other areas of the United States, if the traditional federal authority had to reach more than halfway to meet what finally became the better instincts of the place, then this had to do with the direness of its immemorial past.

William Faulkner, the poet and chronicler of Mississippi, understood how deeply we care for it despite what it was and is—the gulf between its manners and morals, the extraordinary apposition of its violence and kindliness. There is something that matters in a state which elicits in its sons and daughters of both races, wherever they live, such emotions of fidelity and rage and passion. I myself have often felt an ineluctible similarity with Ireland—in the spoken and written language, the telling of tales, the mischief and eccentricity

8

of the imagination, the guilts and blunderings and angers, the religiosity at the base of things, the admiration of the hoax and of strong drink, the relish of company and of idiosyncracy for its own sake, the radiance and fire in the midst of impoverishment. These are qualities, I would discover, which still bounteously exist.

"Time is very important to us because it has dealt with us," Eudora Welty of Mississippi says. "We have suffered and learned and progressed through it." For instance, many of the people I know here of my age had great-grandfathers and great-uncles who fought in the Civil War. Some survived it, some did not, having fallen at Brice's Crossroads or Shiloh or Chancellorsville or Gettysburg, in that near obliteration of the young officer class which rivaled England, France, and Germany of the World War I generation. The experiences of these men have been brought to their great-grandsons and daughters through diaries found in attics, through the words handed down, and through the ancestral relics: a pistol, a sword, old buttons, a shred of grey cloth.

Many Americans, to express it boldly, have remained afraid of Mississippi. I witnessed this fear time and again in the East, and I see it to this day, into the 1980s. It was, after all, not too many years before that D. W. Brogan, who was a British historian but might just as well have been speaking for much of Northern sentiment, could describe Mississippi as the most savage and backward of the forty-eight American commonwealths. The Freedom Summer of 1964, when hundreds of Northerners confronted here the intransigence of the police, the poverty and the cruelty, and went home with stories to tell, was only seventeen years ago. I remember as if it were yesterday sitting in a coffee shop across from my editorial offices in New York City hearing the legendary Bob Moses, the civil rights leader, describing in his gentle way what he had lived through in Mississippi. At this writing—March, 1981—only nineteen years have passed since President Kennedy sent 30,000 federal troops to Ole Miss to assure the admission of its first black student, James Meredith, when Governor Ross Barnett declared: "I refuse to allow this nigra to enter our state university, but I say so politely." These would still be severe realities to Americans who dwell on those embarrassing times and find it almost impossible to comprehend the swift and emphatic transformations in the life of the state, as the Deep South, in the late 1960s and through the 1970s.

Mississippi's most horrific specters have always been racism and poverty. My friend Ed Perry, chairman of the appropriations committee of the state House of Representatives, complains over beer in the Gin Saloon in Oxford of the lack of funds for many essential services. "There's no money!" he shouts. "We have to juggle. There just ain't no money." He recalls what his grandfather, who was a farmer down in the hard land of Choctaw County, once told him: "Mississippi was the last state the Depression hit. Hell, we had a Depression long before the Depression. People were so poor they didn't even know they were in one." The 1980 statistics revealed Mississippi to be so entrenched in fiftieth place in per capita income that it will likely never reach Arkansas in forty-ninth. The state consistently has had the highest proportion of its people on medicaid and food stamps—it was first per capita in getting federal funds—and much of the new industry brought down after World War II tapped the reservoir of unemployment and easy labor by strictly adhering to the minimum wage.

The Governor in 1981 warned that Mississippi was like "an emerging colonial nation" and must begin to be selective about the quality of industry brought into the state: high-skilled industry was desperately needed in an undercapitalized society. In passionate words he warned too against the rampant economic growth which had already ruined large areas of the Deep South, and he deplored the pollution and indiscriminate dumping of hazardous wastes which had made many of the lakes and streams of my boyhood lifeless.

An acquaintance in Yazoo County writes me of the Big Black Swamp, where he had just been deer-hunting. "I felt in a sacred spot," he says, "—a kinship not only with my forebears, but with the land." His father and his uncle hunted in these same woods. So did his grandfather and great-grandfather and great-great-grandfather, the latter having come down here in the 1830s after the Choctaws had ceded their claim to the settlers. Now the Big Black woods are owned by big paper companies which lease out hunting rights. "Big Black Swamp has always been there," he laments, "a fixture, like the moon in the sky. When the paper companies feel they must 'harvest' their 'wood crop' there, will it become Big Black Parking Lot?" This economic colonialism has always been hand-maiden to the poverty.

The returning son, who grew up with these things, needs no statistics to remind him. The dilapidated shacks and the unpainted facades still abound, and although the paved streets and public housing in the older black sections of the towns seem prolific in contrast to the 1940s, a random drive through the rural terrain or the larger cities reveals much of that same abject impoverishment, mainly black but white as well. Out in the Delta, where time often seems not to have moved, the extremes haunt one as they always did (the homes of many of the rich white planters, it must be said, would be cottages in East Hampton, Long Island), but the very land itself seems bereaved with the countless half-collapsed, abandoned tenant shacks set against the copious Delta horizon. These are testimonials to the largest mass exodus of a people in history—the Southern black migration

11

northward since World War II. The triumph of Allis-Chalmers is everywhere, and the farm machinery companies pervade the landscape in such numbers as to astound one who remembers the numberless black silhouettes in these fields a generation ago, picking or chopping, pausing ever so often to wave at the occasional car speeding by.

Brother Will Campbell, the pastor to everyone in the Deep South, claims he was driving down a Delta road not too long ago and sighted a tractor moving up the furrows all by itself, without a driver. The variety and complexity of these prodigious machines overwhelm the eye, tempting one to believe that if they had existed in such prodigality in the 1850s, the North would have seceded from the South. They reaffirm one's intuition, too, that the sheer expense of them must make the Mississippi Delta planter more than he ever was a gambler against the crops and the elements—living high and on mortgage and sending his wives and daughters to the Memphis stores to shop bountifully on credit.

The truth, of course, is that Mississippi has changed phantasmagorically in some ways, and in others it has changed hardly at all. It is a blend of the relentless and the abiding. There are things here now which my grandfather, who was born shortly after the Civil War and who died in 1953, would find unfathomable. If he stepped out of his grave in the old section of the Raymond cemetery and came back to Jackson, I suspect the scene along Interstate 55 with its mile upon mile of franchise establishments would astonish and frighten him. Modern-day Capitol Street and the Metrocenter Mall would leave him mystified, as would the traffic snarls and giant apartment complexes and insurance chains along the quiet streets where we rode the Number Four bus. All around him he would discover a brisk new world, all growth and deracination and touched with the Yankee dollar.

Yet if my grandfather had been with me on a spring

12

morning of 1980, driving from Jackson northeast to Oxford on the country roads, he would have been witness to the sights of his memory. Off the interstates and removed from the resounding nostrums of the New South, lies our remembered world, the world of my childhood: old men in khakis whittling in the shade of a crossroads grocery, a domino game on the back stoop of a service station, an advertisement for a backwoods mortuary on an R.C. Cola sign, an abandoned frame church with piles of used tires in front and a scrawled poster on top of them proclaiming "Fried Chicken, Two Miles," a conversation between an ancient black man and woman in a store which serves also as the Trailways stop:

"How you doin' today, Annie?"

"Not too pretty good, but givin' thanks for bein' here."

Beneath the seeming enigmas, there are a few simple political truths here in these years of which I write which merge the old and the new and which were especially dramatized in the national elections of November, 1980. In less than ten years, Mississippi and its sister states in the Deep South had undergone as fundamental a set of political changes as any in American history. The civil-rights struggles of the 1960s were the catalyst, leading to two of the most crucial pieces of legislation ever passed by the United States Congress—the Civil Rights Act of 1964 and the Voting Rights Act of 1965. All through the late 1960s and into the 1970s federal registrars arrived to help place black voters on the electoral rolls. One consequence of this was the demise of the race issue on the statewide level. The gubernatorial campaign of 1971 was a watershed; it was the first in which the old racial phantoms were not raised. Governor James K. Vardaman, running earlier in the century dressed in his white suit, white hat, and white shoes in a white wagon driven by four white horses, seems a mil-

13

lennium away. From my own childhood I remember Senator Theodore Bilbo at the political rallies, castigating the blacks and demanding that they be sent back to Africa, making jest of the elderly black men who always stood on the fringes of the crowds and responded to Bilbo's perfervid denunciations with self-conscious titters or wild guffaws.

The Democrats now appeal unabashedly for black support, emphasizing economic and educational concerns as a glue to their coalition. The Republicans also seek the black vote while mainly drawing on the young, rich whites of the courthouse squares and the suburbias. The desperate segregationist appeals of the recent past are gone forever. Although much remains to be done, the state of Mississippi, which in 1970 had one of the smallest percentages of registered black voters, leads the nation in the number of elected black officials.

Much was brought to fruition in 1980 in the election of William Winter as Governor. Defeated twice in Democratic run-offs when the traditional segregationists joined forces against him, he was finally elected decisively. He is an eloquent student of history and literature. He is not a Snopes, but a Sartoris. For years he had been the focus for those thousands of Mississipians who represented, in Lincoln's words, "the better angels of our nature"—he stood for racial moderation in the 1950s and 1960s when it was unpopular and even dangerous to do so—and his victory was a cause for reaffirmation among those who had remained steadfast for the civilizing values in the difficult years.

The social acceptibility of being Republican is another phenomenon of these times. When I was a boy, as they were wont to say in Mississippi, the only thing protecting Republicans was the game laws. Mississippi might have gone Republican in Presidential elections, but a dedicated and proselytizing party organization in

14

the state itself was another matter entirely. The New South, whatever it means and wherever it is going, has brought status for the Republicans, and although they may not wish to call themselves the party of Lincoln or of Reconstruction, or for that matter of Teddy Roosevelt, they wear their party badge as serenely as they enjoy their membership in the country clubs. With two of the five U.S. Congressmen and one of the state's U.S. Senators, as the 1980 elections showed, they would be in an upsurge.

Thad Cochran, the Senator who replaced James Eastland was, along with William Winter, a symbol of Mississippi's ascent from bitterness and self-destruction. He would attract a broad swathe of support, including many progressive Democrats. He is an intelligent student of the South who believes in spurning the outmoded legacies. He was in the Ole Miss law school in 1962 during the Meredith episode, a shameful moment which caused many Mississippians to re-examine themselves and the character of the state they wanted here. He recently told David Broder of the day the state's leaders brought in the police dogs:

> I recall sitting on the steps of the law school and one of our professors said, "Oh, I'm glad they brought the dogs. When tanks come over that bridge onto the campus, they're going to get there and say, 'Now, dog, go bite that tank.'"
> And it was sad to walk around the campus after the battle and see the broken concrete benches in the grove there in front of the old Lyceum building. And the tear gas that was used to cut down the riot hung in the air, it seemed, for days. And the large numbers of troops that had to be flown there. It was kind of embarrassing, really.

Cochran would have a promising future nationally. He may even have grown accustomed to the free-spirited jibes of his Ole Miss contemporaries who are Democrats. Several of the latter drove to Holly Springs to find

15

the tombstone of Hiram R. Revels, who along with another black, Blanche Bruce, served in the U.S. Senate during Reconstruction. The tombstone was in questionable condition. Cochran's college mates took a photograph and sent it to him in Washington with the inscription: "To Thad—this is the way we treated the tombstone of one of the *other* Republican Senators from Mississippi."

It is the proximity of Oxford and the Ole Miss campus, each populated by about 10,000 souls, which has given my homecoming its poignance, for both have tender resonances of an older past. Youth and age are in healthy proportion, and the loyalty of the town to the university is both exuberant and touching. The courthouse in the middle of the Square and the Lyceum at the crest of the wooded grove are little more than a mile apart, which is appropriate, for it is impossible to imagine Ole Miss in a big city, and Oxford without the campus would be another struggling northeast Mississippi town. One can drive around the campus and absorb the palpable sophistication of a small Southern state university, and then proceed two or three miles into a countryside which is authentic boondocks terrain upon which the Twentieth Century has only obliquely intruded.*

Shortly after I came here I was sitting on a sofa with Miss Louise, William Faulkner's sister-in-law. We were discussing the histories of some of the people buried in the cemetery. "It's an interesting town," she said. I told Miss Louise that I agreed. "It's so interesting," I suggested, "I think somebody ought to write about it."

Faulkner's presence pervades our place, and living

---

* In the year 1981, people without running water would still bring wooden buckets into town to the ice-house, which had a perpetual flow of water.

here has helped me know him better. His courage was of the Mississippi kind, and as with all great artists, he was a prophet on his own soil—about whites and blacks and the destruction of the land and the American Century and the human heart. W. H. Auden wrote on the death of William Butler Yeats, "Mad Ireland drove him to poetry," and Mississippi worked this way on Mr. Bill, for something moved in him when he finally decided to come back and write about the people and things he knew best, creating his mythical land out of the real fibers of everything around him. Yet in the time he was laboring in solitude on much of the finest work an American ever wrote, he was deeply in debt, Ole Miss had little or nothing to do with him, and the town was baffled and perplexed by him. To many he was a failed and drunken eccentric. When he may have wanted the approbation of the town and the university, in his most solitary and fruitful days, it was not there for him. When the town and the university at last considered it appropriate to sanction him, he had already long before, through his brave commitment to his words and his loneliness there at Rowan Oak, surrendered the expectation of any community benediction. Only after his death is he owned here. To this day an articulate gentleman from out in the county will tell anyone who wishes to listen that he knows for a fact Faulkner did not write those books. He did not have the gumption. They were written by a certain farmer who had a way with words, loved tall tales, and did not want publicity. This is reminiscent of Mark Twain's judgment that Shakespeare himself did not write his plays. It was some fellow with the same name.

"What if he had not had Hollywood to go to and make money?" a friend asked. He would have found *something* to make his stories possible, I suggested.

But he would become an industry in the town, ranking

17

close to soybeans, timber, merchandising, and Southeastern Conference football. Little clusters of Yankee and foreign tourists, including an unusual proportion of Japanese with their ubiquitous cameras, wander out to the grounds at Rowan Oak, or to St. Peter's Cemetery seeking his grave and those of his flamboyant kin, or search the unpaved roads of Beat Two for modern-day Snopeses, or stroll around the Square and the Confederate statue a little wide-eyed, wondering perhaps what might happen to them in Mississippi. A French scholar, asked what had most impressed him in his tour of the county, said: "I was fascinated by your peasants." Ole Miss conducts a sizeable Faulkner seminar every summer and owns his wonderful old house set behind its magnolias and cedars, having won out over the University of Texas which wished to dismantle the house and move it to a site near Austin, trees and all.

This reverence would no doubt bemuse Mr. Bill, but never mind. I find his spirit imperishable in the country people I see here, and in the old black men who sit on their haunches around the Square and banter with the white merchants, and in the proudly individualistic story-tellers of the town, and in the landmarks of his prose—the dank Yocona swamps and the slow-flowing rivers and the piney woods on a dreary winter's day. He died two months before James Meredith came to Ole Miss. I never met him; too many years separated us. I would like to know what he would make of our native state after nearly twenty years. I have a vision of running into him in his tweed jacket and khakis, in front of Shine Morgan's Furniture Store perhaps, or Smitty's Cafe. "Come on, Morris," he will say. "Let's go sit on the porch and drink some whiskey and talk about what's been happenin' in Mississippi since I last left."

I like Calvin Trillin's tripartite definition of a big city—where no member of the city council comes to meetings in white cardigans, where there are at least two places to buy pastrami, and where people eat supper after dark and call it dinner. Oxford, Mississippi, will not qualify. Years from now it may be one of the very last, the last of the way things were here in the lower South. Even now I keep an eye cocked toward the catastrophic suburbia of Memphis only seventy miles away, spreading southward into Mississippi.* Despite the small shopping centers and chain stores on the fringes of town, there is still a patina of time in the graceful streets and wooded open spaces, in the quiet nights of one's childhood with the katydids chirping and the rustlings of the trees and the cool dew on the grass.

My dog Pete, less my dog than my brother, a big black Labrador of warmth and intelligence who once was the official Mayor of Bridgehampton, Long Island, and still is, *in absentia*, likes the blending of the town and the raw country which envelopes it. We are a pair for lonely journeyings. We drive up to Holly Springs, which changed hands forty times during the Civil War and was never burned because the Confederate ladies, realistic as ever, entertained the Federal officers lavishly (*how* lavishly? one wonders) to see the ante-bellum houses. We walk through the woods around Rowan Oak every day, where the old black man who works there and lives in the cabin once occupied by Dilsey, says: "I recognize that dog from his *pictures*." We travel the eighty miles to the battlefield of Shiloh, where we meet Shelby Foote, who knows more about Shiloh than any living man, on the 118th anniversary of the fighting, and where Pete goes swimming in the Bloody Pond. We discover country graveyards set in lonesome hills as far removed from Lexington Avenue and Forty-Ninth Street as any place can be in America.

---

* I hope a reader of this book, residing in Oxford, Mississippi, in the year 2050, does not find himself actually living in the expanded Memphis, but who knows?

19

Pete and I often visit St. Peter's cemetery to see Bill Appleton, the caretaker, and to talk with the gravediggers about the person who has just died on this day. Sometimes my friends come with us to show me the graves of their grandparents and great-grandparents. It is an ineffably Southern place with shimmering magnolias and a circle of cedars, a perfect spot to observe the slow changing of the seasons. Pete and I have been there on limpid mornings of December, in January dusks when the importune grey stones lay enshrouded in snow, at March noontimes when all seems poised for the enraptured spring. One day, after a bitter freeze, the giant magnolias tinkled like the carousels on the playgrounds I once knew in Europe, the ice on the leaves making a melody as it crackled and melted.

On one of our many walks there, Bill Appleton tells of the foreign visitors who come to see Faulkner's grave. One gentleman from Tokyo later sent a Japanese flag in gratitude for his tour, which Bill fetched from his pickup truck and showed to me. "We whupped 'em in the war," he reminds me. I noticed a large new section to the cemetery which was just being opened, crossed by a new road. "Everyone believes the economy is so bad," I said, "and here you are expanding. How do you explain that?" Bill replied: "It comes and goes up here in spurts. We put five down this week, not a single one the week before. It's a pretty good business though." Once I brought a New Orleans friend to St. Peter's, who talked at length with Bill Appleton, then asked him to explain why Mississippi has produced so many writers. "Because the hills around here are so poor and the farmin's no good," he said. "People ain't got nuthin' else to do."

Pete and I also stroll often through the ghostly, deserted Ole Miss football stadium, called Hemingway Stadium in Mr. Bill Faulkner's hometown, just down the hill from the Confederate burial ground. The stands loom empty on all sides, monuments to the old vanished moments of mayhem and glory. It is a place for solitary thinking, about where one is, and where one came from. One November twilight Pete and I walked there while my son ventured high into the stands to take photographs. David later showed me the pictures. There we are on the astroturf, a man and his dog, surrounded by the concrete tiers, while the frosty wind stirs memories, and the Ole Miss campus, tinged with its history of triumph and suffering, stretches away in the dusk.

On the Square one sees the people from their second-story windows, gazing down at the scenes of human commerce. One morning, walking in front of the Gumbo Company with the visting writer, John Knowles, I said, "That's where we ate last night." An old man standing in front added: "And I bet it was mighty good too, wasn't it? Ain't it good to eat in there?" He then proceeded to talk with us about the virtue of soybeans over cotton, and the steadfastness of mules.

I remember the Square at Christmas, and the annual Christmas parade—a black Santa Claus or two, pick-up trucks made into floats for the white and black cub scouts to ride on, and the white and black beauty queens, the fire brigades and a weatherworn tank from the National Guard, a tiny ROTC band and then the high school band playing a little shrill and off-key. Suddenly from around the corner came the strains of "O Come All Ye Faithful," powerful and perfectly pitched, resounding off the facades of the courthouse and far down Lamar Avenue, a majestic new dimension to this small-town parade. What was this, I wondered? Then, row by row, the Ole Miss Band itself appeared, three hundred strong, led by the glamorous majorettes and the black drum major, a panoply of grandness in our midst, so large as to hardly be contained by the narrow streets. The spectators began to applaud and to sing the words—a brief

21

little moment, so swiftly gone, which seized at the heart. Later, at Shine Morgan's Furniture Store on the Square, there is the annual Christmas bachelors' party back among the microwaves and refrigerators, a party that had become an institution, sour-mash flowing prodigiously among the merchants and coaches and the Mayor and the Ole Miss people. Many stories are told in the local rhetoric. Soon the proprietor stands on a table and recounts a bawdy Mississippi story which lasts twenty minutes. The state legislator delivers a paean to the legalization of liquor, which has Celtic rhythms to it. Someone purloins the proprietor's telephone credit card and everyone begins calling all over the nation the memorable Ole Miss players from the past to wish them Merry Christmas—Archie Manning and Charlie "The Roach" Conerly, Wissie Dillard and Bo Ball, Farley Salmon and Ben Williams, Buck Buchanan and Hardwood Kelly, Squirrel Griffing and Larry Grantham. Hotty Toddy yells are offered to the missing comrades, the bedlam drifting out into the night so that the late shoppers press their faces against the plate-glass window and look in for a glimpse of this Christmas enigma. The next morning the owner, on opening the establishment, discovers one of the number still there, sleeping next to a washing machine.

Every native of this county, as in most of rural Mississippi, is still a hunter. The circumstances of 1981, however, are somewhat different from what they once were. Nowadays the hunting season in Lafayette County, Mississippi, is a clear call for a four-wheel drive, 350-horsepower pick-up, high-powered automatic rifle with optional telescopic lens, CB radio, bourbon, and a good old boy's girl friend if she is amenable.

They gather about the Square before the light as they leave; they remind one a little of the Confederacy, although they are better equipped. A typical deer stand will be a friend's barn, with cows stirring at dawn, the good old boy relieving himself behind a haystack while his girl friend, who recently came to town from Etta to work at the Ben Franklin selling cosmetics, with a natural predator's eye and a single 200-grain bullet, brings down a six-point buck who has been nibbling at the salt block. "Whew, I did it!" she says to her boyfriend on his return. It is her first kill, at least of deer.

CB radios announce the event from Hurricane to Toccopola. The sun is just breaking full over the misty landscape as trucks race from everywhere toward the scene. The word is out. "Ronnie Sue—ol' Chick Field's girl—just got one out by Clear Creek!"

By ten a.m., the trucks are returning leisurely to the "deer camp," somewhere along the red clay backroads. It is often the original rough cabin of the fathers and grandfathers, with the new mobile home manufactured in Akron and purchased in Memphis beside it. In contrast to the fresh morning air, the inside of the mobile home is overheated, suffused with the smell of beer and cigarettes and dogs, who laze around scratching and waiting for something to eat. The interior is littered with cartridge boxes, rifles, shotguns, beercans, empty Old Charter bottles, *Playboys*, and a *Hustler* or two. A television set features the early-morning gospel hour and, later, re-runs of *Bonanza* out of Memphis or Tupelo, or a 1950s Doris Day and Rock Hudson movie from Ted Turner's cable station in Atlanta. A filling-station manager, a dry goods salesman, and a boy from Tula who recently went to work for Danver's snore in the bedroom. The deer of Lafayette County are safe with them.

It is Thanksgiving morning, and the married men of the group, red-eyed and unshaven, go back into town to be with their wives and children before returning before dawn the next day. It is almost time for the late-morning

23

poker to begin. Instead of the traditional camp stew of generations gone, prepared for long hours and with loving attention by the cooks in the crowd, or the old black men, and unmercifully tampered with by a drunk or two—"What did he just put in there, Eddie?"—or the rude camp fare as served up in Faulkner's *The Bear* in that time when the Delta woods were dwindling, the hunters are snapping open bags of potato chips, Slim-Jims, and cans of cold chicken-a-la-king. Spurning *The Streets of San Francisco* on the television, they settle briefly into their meal. A red-tail hawk circles the sky. Morning birds call across the frost-crisp fields, and in the desolate Mississippi forenoon the squirrels leap and play among the oaks and elms. In a clearing within sight of the mobile home, a spike-buck paws in the leaves. Inside, a hunter from town cries: "Ante up, boys!"

Observing all the old and new eccentricities within his purview, and contributing to them, is the Mayor of Oxford in our years, John Leslie, who reminds me in his verve of the Jewish mayor of Yazoo when I was growing up, although he does not get out and direct the Saturday night traffic as Mayor Applebaum once did. He was elected in 1973, the year that beer was legalized. "Hell," he says, "I beat beer by twenty-three votes."

Mayor Leslie is a big, cheerful soul of 57. He tries to get people to call him "Your Worship," as they address mayors in England, although the only constituent to do so is Faulkner's one-time bootlegger—a formidable country entrepreneur named Motee Daniels. The Mayor presides over the town from behind the prescription counter of his drug store on the Square. He is a beloved figure here, and a man of sensibility beneath the small-town Dixie facades. "Pharmacist by trade, Mayor by God," a constituent says.

"Look here," he motioned to me on Christmas Eve afternoon. "Here's the last damned Christmas card I'll get from the White House in a long time." His close Democratic friends from Ole Miss college days were John Brademas, the Congressman from Indiana, and Ray Marshall, the Secretary of Labor under President Carter. "Who am I gonna call in Washington now to get strings pulled? You now any Republicans up there? Hey, we still got Thad Cochran." The Mayor started inauspiciously with the Carters. Rosalyn Carter spent the night with him and his family far back in January of 1976. "You're wastin' your time, honey," the Mayor told her. "You may have an outside chance for Number Two, though." One afternoon before that the telephone rang in his drug store and the caller said to him: "I'm Jimmy Carter. I'm coming to Oxford. Will you meet me at your airport?" The Mayor said: "Well, who in the hell *are* you?" When Sargent Shriver, another Presidential candidate, was about to arrive in town for a campaign speech on the Square, several Secret Service men burst into the Mayor's office in the city hall and rushed him to an open window, pointing all the while. "They wanted to know who the fellow was standin' up on the roof of a store. They were fingerin' their guns. Well, it was my opponent for Mayor last time, ol' Crack Wilson, the embalmer. I told 'em who it was, but regretted it pretty quick. I could've had Crack disposed of right then."

It was the Mayor who got the federal money for an interracial community-center complex that was one of the two or three finest in Mississippi. All he asked was that they name the tennis courts after him. These tennis courts would be used by many people, little black boys playing on a court next to Ole Miss coaches' wives and Dean Faulkner Wells. When a referendum for an integrated swimming pool was turned down, he went to Washington and obtained the funds without a matching clause. He supported the expansion of a large, integrated public housing project. "I swapped the old city

25

hall for the old federal building, which we made the new city hall. Then we got $359,000 in federal money to remodel the old federal building. Then I got a third of the land I'd swapped for the post office so I could widen the road. That's good manipulatin'.

"Say, we got to live up to Bill Faulkner's spirit in this town," he says. "We got to be proud of Ole Miss and keep the town and Ole Miss together. We got to understand these black kids and help 'em. This is the best damned state in the Union, don't you know it? I don't give a damn if they don't understand us in the North. They don't know what's happen' down here anyway. We're tryin' to live together, black and white. What the hell do they know about *that?* To hell with 'em, I say.

"We got to try and get a little more industry in this county, don't you see? But *good* industry, not the mean stuff. Look here, will you inscribe one of your books to Tex Thornton? Tell him he can go with you and me and your dog Pete to the Toccopola cemetery. He's a Texan, but his grandparents were from Toccopola." Tex Thornton was the chairman of the board of Litton Industries, and the Mayor wanted one of his plants here.

When one walks into his drug store, the Mayor will be talking with some dirt farmers or with a couple of Hollywood producers. Or one will observe him with the Governor and the Chancellor of Ole Miss and the chairman of the Appropriations Committee of the U.S. House, whose district this is, or telling stories to some pretty coeds.

As part of the mandate, he believes in moving about. One night he and I and Faulkner's old bootlegger were the judges in the Hallowe'en Costume Contest at a big, raucous bar. Scores of contestants of both sexes paraded slowly past our table. Our fellow judge, the intrepid bootlegger, had several free whiskies and wandered off to dance with the coeds. "I trust you boys with my vote," he said as he staggered away. "Let's give top prize to that gal who came as Sex Symbol," the Mayor whispered. "She looks good. I know her. She's a poor gal and needs the money." Our first six selections were about to be announced. "Let's get out of here," the Mayor said. "The mood of this crowd is about to turn angry. It's my business to know about these things. The ones we didn't choose are gonna be mad. Look at Wonder Woman glarin' at us. Look at her boyfriend Robin Hood. He's a big bastard." As the choices were given on the loudspeaker, we stealthily made our way to the back door. An object whizzed by my head, followed by another. "They're throwin' beer bottles at us," the Mayor said. "Let's go!" We emerged into the night to the sound of shattering glass.

In the tradition, and because he is accessible, the citizens play tricks on the Mayor. Many of these are telephone calls. "You can't help it," one of the pranksters says. "It's the way he answers the phone—so innocent and friendly and wantin' to help." A runaway mule has been seen urinating on the Confederate statue, for which the Mayor summons the police; an explosion in Fire House Number Two has set the fire house on fire, and he dispatches Fire House Number One over there; an Old Miss foreign student asks him to give a lecture on pharmacology and sexuality in Finland; a puppy is trapped in a store window on the Square on Christmas Eve night. "Hell, the last one really happened," the Mayor said. "I thought it was Soggy or Representative Perry or Featherstone until they convinced me. It took me a long time to track down the key and let the little dog out. You reckon Ed Koch has to do that as Mayor of New York?" The finest hoax of all was the unidentified man calling moments before the Mayor was closing his drug store for the night. "My wife needs one of those breast-pump machines. You got one? Can you keep the store open a few minutes longer? She'll be right down." Soon a handsome blond came in and began browsing among the counters. The Mayor waited discreetly, then walked over to her. "Do you need a breast-pump?" he inquired. She looked straight at him, then furiously departed. Subsequent telephone calls informed him that the ladies of town were considering a boycott of his store. "Sure, it was a set-up," the Mayor said. "She deserved a breast-pump. But, hell, they couldn't do without this store. This is where we make public policy—good policy, too, I hope, for Mississippi."

In his corpus of fiction Faulkner wrote little about Ole Miss, although he had family antecedents there and he himself was briefly enrolled. He served as postmaster of the university post office until he was fired for not sorting the mail and for playing poker in the back with his friends, declaring after his dismissal that he was "sick and tired of being at the beck and call of every son-of-a-bitch who could afford a two-cent stamp." In his stories he had Temple Drake, a genuine Ole Miss flapper of the Jazz Age, and a few other campus scenes, but I suspect he wished to keep his mythical town and county more or less in its rude state, uncomplicated by such things as a university. Yet he was a familiar figure around the campus and the golf course and at the ball games, and today he would be astonished by many of the changes.

Under the chancellorship of Porter Fortune, a man of integrity, Ole Miss became a different place from its old xenophobic, segregationist image. There is a sophisticated veneer which belies my own memories of it in the late forties and early fifties, when it seemed as rural and struggling as the town itself. Those who remember the political pressures and social inhibitions of even the recent years would be impressed by the extent to which the First Amendment would be working.

A graduate came back not too long ago after an absence of fifteen years. "I can't believe it!" he exclaimed. "It can't be true!" Black and white students mingling in large numbers. Restaurants that serve wines and spirits. Authentic bars. "X-rated movies in *Oxford, Mississippi!*" He was a product of that era when the students had to drive thirty miles across the Tallahatchie River or forty miles into the delta to buy beer, when one of the flourishing callings was selling bootleg whisky under the stairwells of the men's dorms, when the coeds had an eleven o'clock curfew, when a restaurant on the Square which specialized in New Orleans cuisine would have been unheard of, and when the notion of ten young black men together on a basketball court at one time representing Ole Miss and Mississippi State would have been synonymous with revolution.

The alteration in public drinking habits would be especially noteworthy. "As long as the people of Mississippi can stagger to the polls," so went the saying of my boyhood in this hard-drinking society, "they'll vote dry." One could usually buy liquor from the bootleggers (as boys we would have bourbon delivered to the Wednesday afternoon meetings of the church ladies in one private dwelling or another, and hide in the shrubs to watch their reaction), but outside of isolated pockets like the Mississippi River and Gulf Coast towns, liquor was unavailable in bars or restaurants, and legitimate liquor stores were non-existent. Prohibition was in the state constitution, but the legislature defied all legal reason by collecting a ten percent black-market tax. There would still be immense reaches of dry territory, especially in the parched and fundamentalist hills still serviced by the old-style bootleggers, and even the most casual traveller of the Mississippi byways could discern the moment he leaves a dry county for a wet one by the abrupt appearance at the county line of beer parlors or liquor stores with their numerous blinking lights. On a trip to Yazoo, I was intrigued to discover a new bar on Main Street with a Happy Hour right out of Madison Avenue. This establishment had only been open a few days. A companion from New York ordered a double-martini, and the country-girl waitress brought him two martinis.

In those times, the students at Ole Miss with little or nothing to do wandered home on weekends or went up to the Peabody Hotel in Memphis. In the 1940s Faulkner challenged the local preachers on the question of legalized beer in letters to the Oxford *Eagle*, the Memphis *Commercial-Appeal*, and even *The New York Times*, with less success than opprobrium. Now the students have a place to stay on weekends and, who on the Lord's earth knows?, may even be reading books in the process.

Much of the ignoble anti-intellectualism of the institution would also vanish, certainly of the proselytizing kind. The mean-spiritedness inspired by racism was gone. And from my own experience, the best students were as good as the best students anywhere.

I was talking with one of them who had just returned from visiting a Mississippi friend at Harvard. They went to a party in Cambridge and the young man from Ole Miss got into a conversation with a Harvard man.

"Where are you from?" the Mississippian asked.

"What do you mean?"

"Well, where are you from? Where did you go to high school?"

The other young man mentioned an Eastern prep school.

"But where did you grow up? Where are your parents?"

"Well, my father is in Switzerland I think, and my mother is asleep in the next room."

The Ole Miss student told me: "For the first time in

my life, I understood that not all Americans are *from* somewhere."

One thing which has not changed at Ole Miss, and likely never will, are the beauteous sorority girls for which Mississippi has always been famous. The stranger is invariably smitten with them, and they remain to this day the rarest of phenomena. I call them The Goldfish. The experience of gazing for long moments at goldfish in a bowl is mesmerizing. They adore being looked at, and one senses atavistically that they know you are looking at them as they pause momentarily in their bowl. Yet, except for these instants of reflected narcissism, goldfish rarely remain still for very long, darting about swiftly from one to another, rather mindless in their aquarian pursuits. When the observer places his hand in the bowl, they swim together for cover, wriggling their tailfins.

Ah, the Goldfish! One sees them everywhere in their expensive, brightly-colored jogging apparel, or coiffured and made-up for class. At the Warehouse, which, when crowded, is like salmon running upstream to mate, with Goldfish accompanying them, you ask one of them what she is majoring in. She looks you exuberantly in the eye and answers: "Fashion merchandising!" Their best boy-friends are usually named Craig or Wallace, who often are not with them but even in their absence are "neat guys," they say, with a "good personality." Sometime, from the lexicon of the 1950s, they are "sharp" and, on occasion, "real serious about things." The Goldfish are creamy-complexioned and keep their toenails painted. On Sorority Row, three months after the election, their Reagan bumper-stickers are still on their baby-blue Buicks. An Australian movie-maker came down in 1980 and made a film on their Rush Week. When it was shown in the New York Film Festival, one incredulous Yankee reviewer called it "a staggering anthropological document. What screams, what shrieks, what an amplitude of passion. . . . The proceedings are more exotic than the Romsiwarmnarian rites of the primitive Sherentes of Brazil's rain forest."

Yet beware the urge to be jealous of the young, for this interpolation of youth and maturity on a contained Southern campus is fraught with hazards and vague interior recriminations. Smite the temptation to envy the young their wholesomeness; vouchsafe them their endless concourse of golden days. God bless the Goldfish! The Ole Miss landscape would be sullen without them, and the outlander must forever be warned: they are smarter and more tenacious than their sunny countenances suggest. For generations the best of these lustrous cyprinids with double names have grown up to run the Sovereign State of Mississippi, just as their great-grandmothers ran the Old Confederacy, their men dying without shoes in the snows of northern Virginia.

Racism has everlastingly been Mississippi's albatross, of course, and in coming home the native son could no more dwell upon his state without its racial background than he could change the color of his eyes. It takes having grown up here to appreciate the words of the honored Ole Miss law professor, Judge Soggy Sweat, who says one night in the Gin, sharing a pitcher of Moosehead with the Mayor and the State Representative: "This is our greatest period in history here. There's so much to observe. Let's keep our eyes open."

In these times we are seeing a Mississippi that is catching up to the social ideals and values of the older America—the one before Watts or Boston or Detroit, the one of the era when the Eastern liberals considered themselves the black Southerners' best friends before the black Southerners arrived there in such numbers to find that their allies had moved away to Westchester County.

Nowhere has all this been more evident than in the massive integration of the Mississippi public schools, an event which took place in 1970. This has brought dislocations, and considerable local controversy over such issues as aptitude tests and class groupings, and a drift to private academies in many of the populous black counties, yet who a generation ago would have dared predict the day-to-day manifestations of this profound change? It is still so very early, yet the emerging biracialism of Mississippi can be seen everywhere—in the newspapers, television, parent-teacher meetings, sports events; in the friendships white and black youngsters have developed in the schools; in a politeness between the races in public places.

The churches will be the last institutions to integrate, of course—"only the undertaker will take care of that," someone says—and then the civic and social clubs, and the poverty exacerbates everything. But race is no longer the terrible obsession which touched every facet of life as it did, say, in 1965—private discourse, public polity. In the long run, all this to me has been less a result of the Americanization of Mississippi, although the federal presence fostered the process, as of Mississippi itself trying to respond decently to its own genuine heritage.

In 1980 the state as a whole was thirty-five percent black, highest in the nation, and many of the Delta counties were well into the sixties, seventies, and eighties. Lafayette County itself was thirty percent black, and forty percent black in its public schools. In those areas of the state with black populations of no more than thirty-five or forty percent, the integration of the schools has succeeded beyond anyone's imaginings.

At Ole Miss there are about seven hundred black students. The fraternities and sororities are white, with a handful of black Greek organizations. There is a minimum of "social" mingling. In two semesters I have had only one black student. A professor who has been here a long times says that the Ole Miss sorority girl today, with notable exceptions—the one who cares for education and civilization—is little different from her counterpart twenty years ago, with the qualification that "being polite to blacks is part of her repertoire now, just as she had always been polite to the rednecks." Yet the whole story, with all its future implications, is only now emerging.

Outside of the public schools, which have not had a single reported racial incident, the two focuses of integration in the community are the Athletic Department at Ole Miss and, of all places, the bar of the Holiday Inn. This latter establishment, a block off the Square, may not be America's typical Holiday Inn bar, although it is probably the most distinguished, and certainly the most spirited. It draws a loyal clientele, some of whom have been known to invest money in ball games, and its presiding genius is Clyde Goolsby, a black man of 40 who is one of the most popular figures in town, and one of the most powerful. He not only makes "integration" work, Mississippi-style and without any ideological talk about it, he is privy to the secret griefs and mirths of the most accomplished beer-drinkers in Yoknapatawpha County—professors, farmers, bankers, veterinarians, businessmen and women, students, water analysts, horsetraders, lawyers, coaches, pinball-machine salesmen, beauticians, foresters, hospital dietitians, politicians, car mechanics, and a perambulating reprobate or two. "I don't quite know how to say this," a white merchant tells me, "because I'm an old country boy and I grew up the way it was down here, but Clyde's my best friend in the whole world. Damn, I love Clyde! So does everybody else, coloreds and whites. What would this town be without him? If we didn't like the ol' Mayor so much, we'd run Clyde. Hell, still may."

"Lord, in '62 it took 30,000 federal troops to get one black man into Ole Miss," Ed Perry, the state representative, says. "It's Christmas Eve, 1980, and here we are sittin' in this bar, white men and women, black men and women, everybody minglin' and usin' first names, all laughin' and jokin' and havin' a good time, and goin' up to Clyde with our troubles, or to get advised about the bowl games, as if everything that moment in '62 represented never even existed. What the hell *happened*? Why did we go through all that waste of energy and passion? Everytime I see a black and white student walkin' together on the campus, everytime I see black and white folks sittin' in here talkin' and askin' about each other's children, I think of Meredith."

"Hey, Tommy!" Clyde shouts at a white patron. "Get off that beer belly and pay me that ten dollars I loaned you."

"Hey, Clyde!" another white client from out in the county yells, "This here's my boy Clarence, goin' to junior college in Senatobia. Clarence, this here's my buddy Clyde."

"Pleased to meet you," Clarence says. "I heard all about you."

"Hope you're better than your pop," Clyde replies, shaking hands.

Later Clyde announces: "I'm switchin' the TV to the ball game *right now*."

"Aw, come on, Clyde," says one of the several white lawyers who are watching a fight. "I got money on round six."

Clyde switches channels. Two black students and a white policeman are playing liar's poker. "Put on that movie, *The Great Escape*, Clyde."

"We're watchin' the Hawks and the Knicks," Clyde says, then resumes his conversation with an Ole Miss professor on their theory of human history. The jukebox vies with the basketball game:

> The bridge is washed out,
> I can't swim,
> And my baby's on the other side. . . .

Ten years ago, in 1971, I wrote a book about the integration of the public schools in Mississippi; I was in Yazoo on the first day. On re-reading that book now, I believe I was right in my premise that in the long sweep of history that event would prove momentous here. I was wrong on certain things too. I misjudged the efficacy and durability of the white private academies in some areas. I misjudged, likewise, the corrosive effects of bedrock poverty on the efforts toward enlightened progress, such as today in the town of Marks, only forty miles west of Oxford in the Delta. Martin Luther King, in one of his last public appearances, wept over the condition of its black people. Black unemployment has grown apace with the rise of mechanized farming, and racial bitterness still smolders beneath the more serene surfaces of the 1980s.

Although the access to public institutions has been democratized immeasurably in such a short time, only the future will answer the deeper questions of the Mississippi experiment. Yet it is the little things which accumulate, the constant ironies and juxtapositions which wring the soul and tell much. One learns from the bread and circuses of a society:

—a dozen or so black cub scouts at a close Ole Miss basketball game waving Confederate flags, running onto the floor to help the Ole Miss cheerleaders.

—a nocturnal scene, off Highway 7 south of town, little black boys wearing Ole Miss T-shirts shooting baskets by the headlights of a pick-up truck.

—the first black male Ole Miss cheerleader at the Mississippi State football game, lifting a white female cheerleader onto his shoulders before 60,000 spectators.

36

—my black maid Pearline Jones, working the morning shift at Smitty's Cafe to help put her third daughter through Ole Miss.

—second and third-graders, white and black, holding hands on the Square, while that night the white and black high school seniors will have their separate spring dances.

—the basketball team of the University of Alabama, where George Wallace said he would personally block the main entrance to prevent integration, appearing in the Ole Miss coliseum with one white on its travelling squad.

—a black plate umpire at the Ole Miss-State baseball game.

—at a lunch given by the Ole Miss Chancellor, the president of the black students who is also a Rebel tight-end leaning across the table to tell the wife of a new member of the board of trustees: "What I like about you is your quality of enthusiasm."

—white and black ten-year-olds mingling on the front lawn of the town's most eminent private mansion eating birthday cake.

—the State University Press' *Mississippi Heroes* featuring an essay by a black professor on Medgar Evers along with others on Jefferson Davis, L.Q.C. Lamar, and William Alexander Percy, concluding with these words on Evers and his murderer:

> Beckworth could possess the land as a right available only to whites . . . Medgar could claim the land out of duty to all men. Beckworth prompted a selfish preoccupation with the land, exactly as Medgar's allowed great altruism. For this reason, above all else, Beckworth may have taken a life, but Medgar surely gave one for his homeland.

Earlier I tried to describe the acutely physical sensations of my returning in the past to all those disparate places I have lived. When I come back now to Oxford,

Mississippi, my homecoming seems somehow to bring together the shattered fragments of all those old comings and goings. Driving up Highway 7 past the little lost hardscrabble towns, and the roughened exteriors of an isolated America which has been forgotten, I sight the water-towers of Ole Miss and the town silhouetted on the horizon, and then the lights of the Square and Mr. Bill's courthouse, and the loops and groves of the campus with the Lyceum at the top of the hill, and the dark stadium in the distance. All of it seems to have sprung from the hard red earth for me, as the dispirited Roman legionnaire must have felt on re-entering his outpost, his nexus of civilization, after foraging the forlorn stretches of Gaul.

"The writer's vocation," Flaubert wrote, "is perhaps comparable to love of one's native land." If it is true that a writer's world is shaped by the experience of childhood and adolescence, then returning at long last to the scenes of those experiences, remembering them anew and living among their changing heartbeats, gives him, as Marshall Frady said, the primary pulses and shocks he cannot afford to lose. I have never denied the poverty, the smugness, the cruelty which have existed in my native state. Meanness is everywhere, but here the meanness, and the nobility, have for me their own dramatic edge, for the fools are *my* fools, and the heroes are mine too.

Yet, finally, when a writer knows home in his heart, his heart must remain subtly apart from it. He must always be a stranger to the place he loves, and its people. His claim to his home is deep, but there are too many ghosts. He must absorb without being absorbed. When he understands, as few others do, something of his home in America—Mississippi—which is funny, or sad, or tragic, or cruel, or beautiful, or true, he knows he must do so as a stranger.

An Old House on a Hill

ONE WINTER, for how can a Southerner with a growing son be without a big dog, I went up into the Hudson Valley and bought for my boy a black Labrador Retriever puppy by the name of I. H. Crane. Six months later he was the size of a quarter-horse, but without the discipline. My son began to call him "The Monster." The other people in our run-down old apartment building in New York City grew terrorized of our friendly and energetic beast. Coming hell-bent out of our first-floor rooms on his leash, I. H. Crane would quickly disperse the crowd gathered at the elevator; as they dashed and tripped in all directions they reminded me of the famous photograph of the people in the square at St. Petersburg the day the revolution began. On the sidewalks, whenever one of the neighborhood junkies came by howling or moaning or talking enthusiastically to himself, the dog, out of honorable old instincts, would freeze and point, and then let go with a bay ungodly enough to destroy a good fix. One morning, while I was waiting in front of the building with my son for his school bus, I was holding I. H. by the leash, paying little attention to his activities. A sharp-nosed woman with the beginnings of a mustache walked past us to the front door. Suddenly she swung on me and pointed at a respectable pile of dog shit on the sidewalk. *"Did your*

Harper's Magazine, August, 1967.

dog do that?" she demanded. I had always had trouble when people shouted in my face; "No," I replied, "my little boy did." Even the building superintendent, a lovable Puerto Rican named Joe Gonzales who spent his leisure writing new verse to old Spanish songs, was compelled to call for discipline. In addition to this experience, and watching the boy and the monstrous black dog suffer from the usual claustrophobia of the Cave, I had read an article by Jason Epstein in *The New York Review of Books*, one of the most brilliant and acerbic of the city's journals in the 1960s. Epstein categorically advised the readers of the *Review* that it was impossible for people to live in New York City on less than $50,000 a year. I realized with this that it was time to get out, at least for the summer.

We found a big old farmhouse sitting on a hill overlooking a valley seventy miles north of the city; the oldest part of the house went back to the 1740s. I went into hock to publishers, magazines, bankers, and mortgagers, bartered my incorruptible soul for twenty years' labor, buying the house and its six acres, and depositing my family and dog in the house for the summer. Against the full tradition of my boondocks background I became, of all the things I never thought I would be, a summertime commuter.

In the mornings I caught the train at 6:50 A.M., arriving at Grand Central at nine and at my office at nine-fifteen. This was duplicated in the afternoons. By my calculations my travel time from door-to-door was four hours and fifty-six minutes. Leaving my office at the end of a workday was an elaborate and highly contorted process. First I would wait ten minutes for the elevator to reach the eighteenth floor of our building, for we had moved out of the old building which housed the publishing firm into an anonymous skyscraper just across the street, then scramble against the dour insurance

40

salesmen and businessmen from the adjoining offices for a place inside. Once downstairs I could make it easily into the subway on those afternoons when there had not been a tragedy at the unusual corner of Park and 33rd, an intersection where the mad cabs emerging from the secret tunnel wrought their havoc and offset the megapolis' birth rate. A wounded victim and the crowd gawking to see him might postpone my getting to the subway station by three to five minutes, but split-second timing would get me to Grand Central with two minutes to spare. Here I would bound up the two flights of stairs, fighting the strong torrent of Cave-dwellers descending the same stairways, and make it to the platform just as they were closing the gate.

It would be a long haul going home, more than two hours on some days, and I became obsessed with the mood of that commuter run. For three months I watched it as a loner, hardly speaking to anyone except a companion of my age from Mississippi, sidling off to myself in the smoker or the bar-car, observing human nature in that unfamiliar moving culture. For some time, being an editor who was prone to experiment with exotic combinations, I had toyed with the idea of asking Norman Mailer, for $1500 and drinks, to travel for a week in the bar-car of the Harlem River line, standing nose-to-nose with the advertising men, smashing bottles, starting fights, pushing the women executives around a little, and then writing a piece of literary journalism, an article as art, a non-fiction short story, something about that modern American phenomenon of the commute-run that might Stand Up twenty years hence. I had also considered commissioning William Styron to come along for a few rides and describe the landscape between Mount Kisco and Croton Falls, or the way the reservoirs beyond Golden's Bridge looked at sunset, but he was finishing a novel about slave revolts, which had tradi-

41

tionally been kept to a minimum in Thorndale, White Plains, and Pleasantville.

Coming into the city in the early morning mists was always a study in distances. The commuters who got on the train in Brewster, or those who connected up from the little towns of Pawling, Towners, and Patterson to the north, were commuting not from suburbia but from a terrain approximating real country, though I knew that even this, in another decade, would be another extension of the city's lengthening suburbia. But now, in the early morning, through the woods and the purple hills shrouded in fog, riding by the reservoirs which could have passed for authentic lakes, one felt a thousand miles removed from Grand Central, from the East Thirties, from the intersection of Park and 33rd. Bleary-eyed, pulling out cups of coffee or egg sandwiches, the men who got on at Brewster talked about woodchuck, deer, and the elements. The thermometer in the barn, one would say, got down to forty last night. Somebody's spring was running low again. Another shot a rabbit at his back door and had rabbit stew. At Katonah, the first stop down the line, a few of the people who got on would start talking about crab grass. By Chappaqua crab grass seemed the biggest underhanded menace since Eva Braun. Even as early as Mount Kisco the atmosphere had become more distinctly businesslike. The men, brief-cased and meticulous in their expensive suits, shouted robust greetings to each other. Then the bridge boards would come out and the games would be underway. At Pleasantville, home of our modern cultural symbol, *The Reader's Digest*, the relaxed mood of the Brewsterites had been replaced by an aura of self-defense; seats were at a premium now, and there would be occasional exploratory elbow-jabs, and sometimes a few scattered oaths. If Pleasantville was a presage, White Plains was a boundary. From my window I would see the hundreds of passengers on the platform there, employing deft, executive-like stratagems, which included not merely elbows but hips, kneecaps, and other joints depending on the situation and the lateness in the week. As the train moved, non-stop now toward the city, there would be little talk—only the quiet, earnest bridge games, a kind of post-breakfast seance to deaden perceptions in transit. We sped past the acres and acres of gravestones, the closer suburbs, and the Harlem River. We were a lily-white group moving across the narrow dark streets of Harlem; I would look out into Harlem, at the trash piled up on the corners, the old men standing against the broken buildings passing away the morning, the little storefront churches ("Jesus Salva," "Non-Denominational Protestant Church of the World"), so reminiscent of the Deep South. As we entered the bleak tunnel at 96th, a few minutes from Grand Central, swarms of passengers would get up and start walking to the front of the train. At first this curious exodus mystified me; it took me several days to realize that they were getting a head start before the train stopped to get two minutes closer to East 42nd Street.

Coming back in the afternoon would be slightly more relaxed; sometimes people would talk to each other. Once I sat next to a man who specialized in corkscrews, and he talked to me about what a new compound, a deceptive esoteric chemical without taste or smell, had done to his crab grass. Another afternoon I talked with a man who marketed a kind of tinfoil; he talked about the several nuances of the bank mortgage. The hum of the conversation these late afternoons would be of money—its sources, its complications, its fickleness, its wonders—a generalized high-level buzz about purchasing power, generating a rosy affluent glow among the tired men going home. Back in the bar-car, where the train drunkard would be on his fourth Scotch by Pleasantville, the boys would radiate an adolescent Boy Scout cheer, singing songs and swapping sex stories. "Are you on Wall Street?" one of the Boy Scouts shouted across at me at the bar one day. I said no. "Because you sure don't *look* like you are," he said. "Are you a Democrat?" "Not just a Democrat, a *liberal* Democrat," I said, and he and his companions looked at each other, shrugged, and started in again on "Sweet Sixteen."

The car of the train seemed like a safe little island, removed now from the threats of the Cave. Nothing atrocious or disrupting could happen here, with everything so homogeneous and contained. Everyone rustled his afternoon *Post* and scanned the headlines about Vietnam, about nurse-killers, rapists, sadists; it was a particularly violent American summer, the incidents of mass and impersonal homicide seemed everywhere, but we were remote and moving, and I felt some secret, repressed glee, at survival and invulnerability.

It was in such a mood that I learned a sniper had climbed to the top of the Tower at my old university, the same Tower I had stood at the top of my first day there as a freshman, and shot down forty-nine people with a telescopic rifle. Sitting in a commuter car two thousand miles away reading about it, dwelling on the landmarks of the campus I had known so well, filled me with an inexpressible horror, I could hear the other passengers talk of it matter-of-factly, as if it were all a part of coming home. The curious juxtaposition of violence and its incomprehensible banality was becoming more and more a fact of life in America. Who was protected against it? Where would it break out next?

For this man, whose name was Whitman, had also desecrated the symbol of a specific place—The University of Texas—that had once meant for me a liberation from narrowness and self-destruction. He had climbed to the top of that Tower on a hot, lazy summer's morning to try to destroy as many human beings as he could sight through his three-power telescopic lense. His victims lay strewn across the stretch of hill that I wandered on at night, in my Wolfean moods as a college boy. His locus of terror enclosed trees, statues, buildings, and hidden walks etched on my memory. The dead and dying were struck down on that graceful mall where I had courted my girl, read poetry, and sat alone at midnight plotting my private hopes. The horrible act that killed or maimed his victims destroyed something in me. Night after night I would have dreams of that Tower—dark, desolate dreams about death and destruction. Whitman, so coldly rational in his madness that he had not even deigned to waste bullets on the tires of the armored car which tried to rescue the wounded victims, had impressed upon me that nothing—no human being, no symbolic place, no sanctuary of one's loyalty and liberation—was safe from the insane arbitrariness of total hate. One young man had looked around a stone walkway at the Tower, turned to others behind him, and said, "This is for real." Then he looked out again and was shot through the head. The woman receptionist he clubbed to death on the observation deck had pointed out the Balcones Hills to me on my first trip there in 1952. A friend of mine, along with a young boy and girl, was looking at the Tower through a small window of a building 500 yards away; suddenly the man next to him was shot through the arm. The sniper's telescopic lens missed nothing that looked human.

Reading of this now, in a commuter car of the Harlem River Line, I thought less of the terrible endemic violence of Texas than of the abjectness of us all before the mad capricious nihilism of our alienated and disaffected fellow human beings. I thought of the Tower, lit orange on some cold still Saturday night after the next football victory—the observation deck silent, dark, and un-

45

guarded. Then I looked around at my fellow commuters, talking of the sniper as casually as they might talk of some business associate, clinging to life not through terror, but through *dissociation*—a highly developed sense of detachment from the madnesses of our modern existence.

Sometimes on the train I would listen in on conversations between diehard commuters and outlanders who chanced to be riding to more remote outposts in the New England foothills. In these circumstances the talk would be about commuting itself. "Well, how much time do you *travel?*" the outsider would ask, and the commuter would say, "Three hours and ten minutes" or "four hours and twenty, portal-to-portal." "But why do you do it?" "I do it for my family, especially for the kids." The city, you see, had become unlivable, and was getting worse all the time: crowds, noise, pollution, the subways, taxes, Negroes, Puerto Ricans. It was unsafe to go outdoors at night; drug addicts crawled the streets. "*I do it for my family, especially for the kids.*" I heard this phrase more than Mark Twain, in 1861, heard the story about Horace Greeley and Hank Monk in *Roughing It.*

There were the little bedroom towns with Indian names, the names as pathetic as the names one saw on the little lower-class houses in the working districts in England and artificial, so unlike the raw towns with Indian names I had once known in the Mississippi delta, with their grim and dusty exteriors, their closeness to the rich and humming earth from which they sprang. Could a man develop any feel for place along these tracks of the commuter run—identify with Pleasantville or Chappaqua, put roots in Valhalla? For always there was the agglomeration of split-levels and the thin patches of lawn, the rush to the train every day, the hundreds of stationwagons in the sprawling parking lots at the depots. I remembered my first train rides as a boy, the Illinois Central to Memphis and the Negro conductor shouting: "Memphis-town is *heah!*"; and Thomas Wolfe's great expresses roaring through the cold American nights to Asheville or to the Fabulous Rock. This ride, by comparison, was only a daily chore.

Yet these were not "bad" people; they were not much better nor worse than the rest of us. The whole middle-class ethos had suggested to them that to be responsible to their families demanded a house with starched curtains and a piece of lawn as far removed from the disintegrating and ruinous city as possible. Did they want their daughters mugged in the streets? Their wives insulted by derelicts in supermarkets? Their apartments contaminated by the polluted filth sent forth by their city's own incinerators and by their monopolied utility Consolidated Edison? On a dozen occasions in the streets and on the sidewalks of the city I would see one of these middle-class commuters, having just emerged from the subway from Grand Central in starched white shirt, insulted and berated, out of mere chance, by the city's truckdrivers and cabbies. The men with the briefcases would never shout back; they would skulk around a corner avoiding an incident, or red-faced and sheepishly take the abuse as part of the risk involved in coming to work, confirmed even more in their desire to keep their children away.

In the 1960s the big cities of America were falling into extraordinary chaos and decay; New York, being the largest and most crowded, was becoming the worst of all. The middle classes reacted by retreating, as middle classes always had. Their instinct, far from being corrupt, as some writers had suggested, was in human

47

terms perfectly understandable. The man of the family ventured forth each morning into the bowels of the city, leaving his family in a secure and roomier isolation, and returned on the five-twenty-seven. As Pleasantville got pleasanter, the Cave grew darker and more forbidding; its devastation, for the commuter, became more perfunctory and unreal.

One afternoon in late August, as the summer's sun streamed into the car and made little jumping shadows on the windows, I sat gazing out at the tenement-dwellers, who were themselves looking out of their windows from the gray crumbling buildings along the tracks of upper Manhattan. As we crossed into the Bronx, the train unexpectedly slowed down for a few miles. Suddenly from out of my window I saw a large crowd near the tracks, held back by two policemen. Then, on the other side from my window, I saw a sight I would never be able to forget: a little boy almost severed in halves, lying at an incredible angle near the track. The ground was covered with blood, and the boy's eyes were opened wide, strained and disbelieving in his sudden oblivion. A policeman stood next to him, his arms folded, staring straight ahead at the windows of our train. In the orange glow of late afternoon the policemen, the crowd, the corpse of the boy were for a brief moment immobile, motionless, a small tableau to violence and death in the city. Behind me, in the next row of seats, there was a game of bridge. I heard one of the four men say as he looked out at the sight, "God, that's horrible." Another said, in a whisper, "Terrible, terrible." There was a momentary silence, punctuated only by the clicking of the wheels on the track. Then, after the pause, I heard the first man say: "Two hearts."

The old house on the hill reawakened one's awareness

of the land; the yellowed deeds going back by more than a century, their property divides and their descriptions of noticeable landmarks existing yet, were enough to impress upon one that stretches of earth are ours for a brevity, in trust only, and would someday be someone else's, and someone else's again after that. The lovely hill with its hickory and maple and dogwood and apple trees, the ancient stone walls with each stone in its necessary place, the grassy slope tilting at a headlong angle into the woods, these were ours only for the moment, a mere temporary possession, and would one day return again to the commonality before some future bidder. In the winter the wind whistled down from the hollow, and the snow came in its great driven drifts from the taller hill to the north. The autumn here would be spectacular, its colors like none I had ever seen, and spring came forth so suddenly, in such contrast to the grim stark winter that its relief was more emphatic than the springs in the South, which had been a deeper and more fragrant green by far, yet had always been taken more for granted. An old photograph, from the turn of the century, showed an unidentified woman and a little girl in flowing dresses on the big front porch, and under the dogwood tree were two gravestones long since vanished. There was a photograph of the three fantastic figures, the Baldwins, who had once lived here. It was taken in the spring of 1914, the woman huge and phlegmatic, looking like a farmhand's Gertrude Stein, flanked on the same front porch by her two wild-eyed and stern-faced brothers.

The Burton twins, George and Charles, age seventy-eight, now lived down the road, carpenters who practiced their craft with such a skill, pride, and love that when I watched them at labor I felt I was *learning* something about my own work. They had grown up on

"Quaker Hill," across the valley, now occupied by Thomas E. Dewey, Norman Vincent Peale, and a host of Wall Street lawyers, and others of the city's remote executives in big country homes; they loved to talk about Dewey's hill as it was when they were boys. They had known the Baldwin siblings who had once owned our house: Jerome, one of the brothers, had been "mean as hell," and the sister Mary had suffered from asthma and was forced to lean her head out of a window every few minutes during the summer to catch her breath. Now the Baldwins were not only gone, no one knew their burial place, and their photograph in my study seemed their last and only tangible memorial. At Christmas one year, with all the presents scattered under the tree, and evidences of our own affluence everywhere, it occurred to me that the old house had never known such riches. The thought of the Baldwins with their two pot-bellied stoves, their hard existence as simple farmers—their old ledger which had "come with the house" recording their sparse barters and purchases at the country store in Patterson—seemed somehow forbidding; here we were, with a permanent apartment in the city and an eighteenth-century house with central heating, spoiled children of our age.

One day a woman drove by from New York City; she had been raised in the house as a girl, and her father was born in one of the bedrooms in 1865. It was a good old place, the kind of place Thurber had thought of to go away to and read *Huckleberry Finn* and *Tom Sawyer* again, or *Moby Dick* and the *Leatherstocking Tales*. Hound dogs barked in the distance on clear nights, and from the top floor there was a view of the purple range of hills, mountains to anyone who had grown up in the Mississippi delta. The locals of this countryside were laconic and self-contained. Faulkner and his friend Cowley had driven through these hills one matchless Indian summer day. They got lost; they stopped to get directions from two taciturn Connecticut farmers. "Does this road cross the mountain?" Cowley said. "Yes," the man said, with proper courtesy. "Thank you," Cowley said, and they drove on for fifty yards. Then Cowley stopped the car and said, "Wait." He backed the car to the two farmers. "Can I get over it in this car?" Cowley asked. "No," the same farmer said. "I don't think you can."

In melancholy Southern moods I sensed that the great qualities of this country place were doomed; if so, the Big Cave would be the executioner. Often I would catch sight of the developers cruising up our hill in their Chrysler with the city plates, one a fat man named Michaels, his running-mate a thin fellow named Barco. They would get out of their car and unfold their prodigious maps, and then explore the hills and fields, talking and gesturing with great animation. One afternoon they stopped by to give me their business card and to talk with me about land values, for they were engaged in seeking out whatever land was for sale, to buy and resell at $2000 an acre. They had just bought a spectacular wooded hill down the road, sixty acres where the deer and rabbits roamed, to develop half-acre tracts and to contract for crackerbox houses at $18,000 apiece. They talked of the inexorable encroachment of the city's suburbia, seventy miles from Times Square, with a fanatical enthusiasm, and they planned to saw down the grand old trees a couple of hundred yards down the hill and put in a street. Up the hill you could hear the sound of their bulldozers and buzz-saws ripping out some tenacious natural obstacle. There is something agonizingly horrible to me in the rumblings of a bulldozer as it ravishes a lovely hill. Michaels and Barco were like their bulldozers. Rootless sons of the modern city, what did the land matter to them? On Saturday mornings you

51

could see the two of them, stationed on some wonderful high place with their maps, motioning out into the distances. They wanted Thomas E. Dewey's land so badly they would have sprouted mustaches to get it. Once I sat down and wrote Michaels a cryptic note to his office in the city: "Dear Michaels, *No wonder the ruined woods I used to know don't cry for retribution. The people who have destroyed it will accomplish its revenge.* (signed) I. McCaslin."

Yet from their growing suburbia we had a reprieve—five years, ten years?—and it was impossible not to become deeply attached to this old country of the Indians and the Dutch and the Yankees, to the quiet hills and farms of western Connecticut, to the great sweep and flow of the Hudson Valley—Washington Irving country: "A drowsy, dreamy influence seems to hang over the land, and to pervade the very atmosphere. Certain it is, the place still continues under the sway of some witching power, that holds the spell over the minds of the good people, causing them to walk in a continual reverie. They are given to all kinds of marvelous beliefs; are subject to trances and visions; and frequently see strange sights, and hear music and voices in the air." The reveries and superstitions had vanished, but reading such lines to a small boy on some windy night in November generated for the adult his own fantasies, and one was glad for the sake of the child's belonging that a real writer had lived in the neighborhood many years before. For country like this, its changing Yankee seasons, its unexpected shapes and divides, its neat eighteenth-century villages, could take hold of one's imagination, and even one's loyalties. The feeling grew upon me, not apocalyptically but slow as could be, slow as good sourmash gets its mellowing or as a young man matures and finds balance, that in the great chaos of modern existence it was one's work that mattered, work in the broadest and most meaningful sense—this and being close to the people one loved. Here, in the country around this hill, and seventy miles away in the Cave, our fantastic cultural capital, was where one's work was, one's family, and friends—friends whose own work was important to the national life. The feeling had been a long time in coming: you did not have to go to your sources again to survive; one's past was inside of a man anyway; it would remain there forever.

* * * * *

MISSISSIPPI. In the little frame house on Grand Avenue, where we were to stay one night, I showed my son the mementos from my high school: the framed scrolls and certificates and documents on the walls of my room, testifying still that I had once indulged myself in all the official trinkets and the glittering medals. Under the bed I discovered a whole shoebox full of love letters from a blond majorette from Belle Prairie Plantation: I took them into the back yard, arranged them in a neat pile near the place where my dog Skip was buried and where my father once hid from the visiting preachers, and put a match to them, gazing down at one phrase not yet burned: *"I'll meet you in front of the drugstore at 7:30 in my green sweater."* My mother and my grandmother Mamie fixed fried chicken and huge steaming casseroles, and chocolate cake and meringue pie, and while we digested this feast, spurning "Bonanza" on television, my mother played, on the grand piano, some of the old hymns: "Faith of Our Fathers," "Bringing in the Sheaves," "Living with Jesus," "Abide with Me." Outside, on the street, the teen-agers sped by, shouting and blowing the horns of their family cars, and the pecan trees in the yard rustled and moaned in the wind, stirring up too many ghosts.

Our plane for New York was to leave Jackson, forty miles away, at noon the next day, and since I had resolved not to see anyone, since old friendships suddenly brought together again had always embarrassed me, we got up at dawn to drive around town. The streets of Yazoo were so settled in my consciousness after all those years that the drive was unnecessary, for I still knew where every tree was, the angles on the roofs of every house, the hidden alleys and paths and streams. Coming around some bend I would know exactly the sights that would be there—and there they were, the memory of them even more real than the blurred shapes of reality. We drove through niggertown, some of its old dirt roads now paved and with curbs and sewers, past the grocery store where the colored men had seen my dog propped against the steering wheel of my car and shouted: "Look at that ol' dog drivin' a car!" Back again in the white section, every street corner and side street had meanings for me; I had sat on the curb at Grand Avenue and Second Street, near Bubba Barrier's house, one summer afternoon in 1943, wearing a Brooklyn Dodger baseball cap, dreaming of the mythical cities of the North, and bemoaning my own helpless condition. Grand Avenue, with the same towering elms and oaks, had changed hardly at all, and only the occasional new chain store or supermarket marred my memory of it. Driving down that broad boulevard, my mother pointed out the houses in which people I had known had died, by simple attrition or by violent, tragic causes; each house represented a death or more, and the knowledge of it, after my having been away so long, gave to the whole town a vague presence of inevitable death. My old schoolhouse on Main Street, where the ineffable Miss Abbott had taught my fourth-grade class enough Bible verses to assure our salvation, had a new coat of paint; the schoolyard where I had played football against the Graball boys still had its Confederate monument; the soldier on top with the gun in one hand and the other hand extended to take the flag from the Confederate lady had not moved an inch since 1939. On Main Street the Dixie Theater had vanished from the face of the earth, as had some of the smaller stores, replaced now by the Yankee chains advertised on national television; but many of the familiar places remained: the *Yazoo Herald*, where I had turned in my first sports articles at the age of twelve, the radio station where I had played Beethoven instead of Tennessee Ernie Ford, Tommy Norman's, Henick's Store, where my taps-playing colleague Henjie now sold tires and tire accessories. But most of the young people I had known here, in the 1940s, were gone long before, living now in the prosperous 1960s in the sprawling and suburbanized cities of the New South—Atlanta, Memphis, New Orleans, Birmingham, Nashville. Out on the edges of town, where the bootleggers had once flourished before Mississippi legalized liquor, I noticed that Yazoo had even developed its own suburbia. I was suffused with a physical feeling of lost things, with a tangible hovering presence of old dead moments; it was time to get out, and I drove as fast as I could up Broadway, that fantastic hill, for Highway 49 and Jackson.

We drove through the lush rolling hills toward Jackson. Along the highway a huge billboard had a picture of Martin Luther King, surrounded by throngs of Negroes, and the words on the sign said: "M. L. King Meets His Fellow Commies." Near Jackson I saw a more ambitious suburbia, sprung up now from the pastures and cottonfields I remembered from my childhood, row after row of split-levels that seemed not much different from Pleasantville or Hawthorne on the Harlem River Line.

Mamie said, "Let's drive by the old house and see what they've done with it." We headed down Jefferson

Street, and there was the brick house just as it was, the same magnolia tree, the sticker bushes where my great-aunts had gotten trapped in their endless peregrinations, the rickety garage where my grandfather Percy had built for me the miniature steamboats with names like *The Robert E. Lee* and *The Belle of Memphis*. Then down the street Percy and I had walked to the Jackson Senator baseball games, past the old house where the man who "stole the money from the state" had once lived, to the old capitol building at the corner of Capitol and State. Mamie turned to my son, who had been looking at many of these unfamiliar landmarks with a Yankee's skepticism. "Son," she said, "you see that building there? My father—your great-great-grandfather Harper—was in the legislature there, and one day when I was a little girl my brother Winter took me inside and told the guards, 'She's Mr. George's girl, and I want her to sit in our Papa's chair.' See that balcony yonder? That's where your uncle Henry Foote—he was Governor of Mississippi many years ago—made a speech in 18-and-50, tellin' folks not to believe a word ol' Jefferson Davis said." The boy looked out at the object of these words, the graceful building that had been restored by the State to its previous grace and eminence, and then smiled sheepishly at me, still a trifle disbelieving.

We took the road out to Raymond and drove by the Harper house, also restored so that its picture now appeared in the travelogues, and then on to the town cemetery; neither my mother nor my grandmother had visited here in years. The old section was overgrown with weeds and Johnson grass, the iron fences rusted and fallen, the tombstones crumbled or vanished entirely. I parked the car on a ridge and the four of us, of our four different generations, got out and walked around. It was a bright, crisp October morning, but the terrain itself was damp and gray, casting an odor heavy

56

with decay and ruin. We looked hard enough, but we could not find the Harpers, not a single one of them—not my great-grandfather or great-grandmother, nor my great-aunts, nor even my grandfather Percy. We searched in the weeds and stickers on the hill where Mamie thought they had been laid away. "Well, I *thought* they were around here somewhere," she said. Fifty yards away was a well-kept plot of graves, soldiers who had been killed in some minor skirmish attendant to the siege of Vicksburg, watered and manicured now by the ladies of the town, and my son went over to look at these while we explored the countryside for our vanished kin. Finally, we found what must have been the plot—the remnants of a fence, the unrecognizable stumps of gravestones, covered over now with the dank, moist weeds. "I guess they're here somewhere," Mamie said, "but you'd never know it."

I took Mamie by the arm and we wandered farther down the hill, stumbling occasionally over a stretch of barbed wire or what remained of a tombstone. One of the old broken stones marked the grave of Miss Lucy McGee, born in 1820, died in 1850. "Mamie," I said, "this is where Miss Lucy McGee is. Did you ever hear of her?" "*Lucy McGee!*" she said. "Why, of course, son. I remember Papa and Mamma talkin' about the McGees when I was a girl. I believe she died very young for her age."

The airport was a new one, bright and shining and strangely quiet on this morning. As I confirmed our tickets back to New York, my mother and grandmother spotted some TV star on "Hollywood Circus" having coffee in the restaurant, and went up near to his table to get a closer look. Then we walked down the broad corridor toward the landing field, waiting near the door in that awkward moment that always precedes some long departure for me. The loudspeaker announced the flight, and we made our goodbyes. "You come back now, you *heah?*" my mother said, and my son and I walked down the ramp and got on the plane.

Why was it, in such moments just before I leave the South, did I always feel some easing of a great burden? It was as if someone had taken some terrible weight off my shoulders, or as if some old grievance had suddenly fallen away. The big plane took off, and circled in widening arcs over the city, over the landmarks of my past, and my people's. Then, slowly, with a lifting heavy as steel, it circled once more, and turned north toward home.

Loving and Hating It

November, 1969
The last time I had been there, I had gone to see my grandmother, whom I call Mamie. She is ninety-five years old, the youngest of seventeen children and the only one of them still alive. My mother, who lives alone with her now, telephoned me in New York to say that Mamie had just had a stroke and I should come right away; it might be my last time to see her.

Her great-great-uncle had been the first territorial governor of Mississippi, before it was admitted to the Union, and her people had settled the state when it was still called "the Southwest." Another uncle had been the United States senator through the 1840s, had given the dedication address at the Washington Monument, and had defeated his blood enemy, Jefferson Davis, for governor in 1851; all over the South before the final break, he defended "the good old Union, the fruit of the sage counsels of our immortal ancestors." Her father had been a Confederate major and a newspaper editor; an obscure and unidentified Federal captain, under direct orders from Sherman, had deposited his printing presses in a well when his troops marched through his little town, Raymond, on the way to Jackson, which was considerably larger game. She was born not long after the Federal soldiers pulled out of Mississippi.

Harper's Magazine, May, 1970

Now Mamie lies in the back room of the house where I grew up in Yazoo. She is completely blind and almost completely deaf. Some of the time she is with us here in the present, as lucid and full of good humors as she was when I was a boy; but mostly she inhabits an old woman's whirling misty shadows and premonitions, mistaking me for her brother Samuel Dawson Harper, who has been dead sixty years, talking with the spirits of her dead sisters when they were children in Raymond, asking my grandfather Percy if he wants his chicken fried or broiled for supper in the tiny brick house across from the Jitney Jungle on North Jefferson Street in Jackson. Sometimes she thinks my son David is me.

I have brought David with me on this trip. I want him to have the chance to remember her. He is a New York City boy. He is ten years old, and he has been riding the subways alone for three years, loving the noise and speed of those subterranean phenomena which for his father are only dark monstrosities. Occasionally he makes fun of my Southern accent, though he asks me more and more as he gets older about where his people came from. For a present three years ago, he typed away secretly for two days on my typewriter and later came out with a framed copy of the Gettysburg Address, done with his own fine Yankee hand. It had its share of typos, and it began, "Dear Daddy—The Gettyburg: Four score and seeven year ago . . ." and concluded, "The Ent— Love, David." I took him to Gettysburg after that, showing him Cemetery Ridge, Big Round Top and Little Round Top, the Wheat Field, Seminary Ridge, and the rounded green valley where on the afternoon of July 3, 1863, the idea that we were to become, after all, a mass multiracial democracy may have been decided, among American boys tearing each other to death with canister, bayonets, rifle butts, and big old stones. He wanted a present for himself, and when I took him into a store close to where Longstreet had set up his artillery, he decided, among all the modern artifacts of what happened there, on a gray infantry hat. While I was paying the clerk, $1.75 plus three cents Pennsylvania sales tax, I noticed he was pondering the gray hat, finally putting it back in place and taking a blue one instead, which he calmly put on his head. When we got in the car, I said nothing for a few minutes. The road we were driving traced the line of Lee's great retreat, and the sun's late-summer glow caught the monuments and the cannon in the splendid battlefield tableau that fills every Southern boy's heart with a wonderful dread and excitement. Finally I said, "Why did you pick the blue hat instead of the gray one?" He replied, "Because I don't want to be nobody's slave."

We had driven now the forty-eight miles from Jackson in a rented car, across the hills in autumn, and we reached the town after dark. I had timed it deliberately, because we were leaving again the next morning, and for several quite good reasons I did not want anyone to know I was home. My mother was there, and Mamie sat up in the bed and reached out to embrace us. I had forgotten my own fears as a child of sick old people, fear of their smells, of their tenacity and irascible durability, and the boy went away for a while. Viola was there too—the Negro woman almost as old as my grandmother, frail and very gray now but still quite healthy, who had worked for the family for more than a generation, had slept and lived in the house during its times of crisis, who had come to know us in our several disasters of the flesh, and who now sat in a chair several hours every day next to the bed. She was a sturdy physical presence in this place of decay, and even though three others of us were here in the room with her, Mamie would extend her hand every so often, stretch out her entire gnarled and skinny old arm, and cry, "*Viola!*

Viola! Where's Viola?" "I'm right here, honey," Viola would say, taking her hand and stroking it, carrying on a steady half-monologue all the while. This scene, my mother said to me, took place all day long. A few days later, at a fine sophisticated dinner party given by friends on the Upper East Side, I described what I had seen. A well-known New York writer said, "That's the most racist description I've ever heard." And the writer's wife added, "It's a racist description of a corrupt and racist society."

January, 1970
My grandmother had survived the stroke, and this time, in January and later in March, I went back to Yazoo for different reasons. The United States Supreme Court had ordered thirty school districts in Mississippi* to completely integrate their schools immediately—a harbinger, sixteen years after the *Brown* decision, for the rest of the South and, presumably, the nation. Compliance with the latest Supreme Court decision, or even a substantial degree of compliance, meant, as any Southerner would tell you, the beginnings of a true revolution, revolution of a kind that had not so much as touched the South, not to mention other Americans. Yazoo, sitting incongruously on the edge of the great delta, half white and half black, was one of the thirty districts.

I did not want to go back. I conjured many elaborate reasons, a dozen dramatic interior motives, for avoiding it. At least five times I promised myself, firmly and irrevocably, that I would not go. My office friends will testify to these curious emotional gyrations, these jolting peregrinations of a vainglorious heart, which tormented

---

*Under *Alexander v. Holmes*, October 28, 1969, the existence of any all-black school in a school district was proof that the dual system was still in effect. The "all deliberate speed" of the 1954 *Brown* decision was no longer permissible.

me relentlessly during a wintry Manhattan fortnight. *I did not want to go.* I had written a book a couple of years before, *North Toward Home*, which was about myself and about the people I had grown up among in Yazoo, and except for the one brief secret nocturnal visit, I had not been back since. My book, as such things always do in our country, had deeply disturbed the town. Many people there thought I had damaged and condemned it. One person wrote me that I had besmirched the memory of my father. Another wrote a letter published on the front page of the Yazoo *Herald* that I had embarrassed my church, my school, and my friends. My mother received a few threatening calls. I got pointed warnings about what would happen if I ever came back. Since Yazoo did not have a bookstore, the publishers had placed a substantial number of copies in the P & S Pharmacy on Main Street, which had sold out in short order. My old friend Bubba Barrier, my best friend since we were three years old, who now helps run his father Hibbie's plantation, telephoned me long distance in New York. Bubba said, "I just want you to know one thing. This book of yours is the biggest thing to hit town since the Civil War." You couldn't walk twenty feet, Bubba said, without hearing an earnest conversation about it. People were standing in line to get it at the library. "I think half the people in town kind of likes it," Bubba said, "and may be a little proud of it. The other half of the town is extremely agitated." Bubba went on to say he had the impression that the half which was so agitated consisted mainly of the people who were not in the book.

After a while, I believe, this reaction, which amazed, baffled, and for a time deeply disturbed me, though I of all people should have appreciated its origins, softened considerably. This too is a very American phenomenon. For a number of people there—Bubba, and my old English teacher Mrs. Parker, and the editor of the paper, and the librarian, and especially the boys with whom I grew up, some now scattered all over the South (Henjie Henick, Muttonhead Shepherd, Ralph Atkinson, Big Boy Wilkinson, Peewee Baskin, Honest Ed Upton, Van Jon Ward, Robert Pugh, Billy Rhodes, Moose Moorhead, good old Mississippi boys)—realized, I believe, that my book had been written as an act of love; sensed, perhaps, Faulkner's understanding that one loves a place not just because of but despite.

Yet all this was not my only excuse. The most terrible burden of the writer, the common burden that makes writers a fraternity in blood despite their seasonal expressions of malice, jealousy, antagonism, suspicion, rage, venom, perfidy, competition over the size of publishers' advances—that common burden is the burden of memory. It is an awesome weight, and if one isn't careful it can sometimes drive you quite mad. It comes during moments when one is half asleep, or after a reverie in the middle of the day, or in the stark waking hours: a remembrance of everything in the most acute detail from one's past, together with a fine sense of the nuances of old happenings and the most painful reconsideration of old mistakes, cruelties, embarrassments, and sufferings, and all this embroidered and buttressed by one of the deepest of urges, the urge to dramatize to yourself about yourself, which is the beginning of at least part of the urge to create. Since my town is the place which shaped me, for better or worse, into the creature I now am, since it nurtured me and gave me much of whatever sensibility I now possess, since it is a small Deep-Southern place where the land and the remembered places have changed very little, where the generations come and go in the context of these common and remembered places and amidst the same drawn-out seasons, where mortality itself grips and maddens one's consciousness in the missing faces, in all the children who have grown up toward middle age and all the middle-aged adults who dominated your boyhood and are now terribly, painfully old—I knew, as I had known for some time, that going back for me, even more than exposing myself in some new notoriety, would bring the most intense emotional pain.

Given all these circumstances, one should not be surprised to hear that a premonition had been working its way up my frontal lobe; at first it was a mere grain of sand, but eventually it grew to enormous proportions. This premonition was that I would meet there, on my home ground, a violent death, perhaps even a death accompanied by mutilation and unfathomable horror. My premonition had an animal force to it, unlike all the other premonitions in my life. *Some bastard is going to kill me in Yazoo.* Although I may not be one's paradigm of heroic courage, I am not easily frightened, having indeed sometimes courted danger, and as a somewhat harried editor working in the state of Texas, found myself often in situations full of potential violence, danger, and mayhem. I know a great deal more about violence, say, than the perfervid nihilists and pop-art guerrilla fighters of the New Left, on Manhattan Island and elsewhere, who were all for it as the prevailing fashion—confrontation tactics, some call it—and who had yet to dwell for any considerable time in certain places in America where if you talk violence with any consistency, you are sure to get it in whatever form you want it to come at you. Yet there was no avoiding that I had this on my mind, and it provided another among the several highly valid excuses to remain right here on safe, sane Manhattan Island. I finally went home because the urge to be there during Yazoo's most critical moment was too elemental to resist, and because I would have been ashamed of myself if I had not.

One of the more perplexing ironies of my life is that the longer I live in Manhattan, the more Southern I seem to become, the more obsessed with the old warring impulses of one's sensibility to be both Southern and American. It is an irony I take neither lightly nor fashionably; it is an honest obsession. Why, after all my generation of Americans has grown with in our coming to maturity—Auschwitz, Leningrad, Hiroshima, the Cold War, Vietnam, the assassinations of our finest young leaders, the enormous wastes and failures which haunt the greater American society—does this special part of America continue to engage my imagination, to touch me in the heart as no other can? Why, after seven years in Texas, three and a half in England and Europe, four as editor of a magazine with one of the most distinguished histories in the nation, am I still a son of that bedeviled and mystifying and exasperating region, and sense in the experience of it something of immense value and significance to the Great Republic? "Aren't we over all that shit?" a New Yorker asked me only a few nights ago.

Mississippi and Texas are the two places in America I know the best, or used to, yet even with Texas I find myself losing my old easy wonder and involvement. In the fifteen years since my friends and I on the student daily were censored by the established powers for concerning ourselves with issues which mattered in those days of McCarthy and Dulles, Texas at the true sources seemed to have changed hardly at all, so that after a time it struck one from afar who once cared deeply for its fractured, extravagant façades as something of a parody of itself. It lacked the blood and darkness and, yes, *character* of Mississippi, which despite its great despairs was slowly forming deeper strata, in torment and incertitude—deepening and extending itself toward something at once rich, various, and distinctive. Mississippi was maddened and bewitched; Texas, in its institutional aspects, was merely beholden. Once again its state university was in the hands of the xenophobic know-nothings, and the Texans who made the rules remained, toward the slightest hint of outside questioning, as everlastingly paranoiac as they had always been. *"We're doin' all right. We've succeeded in runnin' out almost everybody down here like you,"* a powerful Texas wheeler-dealer said to Bill Moyers in Austin. It all came down to the quality of the money that controlled, and Texas as a society, despite some of the most articulate dissenters in the nation, remained as firmly the domain of the most uncivilized wealth in America as it had been two generations before. So Texas seemed more bereft than ever of that brooding generosity of the soul out of which the things that matter always derive; it had not summoned the courage to try itself, for in the end it had been corrupted by the narcissism that powerful and established greed entails.

But I am being unfair, and have not answered my own question.

When I came up from the South by way of a Greyhound bus across the continent to work for the magazine I would later edit, I was in awe of it, just as I was of the city itself, for all it had meant in our literature to ambitious young outlanders such as I. I loved to wander its neighborhoods from Battery Park to Baker Field on weekends; or to take a new issue of our magazine the day it came off the press, hide in some bar by myself, and read it from cover to cover with a fine light glow of satisfaction and fulfillment; or to come to know the finest writers of one's day, to watch them as they finished some work which would be read a hundred years hence. One could come to terms with this extraordinary, driven, mad, and wondrous city if there were something to care for in it, something to engage one's calling and one's feeling for America.

Who, indeed, needed to be a Southerner? Here was the oldest journal in the nation, a durable institution which had seldom hesitated to change as the times had changed, to speak in the accents of its own age. The pioneers had carried its bound volumes across the country in their covered wagons, and contemporary migrants from New England to Orange County, California, still carried them in the trunks of their Mustangs, Falcons, Cougars, Jaguars, and Barracudas. So a magazine became a living thing to me. Sometimes on rainy Saturdays, I would go to my office and take down from its library back issues a century old: to see what William Dean Howells had to say in 1898, or what the table of contents was in the issue which came out in the month of my birth.* I would go to the file which had the records, card by card, of each story, article, or poem published since 1850, done alphabetically by the last name of the author, with the dates of acceptance and publication, the length of the manuscript, and the money paid. C: *Clemens, Samuel.* J: *James, Henry; James, William.* D: *Dickens, Charles.* E: *Eliot, George.* S: *Sartre, Jean Paul.* F: *Faulkner, William.* T: *Thackeray, W. M.* J: *Jones, James.* M: *Mann, Thomas.* R: *Roosevelt, Theodore.* K: *Kennedy, John F.; King, M. L.* C: *Crane, Stephen.* L: *Lewis, Sinclair.* P: *Porter, K. A.* K: *Kipling, Rudyard.* D: *Dickinson, Emily.* W: *Wilson, Woodrow.* All this was heady and exhilarating; it made me a little proud. Hundreds of letters, some of them hostile, most of them long and thoughtful, had come in after the publication of Norman Mailer's *Armies of the Night* in 1968. Mailer came to our office to read them. It took a few hours, but he looked over every one, and said: "All these peo-

---

* It included pieces on the dangers of federal crime control, the Russian economy, population increases, and racism in America.

68

ple sitting all over America writing these letters. They're carrying on a conversation with a magazine as if a magazine itself were a human being."

It *was* a human being. At its best, it was encouraging and defending those of our contemporaries who were our best writers and journalists against the distractions and the philistinisms of modern America. It was seeking to draw on some of the flamboyance, the creativity, the richness of the language of the country. It was hoping to suggest that America still had the genius and courage to someday achieve its original promise as the hope of mankind. It had made mistakes. Sometimes it had gone too far, and at others it had said too little, but it was nothing if not American.

And it was to this city, whenever I went home, that I always knew I must return, for it was mistress of one's wildest hopes, protector of one's deepest privacies. It was half insane with its noise, violence, and decay, but it gave one the tender security of fulfillment. On winter afternoons, from my office, there were sunsets across Manhattan when the smog itself shimmered and glowed; later there would be long talks with colleagues, with gossip and plans for the next issue—*Vol. 241, No. 1450*—or how the cancellations stood in November as against the renewals, or when one of the writers would be back from Israel or California or Washington, or whether some others of them, whose deadlines were tomorrow, were drinking beer at this very instant at the Empire or at Greenstreet's. Despite its difficulties, which become more obvious all the time, one was constantly put to the test by this city, which finally came down to its people; no other place in America quite had such people, and they would not allow you to go stale; in the end they were its triumph and its reward.

The two places in America that more than any others are the nation writ large, as many an exile has finally discovered, are New York City and the South.

I go back to the South, physically and in my memories, to remind myself who I am, for the South keeps me going; it is an organizing principle, a feeling in the blood which pervades my awareness of my country and my civilization, and I know that Southerners are the most intensely incorrigible of all Americans. In the end, being what I am, I have no other choice; only New York could raise the question. When I am in the South and am driven by the old urge to escape again to the city, I still feel sorry for most of my contemporaries who do not have a place like mine to go back to, or to leave.

November 17, 1970
The last night I was in Mississippi, I had dinner with Hodding Carter III, editor of the paper in Greenville, the *Delta Democrat-Times*. Hodding's father, whom people call "Big Hodding" or sometimes just "Big," had retired now from the paper; he was one of my special heroes back when I was editing the daily at the University of Texas. Big Hodding had made a stop in Austin then on a lecture tour, and before an overflow crowd had said: "There is a young man from my native state who is the editor of your newspaper. It is an outstanding paper and he is doing a good job. All Mississippi boys are mean and rambunctious, so don't play around with him. He is in trouble now because all editors worthy of their calling get into trouble sooner or later." Then he proceeded from personal experience and with much gusto to defend the beleaguered notion of independent and courageous newspapers.

Shortly before I met young Hodding on my final night in Mississippi, I had driven from Jackson to Greenville for a visit in that remarkable, civilized river town. I had started out on the narrow old highway which parallels the river into the delta, and my rented Hertz had skidded and bumped all the way, and seemed to be balking a little at entering this ghostly terrain. Only a few miles into the delta, just as the sun disappeared out over the river, a storm descended, the rain came down in great torrents driven by a terrible whistling and moving wind, and beyond the edges of the highway I could see nothing but bayous and gullies and an occasional little creek or river suddenly swollen and eddying with the rain. This, I knew from my boyhood, was one of the most desolate and treacherous drives in the whole state. My gasoline gauge pointed to empty, and I beseeched the Lord that I would not be stranded here in a storm, with not even a road shoulder to drive the car to, much less a Seven-Eleven or a Bun 'N Burger. I drove for miles in a mindless fright until, there was the town of Onward, Mississippi, with a general store plastered with patent-medicine posters and a gas pump sitting precariously on the edge of the swamp. Back in the car again, stopping ever so often to read in the eerie glow of the headlights the historical markers about the early Indians, the Spanish explorers, or the French settlers, I felt for the hundredth time the pull of that powerful delta land, its abiding mysteries and strengths—retrieved from the ocean and later the interminable swamp—and the men of all colors and gradations known to the species who had fought it into its reluctant and tentative submission. No wonder there is no other state remotely like this one, I thought, no other so eternally wild, so savagely unpredictable, so fraught with contradictory deceits and nobilities; societies are shaped by the land from which they emerge, and on this night in a dark and relentless November storm, the land from which I and my blood-kin had emerged was scaring the unholy hell out of me.

Now young Hodding and I were in the old Southern Tearoom in Vicksburg, being served catfish by Negro mammies dressed for the role, only a few hundred yards from the great battlefield where 20,000 American boys—average age 20—died in Vicksburg's gullies and ravines and swamps 107 years before. We had refused the "Yazoo Razoo," the "Mississippi Grasshopper," and the "Rebel on the Rocks" and had settled down with some serious Yankee martinis. Hodding and I are almost precisely the same age, but he came back and I went away, so we approach our common place like two radiants in the same prism, but with the same impetuosity, and the same maniacal blend of fidelity, rage, affection, and despair. I had my plane out the next day, and so I was loosening up with no effort at all. I had been back six times since my first trepidations about death on native soil; I had not been murdered, had not been shot at, had not even been treated rudely or narrowly, as I should have had the good sense to know all along; my Manhattan premonition was in truth the old endemic heart's fear of too deep an involvement in this place I came out of, where by the simple pristine intensity of emotion, the people in it have always been somewhat more than human to me, and hence confront me nostril-to-nostril with my own humanity.

A few days before, Hodding had been jumped, for the first time in a long while, by some hard-noses in a restaurant in Greenville called Doe's. There were five of them—from Prentiss, Mississippi, it turned out—and they had asked him over to their table. "*So you're Hodding Carter,*" one of the hard-noses said, with a sneer from his lips to the beginning of his left ear lobe. Hodding had tried to be friendly, in a kind of collegiate Southern way, a rather tentative amalgam of Princeton and Greenville High School: to kill them, as we are taught here, with kindness, "because," he said later, "people like that down here are worth winning over." But within earshot of his beautiful blond wife Peggy, sitting at his table, they had called him a "mother-fucker," "son of a bitch," and "nigger-lover," and perhaps even accused him of being out for the Yankee dollar. There is a certain strain of violence in Hodding's molecular composition. Most of his qualities derive from gentlemanly sources, but a remaining few have some remembrance of precisely what it took in blood for the rest to be gentlemanly; so beneath the dark good looks and the Mississippi charm, there is a lurking touchy quality, as in me, that would allow him to damage a man very badly if he lost part of the prepossession they taught him in Old Nassau Hall. But this time there were five of them, and he was with his wife, so he left, feeling a little guilty for leaving, saying, "If I were in the kind of shape I was in when I was in the Marines. . . ," but still not too proud of the encounter, and even less so when his wife got an obscene phone call that night from one of them.

He had once told me that when he took over the paper from his father several years before and got the usual threatening letters and phone calls, he would sometimes spend all night in the shrubs in front of his house with a gun. Or he would put a strip of Scotch tape on the crack of the hood of his car, and check each morning to see if it had been broken. He was even reluctant to go out into the little towns of the delta, the same dusty hamlets where I had been knocked around, often humiliated spiritually as well as manhandled physically, when playing sports in high school. Now he no longer sits in the shrubs or bothers with the Scotch tape, and he goes out into the little delta towns all the time on stories or to give speeches. He is a friend of Charles Evers, Aaron Henry, and the Negro leadership; he edits the best paper in Mississippi and one of the best in the South; he is blood-proud and quirky, with a high quotient for recognizing nonsense in whatever form it comes his way. "Mississippi by any human measure has had to reform," he once said. "But in the very process of reforming, and all that that entails, we may become like the rest of the country." Adding: "You're obsessed with the South and went away. I'm not and I stayed."

"It's *insane*," Hodding was saying, having previously lied to me that he had an uncle and a grandfather who fell here in Vicksburg, carrying tattered flags punctured with several dozen miniballs and riddled with New Jersey canister. "*Mississippi!* The one very damned place where Yankees and everybody else say this can't work, and it's become the battlefront. It's part of the screwy system in this nation that the one state least equipped, financially and emotionally, to deal with all the implications of it is finally havin' to do it first.

"People could have helped us, maybe could have saved us with their impeccable white Mississippi credentials. They could have helped move things in a civilized way, but they took their refuge in the thickets of the law. One thing's for sure, there won't be any flight to white suburbia down here. Where do you go? Hollandale? It's 80 per cent black. Itta Bena? It's more. I've got cousins up in Scarsdale who are very happy."

Why, then, did it finally get here first? Now he gesticulates a little, raising his voice, and the Negro mammies look over our way, and for all I know even some of the rotted gray ghosts of our people in the big cemetery up the river bluffs. "Through *stupidity! Sheer stupidity.* Sheer *unyielding conservatism!* That's why. All the state had to do was talk quietly and try to accommodate, and be a typical hypocritical American state. But there's no halfway measures in *this* place." He flourished his knife at the catfish. "Hell, it just might work here someday. Wouldn't *that* surprise 'em?"

Now the oracles in the Georgetown precincts of Washington would have us rest in peace. Stewart Alsop writes in *Newsweek* that "integration is a failure . . . it has become impossible to hide from view any longer the fact that school integration, although it has certainly been 'an experiment noble in purpose,' has tragically failed about everywhere." The crafty and cynical policy of the Nixon Administration would give further endorsement to what the disillusioned Yankee liberals and the Northern black separatists have given their benediction, not to so much as suggest all the racists everywhere. It takes a Southerner to know the extent to which the South has always been the toy and the pawn, in greed and in righteousness, of all the rest of America: the palliative of the national guilt, the playing field for all the nation's oscillations of idealism and idealism's retrenchments. The Yankee's Southern retainers have always been the worst of a breed, and now the new absenteeism was the federal government's retreat from our most difficult hopes for ourselves.

I believe that what happens in a small Mississippi town with less of a population than three or four apartment complexes on the West Side of Manhattan Island will be of enduring importance to America. It is people trying: loving, hating, enduring cruelties and perpetrating them, all caught, bedeviled, and dramatized by our brighter and darker impulses. Its best instincts only barely carried the day, and still may fall before anything really gets started (for we are mature enough in our failures by now to know how thin is the skein of our civilization), but nonetheless these instincts responded in ways that served us all. How many other little towns in America would have done nearly so well? Southerners of both races share a rootedness that even in moments of anger and pain we have been unable to repudiate or ignore, for the South—all of what it is—is in us all. As with Quentin Compson speaking in his pent-up frenzy to his Canadian roommate at Harvard, we love it and we hate it, and we cannot turn our backs upon it.

75

Where Does the South End?

WHERE DOES the South end and the West begin? A young man from Sweden was in Austin last week and wanted to know. He had been doing the South, talking to Freedom Riders on bail and in jail. By the time he reached CenTex, he wondered if he had imperceptively passed the barrier, silently and in the dark of night, or if the South were still upon him.

Larry Goodwyn, for instance, says the South ends at the Balcones Fault. We were sitting at Scholz' Beer Garden late one afternoon and Larry, in one of his dramatic flourishes, pointed out toward the gathering blue mists along the ridges and said, "The South ends two miles from here." A slightly intoxicated colleague demurred. "The South ends right here at Scholz'," he said. "This is the last outpost of civility. It is an enclave in a bad, bad land."

Another friend says the South ends on the other side of Lampasas. We were driving out to far West Texas and he advised me as we went through Lampasas that the Confederate soldier lounging in that familiar frozen posture on the inappropriate rocky lawn was the last we would see. After him, as we drove west, the old dignities and graces give way to the land of the vanished Indians and guerilla fighters, the oil and cattle people, and the Amarillo Globe-Times-News.

The Texas Observer, September 12, 1961

Ronnie Dugger says the South ends to the northeast of Austin, where East Texas finally gives way to scraggly trees and impoverished cotton. He once told me there is a stretch in the highway from Hearne to Austin: the mists around the horizon grow thinner, things suddenly get less intense. The South ends for Dugger about three miles southwest of a certain Humble filling station on Highway 79.

Another perceptive student of the South at the University believes the South ends at Conroe. He says he has a friend in the Texas Rangers who contends that in the South roadhouse brawls always take place outdoors, whereas in the Southwest they invariably occur indoors. "Conroe is the last place where these brawls take place inside," this friend observes. "Everywhere east of there you see them outside, around parked cars."

Where *does* the South end? When I was seventeen and got on a Continental Trailways bus in Vicksburg, Mississippi, to come to the University of Texas, my first reaction was that the South ended just west of Shreveport, Louisiana, along a stretch of road where you could only see service stations as far as the naked eye; in short, the South ended for me where Texas began. My first semester at the University I thought I was trapped in a nest of frost-bitten Yankees. Not only were the accents too twangy, there was a disproportionate interest in the origins and uses of money, which for me has always remained acutely un-Southern, since Mississippi has never had occasion to be obsessed, in any institutional way, with either. But in my second year, after a great deal of traveling between Austin and Yazoo City, Mississippi, I became firmly committed to the idea that the South ends where a man's feel for the guilt of the land fades away, wherever that might be.

Bob Sherrill, the associate editor of the Observer and only known survivor of Frogville, Georgia, a metropolis which apparently ceased to exist in the 'thirties, takes the cynical view of the question. He answers it, in fact, in reverse: "where does the South begin?" Although I am not in total agreement with Sherrill, since I am sending this clipping to my young friend from Sweden, it might be appropriate to conclude with his observations, in the hope that our young Swede will in the future take his queries on the Southland to a compatriot named Gunnar Myrdal:

That's Where the South Begins

Back where might makes right a little far-righter,
Back where the race blights a little blighter,
And where the benighted are a little benighter—
That's where the South begins.

Back where the cops' boots are a little flashier,
Back where the white trash is a little trashier,
And where Cash rings a little Cashier—
That's where the South begins.

Back where the grits are a little grittier,
Back where the loungers are a little spittier,
And the illiterates are a little illittier,—
That's where the South begins.

The Other Oxford

I REMEMBER the first essay I wrote at Oxford as a Rhodes Scholar fresh from the University of Texas. The tutor, whose habit was to sink into an easy chair near the fire, cross his legs, and look out at his students with bemused suspicion from his vantage point slightly above the floor, had assigned me something on the Reform Act of 1832. I had stayed up through a cold, windy October night polishing this mighty effort to its Wagnerian conclusion. I read the next-to-last sentence, "Just how close the people of England came to revolution in 1832 is a question we shall leave with the historians," and was about to move on to the closing statement. "But Morris," interrupted the tutor, subversive as Socrates, "we *are* the historians."

There it was, right at the start, the stark assumption, the monumental confrontation that Oxford embraces the young student as an individual, a participant—not as an outsider or an interloper—in the process of learning. This was my earliest and most valuable lesson. It was also the hardest.

It was remarked some months ago by Lord Elton, in his valedictory as secretary of the Rhodes Trustees, that above all else an Oxford education aims to teach a man to recognize nonsense when he sees it, especially in himself. Considering the rampant romanticism the place has

The Texas Quarterly, Winter 1980.

inspired, I would do well to keep this aphorism in mind here. Every year or so a new set of reminiscences comes off the presses, dealing more often than not with the peculiar color of the dawn after the commemoration ball, the smell of the Meadows in a spring rain, or the spry footwork of the bulldogs chasing some dear and now slightly mildewed old contemporary down Magpie Lane on Guy Fawkes night after the Turl Tavern has closed.

I would prefer to avoid the gentle stereotype, even though it represents a very real part of Oxford. But being fresh out of the place and caring greatly for it, I still remember the strange, bewildering, and sometimes oppressive Oxford that confronts an American student just emerged from the provinces. The adjustment is often traumatic. If, from the academic perspective alone, I leave no other impression than that of the challenge of my first tutor, Herbert Nicholas, my job will have been done.

We Americans found ourselves, quite suddenly, taking meals in those darkened medieval dining halls, surrounded by portraits of heroes and warriors and kings, princes and scholars and poets, prime ministers and parliamentarians and ecclesiastics; living for the first time amid crumbling walls and towers predating the discovery of America; eating at society dinners with silver two or three centuries old; humbly served as gentlemen-scholars, we aggressive democrats, by distinguished greying scouts who shined our shoes, replaced our bicycle chains, brewed our coffee, and called us "sir," even though back home they might have passed as Rotary officials or associate professors of English. In college quads we heard the sounds of echoed footsteps; we saw in the stairs leading to the dining hall the deepened grooves made by two-score generations like us. In college chapels we read the memorials to the dead of several wars, inscribed with names by the tens and hundreds. On those first Sunday afternoons, after the sun had disappeared, sometime in late morning, all the bells in the old town rang—wild hymns to loneliness and the years.

Under these circumstances, as I understand now, every day those first few months involved an often frenzied search, somewhere down in the subconscious, for self-identification. In that first winter, had it not been for Suez and Budapest and Adlai Stevenson's second defeat, America for us might just as well have been nonexistent amidst the memorials to centuries of English greatness; our own history seemed comparatively insignificant and all too easy to deny.

The dons were shadowy, rather terrifying figures who dwelt somewhere on the peripheries of ordinary human existence. They looked as if they might be judging the rest of us as subjects for some massive yet clever history to be written for the sober edification and entertainment of equally illustrious Oxford dons of the early twenty-fourth century. Within a twenty-five yard radius of one of these Olympian gentlemen, my claims to seriousness only barely exceeded those of Abimelech V. Oover, Max Beerbohm's Anabaptist from Pittsburgh. Their table in the dining hall was a foot or so above the undergraduates, just under the portrait of the founder, with whom they seemed to share some cosmic exemption from human frailty. William of Wykeham, looking down from above during our nightly bouts with vintage potatoes and alleged roast beef, might have asked the college classicist to pass the claret, and I, Abimelech, would merely have noted the event in order to describe it in my next letter home.

Those weekly or twice-weekly essays, some of them written after reading seven or eight books, others hastily contrived two hours before tutorial time after perusing three chapters of George M. Trevelyan's *Illustrated History of England*, were at the start frightening intellectual exercises. After six typewritten pages of sometimes unmitigated nonsense, an Oxford don's "Yes, hmmmmm," an expression whose meaning—like the English "thank you"—depends largely on intonation and accompanying bodily rhythm, was the stern rebuke of the ages not only for the reader of the essay, but presumably for Columbus' voyage and the subsequent appeasement policies of various Indian chieftains.

The English students, moreover, seemed uniformly brilliant, articulate, and informed. Even in casual conversations they used the language beautifully, with a fine regard for all the nuances of the English idiom. I have never heard infinitives, for instance, used with such poetic intensity as in those first few days at Oxford: infinitives as subjects, as objects, and as verbs, split only rarely and then on principle and for the sound of it. These students could talk at discreet length on a broad range of subjects which usually included various fine points in American politics, literature, and diplomacy. Were they some superbreed of the intellectual man? So they seemed, and so, indeed, many of them turned out to be.

The warden of Rhodes House, one of the great sons of modern Oxford, had been advising us to feel out the terrain warily, to take things rather easy for a time. On the face of it, this might seem the simplest approach of them all. But the problem involved in accepting an expansive leisure as the core of the system of education was a problem not to be surmounted overnight, not after the furious daily pace of an American university. A West Point graduate said he spent most of his first two weeks going to bulletin boards looking for an order. There was, of course, no compulsion to attend lectures, many of which were as exciting as television weather surveys; indeed, according to one of her many biographers, Christopher Hobhouse, Oxford has looked with some disdain upon lectures as somewhat obsolete since the invention of the printing press in the mid-fifteenth century.

Examinations were comprehensive and came at the end of three years. With the weekly or twice-weekly essay the only formal requirement, a student could do very much as he pleased: read Hemingway novels, take walks along the river, sleep till noon, go to London, patronize the pubs, or spend sixteen hours a day reading for the next tutorial. The necessity for gradual adjustment to this venerable technique in learning, with the student the sole master of his fate, incited an occasional puritanical apprehension that one was being slowly subverted, alienated from the old Jeffersonian urge to get things done. If Eugene Gant's professor (Merton, '04) in *Look Homeward, Angel* had boasted that Oxford discourages the "useless enthusiasms," might not the place in the long run annihilate the useful ones as well?

Lest this seem a confessional on the inherent psychic inferiority of the American student, let it be said that happy adjustment came with time. A poet from some deep Southern state had coined the plea in November, "Oh to be in April now that England's here." By the time April came, we dexterous products of John Dewey's genius had not only transcended many of the early difficulties; we had become so immured in the tight little community, a world in itself, that we speculated whether it might not be exceedingly difficult to get us out again. Already the most brilliant in our group were being informally groomed for the expected First. The walls and towers of the town, once such grey and forbidding structures, became friendly and familiar landmarks. Even the dons grew mellow and gracious, human enough for their alleged eccentricities to be widely discussed. One of them used breadcrusts for bookmarks. At the high-table, under the portrait of the founder, I dined one evening late in

83

the year, drank claret and watched the faint shadows from the candles dance across the woodwork on the high arched ceiling, and eavesdropped on a conversation across the table: "Are you by any chance writing his obituary for the Academy?" It was a long way from the Yazoo City High School cafeteria.

Behind their facade of exquisite language, we began to see that the English students had great chasms in their learning as well, that in some instances our American education had encouraged us to be more flexible, imaginative, and wary of preciosity. We discovered that as Americans we could skirt the class distinctions which separated some groups among the undergraduates, those subtle distinctions which inspired a clannishness we found surprising; we were equally welcomed socially by the Tories and the Socialists. We realized, finally, that our presence was the result of a decision arrived at years before, the decision to make of Oxford a genuine academic center of the English-speaking world. For when it accepted the principle of the Rhodes Scholarships, the ancient university was gambling that a large community of exuberant aliens would contribute to the excitement and intensity of life there.

By the late fifties, of course, Oxford had undergone far greater domestic changes than the annual influx of three-score or so Rhodes Scholars could ever have brought about. Preserving many of the outward forms and much of the old elegance, the university has actually experienced since the war a quiet revolution. Oxford, with Cambridge, is today at the apex of welfare-state education. In a national system of education with entry and advancement based on the merits of the individual student, the competition for places in the two oldest universities has grown increasingly keen. Both universities will retain their monopoly on the best young scholars in the country—for the very simple reason that the able student with the opportunity of choosing between Oxford and Leeds, or Cambridge and Nottingham, will continue to choose on the basis of age, excellence, and respectability. The persistence of the old gentleman-scholar motif embodied in the two universities may seem somewhat anachronistic in a country becoming more and more devoted to the idea of democracy in education. But the paradox has been in some measure resolved; and the manner in which this resolution has occurred over the last decade or so has been one of the interesting features of contemporary English society.

Just about destroyed is the old stereotype of prewar Oxford, where the young sons of the gentry consumed immense quantities of champagne, followed the hounds in the afternoons, and courted London debutantes while treading at a gentleman's pace the respectable surface of history or the law. In the Oxford of today, the shooting of a deer in Magdalen Park by the son of a lord (promptly "sent down" for it) is as exotic as the presence of a coal miner's son at Christ Church would have been in 1928. The majority of students now are on state grants of one kind or another. More and more are coming from state grammar schools, the sons and daughters of lower-middle class and working-class parents. Confronted at the start with venerable college tradition, attended by deferential college servants, raised far above their parents' status by virtue of the social prestige of being an Oxford student, many of them—perhaps most of them—will soon join the ranks of the new English middle class, composed of those growing numbers of young people discovered, trained, and rewarded in the postwar welfare-state democracy.

The old stereotype has been further modified. With existing college facilities unable to accommodate the increasing enrollments, most students must move into digs in the town their second year. The old and admirable idea of the closely-knit college society, the leisurely community of gentlemen-scholars living within the walls of the college, has suffered immeasurably. Many of the poorer students spend their last two or three years in two-pound-a-week bed-sitting rooms, often dismal places three or four miles from college in working districts like Cowley, or in dingy quarters along Walton Street near the gasworks.

One could hardly avoid noting, after vacation time, the quiet frustration of many of those students whose parents had left school at fourteen or before. They went home at the end of term, these boys, to the dismal, restricted life of the provincial town or the Midlands industrial city; they sat in their cramped parlors and watched the "telly" by the hour; they felt the growing and perhaps inevitable alienation from their families and from their parents' limited vistas. These young people themselves are victims, as many of them well understood, of the relentless welfare-state pursuit of talent and ability. The mixed feelings of alienation, gratitude, and guilt which this situation engenders sometimes produce bitterness.

One of the most stimulating of my college friends was Dennis Potter, author of the widely praised diatribe, *The Glittering Coffin*. Potter, the son of a coal miner, was a brilliant and dedicated young socialist who spent a good part of his three years at Oxford writing and debating on the cultural shortcomings of the new welfare-state society. When he brought his fiancee to Oxford, daughter of a coal miner from the same village, I remember he took pains to invite only Americans and his more committed socialist friends to meet her. Yet it is a commentary on the tenacity of the old institutions, as well as on the direction the paths toward reward and accomplishment are taking in modern England, that when Potter left Oxford he took a position with the B.B.C., since the twenties one of the unerring symbols of the Establishment and its values.

The paradox and variety of contemporary Oxford are curiously illustrated in its social life. There are social functions right out of Edwardian Oxford—from sherry in a don's room on Sunday morning to the raucous society dinners with their four or five wines or the fabulous commemoration balls with the all-night champagne and array of London orchestras. Perhaps the most elegant party I attended was given by the warden of our college in honor of graduating students. At twilight one June evening, in the medieval atmosphere of the college cloisters, the guests—ranging from recent graduates to lords and ladies of Her Majesty's realm—sipped champagne and heard madrigals sung by a boys' choir. I thought of the monks who had known and loved those walks in more solemn moments and I felt they were blessing us that evening with a smiling indulgence if their hovering spirits were agile enough to avoid the steady crossfire of champagne corks.

There was a time, also, for pork pie and cheap red wine at someone's digs in Cowley. There was a time for the Saturday night parties given by the poorer students where, in one or two close and smoky rooms, dozens of undergraduates were crowded beyond escape. Here invariably was the white wine concoction, the sound of American jazz from the gramophone in a corner, the shy and awkward talk between boy and girl, the quaint and incongruous offerings of the white-coated college scout: "Fill it up, sir?"

Perhaps the truest impression an American can take from Oxford, and the one he may most deeply appreciate because of its absence in his own society, is the almost universal deference paid there to privacy—privacy in the broad, human sense. At Oxford, more than any place I have ever known, every person has it; and it is his own domain, not to be invaded lightly. In an institution of learning, this uncompromising homage to privacy implies a kind of informal recognition of self-sufficiency and maturity in the individual student, as well as a faith in isolation itself as a way of treating problems of adjustment. In encouraging that genuine participation in one's discipline on which my tutor had insisted at the very start, this privacy is regarded as an essential for the independently rational person the University seeks to develop. It is the student's physical privacy, the separateness of always separate rooms, and it finds expression in the haunting loneliness of the place. Further, the community does not interfere with, does not choose to judge, one's personal habits. In fads and eccentricities, as in the paths the mind takes, the Oxford student is protected by a soft, gentle tolerance. The young Trotskyite who wore the same maroon pullover every day during winter and refused to wear his false front tooth when the Tories had aggravated him, and the young lord with the pince-nez and black cape and cane who engaged in writing a history of European dungeons, felt no compunction whatever to conform.

On Sunday afternoons in early spring the tourists, in their streamlined American Express buses with the expansive glass domes, touched down long enough to see their two typical Oxford colleges en route to a typical play by Shakespeare, in his home town to the north. Laden with cameras, light meters, and tripods, they would remain for the requisite half-hour, diligently exposing themselves between poses to the fleeting, grey sensual impressions of the old town. Then, with a monumental rattle of paraphernalia, they were off again.

In the end, of course, like the tourists we were temporary to Oxford. We too collected our paraphernalia, mostly books, leaving behind healthy deficits with Mr.

Blackwell, and returned home again to America. The Yoders, the Oomses, the Sniegowskis, the Hammonds—from Carolina and Illinois, Kansas and California—all of us knew it had been the freest time of our lives, and rare was the scholar who had not sooner or later discovered there what kind of person he was, his abilities, his faults, his deepest convictions, and his darkest prejudices.

Weep No More, My Lady

FOR THE LAST three years Mamie had been in a nursing home in my hometown, right around the corner from my mother's house. All day long, over and over, she would cry "Momma, Papa" and talk with people four generations gone. The last time I saw her, tiny and shriveled in her bed, completely blind and almost wholly deaf, she took my hand and said, "Is that the boy? My boy always was a rascal." In her final lucid moment she whispered to my mother, "Put me in the ground next to Percy and close the gate behind you. I want to go home." She was weeping when she died.

She was 97, the repository of vanished times for me. Although she would not have understood had I told her, she helped me to have feeling for the few things that matter. I was nourished in the echoes of her laughter.

When I was a boy, she and I took long walks around town in the gold summer dusk, out to the cemetery or miles and miles to the Old Ladies' Home, talking in torrents between the long silences. All about us were forests of crape myrtles and old houses fairly ruined. Widow ladies and spinsters sat on the galleries of the dark houses cooling themselves with paper fans, and we greeted each lady by turn, and then she told me who they were and what had happened to their people. We must have been an unlikely pair on those long-ago journeys, she in her flowing dress and straw hat, I barefoot in a T-shirt and blue jeans, with a sailor's cap on my head, separated by our sixty years. Only when I grew older did I comprehend that it was the years between us that made us close; ours was a symbiosis forged by time. *What are hills? How old are horses? Where do people go when they die?* She always tried to answer me. But mostly she told me stories. Since she was the seventeenth child, she told me, her mother was so ashamed that she hid her as a baby under the blankets of the wagon when friends approached on the road. During a race riot after a political barbecue, five or six Negro men asked her to hide them, so she kept them in a deserted chickenhouse for two days and fetched them cornbread and buttermilk from the kitchen. One autumn twilight she took me to the old family home, sold to pay taxes long before, and under the house she sighted a beautiful white pebble, quite large, and she told me she had found it down by the town well when she was ten years old.

To my grandfather Percy, who made potato chips at the potato-chip factory, she was the sustenance of life; she was ever patient also with my two outrageous old-maid aunts, who in their blindness peregrinated about the house at all hours, carrying on conversations with garbage cans or brooms standing in corners or the hall furnace, waiting for the food to be served. One hot summer night many years ago, she went to get me a glass of water, and in the darkness broke her big toe on a rocker. To ease the pain until the doctor came, she smoked the only cigarette of her life, a rolled-up Bull Durham, saying to me, "I could get *addicted*." When I had my tonsils out in the hospital, I fought my way from under the ether, spitting blood on the bed, and then I saw her next to me, whispering, "My poor, poor boy." At nights, half asleep on the couch, drowsy in the cadences of the katydids, I absorbed in a reverie her aimless talk with her sisters—disasters of the flesh, people long forgotten, her Momma and Poppa—and heard the big clock on the mantel chime each quarter-hour. She made her first trip to New York, to see me, when she was 87. It bemused her that the magazine I edited bore her family name, Harper, though she deemed it the Northern branch. She and my mother and I sat one evening at a sidewalk café in Greenwich Village; a number of racially mixed couples strolled past us, hand-in-hand. "I've never seen people carry on like that," my mother said. I attempted a reply. Then, quite gently, Mamie said, "It's a long way from home, son. *You* know that." Then she paused for a moment, looking across Sixth Avenue at nothing in particular, and added, "Maybe when we all get to heaven, *they'll* be white and *we'll* be black."

When the call came to me on Long Island that she had died, my son David and I rushed to LaGuardia and made the last flight back. It took us just eight hours to be in Yazoo, although we seemed in many ways to have traveled considerably farther than that.

Spring was on its way; the jonquils and burning bushes and Japanese magnolias were in bloom, and out in the delta the black land hummed with motion. But we were immersed in a web of death, for death in a small Southern town is like death in no other place. Everyone knows right away when someone has died, and there is a community apparatus to deal with the situation, old bonds of institutional grief almost primal in their unfolding. Having lived away so long, I had forgotten how they cope with it, death every day, death everlasting.

But they do. They bring food and they talk among themselves about this death and others. They hover close in the web of death; they try hard to make mortality natural. Here in Yazoo, at the age of 39, I looked

92

death in the face with stark comprehension for the first time.

In the funeral home she lay in the next room. I watched my son looking furtively from time to time in her direction. It was his first funeral. The sight of him there made me remember my first one, and looking at him now helped me know my son better. He lurked now in corners watching the whole town come through, my mother's church ladies, my father's fishing and domino friends. "He looks just like you did," they said. "He favors you." They admired his Yankee accent.

Later, when Mamie's funeral procession approached the church, turning east at the courthouse, a black policeman stood in the center of the street at attention, holding his cap over his heart. We were to bury her in Raymond, fifty miles away, and now only five or six cars followed us, a meager parade, as we drove past the suburbs and shopping centers of old Mississippi, a lovely terrain of abrupt hills and green vines being ripped away whole, and mammoth new expressways making something else entirely of the land she once knew.

We reached the old section of the Raymond cemetery before the hearse, and everyone got out to look around. Desolation awaited us. On this isolated and forlorn hill, the people who had settled her town were buried. I saw my son strolling among them, and among the older graves across the way, and a few moments later he walked up to me carrying a small broken tombstone, wordlessly laying it at my feet: "To Richard Edwards, 1828–1863, From His Friends the Confederate Soldiers." He was upset when I told him he could not take it back to New York.

"I hate to leave her in this awful place," my mother said; as she said it the hearse arrived. The men put the coffin and the flowers on the open grave, and we gathered about against the heavy wind and said "The Lord's

Prayer." It was over in moments.

Yet people stayed, as if riveted to that place and time; they moved a distance from the grave to talk. I saw my son with the undertaker, watching the coffin slowly descend into the ground. In the crowd a tall, angular man I did not know, a local man, caught me by the arm. "By God, you're Ray." Not Ray, I said. "Yes, by damn, you're *Ray*. You're the image of your father. You're Ray's boy."

I walked away from this strange lingering, and drifted alone up the hill. Wisps of clouds cast the terrain before me in gloom. Far below stretched the streets of the old town. The bell on the courthouse struck four, and, in a lane beyond, a child ran after a car tire that was rolling along. A dog barked in pursuit of the child; from near the grave there was laughter, and the minglings of a dozen voices.

In a rush I knew in my heart the sweetness and simplicity of her days on this earth. Alone on the hill, in a February wind, I grieved for Mamie.

Christmases Gone

THE TOWN was so wonderfully contained for me in those Christmases of childhood that I could hardly have asked for anything else: the lights aglitter in front of the established homes on the hills and down in the flat places, the main street with its decorations stretching away to the bend in the river—a different place altogether from the scorched vistas the town gave us in summer. There was an electricity in the very atmosphere then, having to do, I know now, with pride in the town's sudden luster, and when we went caroling and gave our Christmas baskets to the poor white people in the neglected apartment houses and the Negroes in the shacks on stilts in the swamp-bottoms, on those cool crisp nights after school had turned out for the holidays, I would look into the delta at the evening star bright and high in the skies and think to myself: There is The Star itself, the one that guided them there to the new child. To this day when I hear "O Little Town of Bethlehem," that town for me is really Yazoo.

When does memory begin? I remember a Christmas pageant in the church when we were 5 years old. Our teacher had borrowed one of the Turner twins to be Jesus, promising the Turners that no one would drop her on the floor. Kay King was Mary, I was Joseph, and Bubba Barrier was the innkeeper. When I knocked on the door, Bubba Barrier was supposed to open it, thrust his head out, and say, in a booming injunction: "*No room in the inn!*" We had practiced this to adult perfection. But when the night came, Bubba was flustered by the dozens of parents and relatives crowding the church sanctuary. When I knocked on the door of the inn, he opened it with diffidence and said: "Willie, we done run out of space."

For me those mornings of Christmas were warm with the familiar ritual. We would wake up at dawn in our house in Yazoo—my mother, my father, my dog Old Skip, and I—and open the presents. My mother would play two or three carols on the baby-grand—then we would have the sparsest of breakfasts to keep room for the feast to come. Under the purple Mississippi clouds which, much as we prayed for it, never brought snow, we drove the forty miles south to Jackson to be with my grandmother, Mamie, my grandfather, Percy, and my two old incorrigible great-aunts, Maggie and Susie. The drive itself is etched in my heart, the tiny hamlets of the plain where white and black children played outside with their acquisitions of the day, the sad unpainted country stores with the patent medicine posters trimmed in tinsel, and finally the splendid glimpse of the capitol dome and the ride up State Street to the little house on North Jefferson.

They would be there on the gallery waiting for us, the four of them, and we would all go inside to exultant embracings to exchange our gifts—modest things for sure, because we were not rich—and examine what we had given each other in much detail, and then sit down and catch up on our tidings. And the smells from the kitchen! The fat turkey and giblet gravy and corn-bread stuffing and sweet potatoes with melted marshmallows and the nectar and ambrosia and roasted pecans and mince-meat pies! My two great-aunts bumped into each other every now and again and wished each other Merry Christmas, while the rest of us sank into the chairs by the fire and awaited what my grandmother Mamie was making for us. Christmas songs wafted from the chimes of the church down the way, and my grandmother would dart out of the kitchen and say: "Almost done now!"

Then, at eleven in the morning, never later, we would sit at the ancient table which had been my great-great grandmother's: my grandfather Percy and my father at opposite ends, my mother and great-aunts on one side of it, my grandmother and I on the other, Old Skip poised next to my chair expecting his favors. We would sit there for two hours, it seemed, all of them talking about people long since departed from the earth, about vanished Christmases. The clock on the mantle in the parlor would sound each quarter-hour, and my great-aunts would ask for more servings and say: "My, ain't this *good?*"

I would look around me every year at each of them, and feel Old Skip's wet nose on my hand, as if all this were designed for me alone. Then, after the rattling of dishes, we would settle in the parlor again, drowsy and fulfilled, and talk away the dreamy afternoon. Finally my grandmother, standing before us by the fire, would gaze about the room and always say, in her tone at once poignant and bemused: "Oh, well, another Christmas come and gone."

They are all dead now, each one of them: Mamie and Percy and my great-aunts Maggie and Susie, buried in a crumbling graveyard on a hill; my mother and father in the cemetery in Yazoo; Old Skip behind the house.

Only I remain, and on Christmases now far away from home, I remember.

Vignettes of Washington

1.

MANY YOUNG women migrate to New York from the provinces to try to prove themselves, and this has become part of the mythology of America—the office girl living in the walk-up in the Village or on the West Side, hoping in these inauspicious beginnings to follow a dream. Less dramatic, not so familiar to our literature but no less true of our national experience, are the girls who come to Washington to find their way, and who give to this city something of its unique temper.

The fiction of this country is filled with those of them who are drawn to Manhattan. Perhaps it says something about Washington that practically no serious novelists have ever settled in this "vain and noble city," as Henry Adams called it in *Democracy*, and hence there is nothing in our imaginative writing to do quite justice to them, these young people who come here out of the same impulses of ambition and the imperatives of escape to find some measure of belonging.

One night this week I had dinner in one of those criminally expensive restaurants in Georgetown with a Southern girl, a friend of mutual friends, noted among them for her warmth and candor, whom I had asked to tell something of herself, and of her life here. It is just a Washington story, no more, no less, a vignette about the sexual revolution, and I wanted to put it down.

The Washington Star, February and March, 1976

Her name is Nancy Battle, or that is close enough. She is soon to turn 27, a wholesome brunette beauty who works for one of the government agencies that has a familiarly recognized name, if not a familiarly acknowledged set of functions, which deals among other things in the creative arts. She was born and grew up in Charlottesville, Va., her father being a prominent lawyer, and, although she loved it, she does not look back on it now as an authentic American childhood, because the town was dominated by the University of Virginia, the exotic flavor of it, by the outsiders who dwelled there and by the strangers who came to see the Old Colonnade and Tom Jefferson's house on the hill. She stayed for college there, to study history at U Va, and before she graduated and moved to Washington she had only been here twice, and then on school weekends in cherry blossom time.

She came to Washington rather than New York, she says, "because I was intrigued by government, by the things I'd read of government, by the people who made government work." From a distance she thought politicians a more interesting breed than, say, publishers, or television people, or Wall Street brokers. She was 21 years old when she went to the office of a Virginia congressman she admired to ask for a job. She got a temporary one helping the congressman's wife address Christmas cards, and then they took her on permanently at $110 a week, doing odd chores, writing mundane letters, and sometimes being a back-up receptionist to an old woman named Mrs. Grumsby who had been there thirty years.

She adored Capitol Hill at first, sandwiches on the lawns at lunch that first Indian Summer, discussions with other young people about committee work and all the rest, absorbing herself in the life of that peculiar cosmos. She took a house on Duke Street in Alexandria with four other girls her age, all from Virginia, girls she had known for a while, and she remembers John and Maureen Dean and Barry Goldwater Jr. and "a whole slew of people from Chapel Hill" who went to the same parties she and her friends did.

One of the girls did not last very long; she stayed up all night in the house on Duke Street drinking scotch and entertaining boys a little older than she from the Hill, in an alcove under the stairs, and she got frightened and went home to Danville to marry her high school sweetheart, an enormous wedding at the Presbyterian Church and reception at the country club, a marriage that started in fear of the ambivalence of Washington and ended in divorce, as indeed already have the marriages of all the girls except one with whom she grew up.

Another of the girls she lived with, the beauty of the group, Nancy says, left the congressman she worked for because his A.A. was a 40-year-old drunk and lecher who made life miserable for her—banging on the door at 3 a.m., trying to take her on weekends to the country away from his wife and family, claiming that he kept a permanent room in a motel in Harpers Ferry. She took a job as a glorified copygirl with Time Magazine, and is now one of those thousands of young ladies who disappear every morning into the Time-Life Building.

The third girl among her housemates got pregnant by one of the older men down the hall in the Rayburn Building, went to New York to have an abortion, and now teaches fourth grade in Pottstown, Pa.

And the fourth, who was the daughter of a banker who was the biggest financial backer of the congressman she worked for, lasted two years and then went off with an unemployed rock singer to live in the hills around the Blue Ridge, where she took up pottery and promptly changed her name, for reasons largely inexplicable to Nancy, from Lois Ann Simkins to Chloe Starr. So she is the last of the group to stay on here. "They talk about this being a city of transients," Nancy says. "For every old biddy who stays forever on the Hill to make life difficult for everybody else, there are twenty girls who leave before they're my age. There seemed to be a farewell party every day."

Nancy herself says she learned less about governance in those early days, although she became adept in handling boorish constituents, than about the Hill's obsession with sex.

"They just came at me from all sides," she says. "They were relentless. The younger guys weren't so bad. At least we came from the same generation and had something in common. But the older married men were another matter. It left me with a sour feeling about marriage. Why bother? I'd had affairs in college, but I worried for a long time here that I might've turned frigid. Jesus Christ, some of those men on the Hill were desperate. I'd have felt sorry for them if I'd had any time left from fending them off."

After almost two years in the congressman's office, with his help she got a good job—"lower to middle-level responsibility"—with her present agency.

She makes $13,000 a year and rents a small two-floor apartment off Dupont Circle, bedroom downstairs, kitchen and sitting room upstairs, at $300 a month. She did not want to stay in the suburbs, or to move into one of those tall new buildings out there that caters to young people, and where unusual arrangements are said to take place. (People advised her, of course, against walking around much after twilight around Dupont Circle, and to always have enough gas in her Saab when she drives home alone from one of the Georgetown bars, and to gaze around her at all times, and to be chary of footsteps, but she has only been troubled once on the streets, when a teen-age boy stole up from an angle and pinched her on the rear, but even he dashed away at great speed when she screamed for help.) She writes position papers, goes to New York about once a month to confer with her agency's staff there, and feels her work is creative enough to engage her interest and to make her feel she matters.

She has dated younger men, divorced and single, slept with one or two of them in her apartment or theirs, and she says her parents for the last year or so have been subtly suggesting that she come on back to Charlottesville and give some pattern to her life.

"I think my life has a pattern," she says. "But I can feel how much they want me to get married and have a child. They don't seem to understand my living alone in the big city. They try, but I can tell they can't comprehend it."

Still, there has been real loneliness for her, she says— the loneliness of returning to a dirty apartment after work, of driftless weekends when she thinks she wants to be alone but isn't sure, of that fitful melancholia which can torment all of us who live more or less by our own devices, of those days of early dark when she does indeed wonder if her life has much substance, or if she may be missing out on something.

"I think the trouble with my generation," she says, "is that even with all the freedom, the lack of guilt, we don't have any ground rules, nothing to fall back on in the middle of the revolution. I guess we're having to make our own rules as we go along." And that is compounded by something in the life of Washington itself, she believes, something that she senses in the atmosphere of it but cannot quite put her finger on, having to do with a lack of cohesion—or perhaps the word is community.

She has taken to spending some time after work in a bar and restaurant called Columbia Station, on Columbia Road at 18th Street, which has a flavor and a feel of belonging she likes.

"It's not like a Georgetown place, it doesn't have that Georgetown set, affluent, young, single, not really into anything but themselves. It's not like the Bachelors and Spinsters, which is only for young singles and is nice enough, but gets boring because finally no one has anything to say."

There is Childe Harold, around Dupont Circle, which appeals somewhat to "cause-oriented young people" who work for agencies like the Civil Rights Commission, young actors and actresses, more committed to things. Columbia Station gets "a real amalgam of people, unpredictable, of all ages. People come in in blue jeans if they feel like it. It's a casual kind of place. You come in and read the newspaper if you're lonely at home—people who write a little bit, and God knows what they write about, and play backgammon. It's a little like an Upper West Side place. You don't know who's who or what people are up to. I like that all right."

And in addition to all this, best perhaps for last, she has taken a fairly serious lover, a married man whom she met on one of her New York trips, fifteen years older than she. They meet in New York, and occasionally he comes here in the middle of the week, and she says she is the happiest she has been with a man.

She had never spent any time with a married man before, "but it's perfectly natural, thank God. We never talk about his family, and I think we care about each other. It's the first time I've wanted to run up to someone after we've been apart and embrace, the way they do in the movies. It's fun when he's here. It makes things matter more. It takes the nervous edge off things. I know it won't last, but one thing I've learned is that you can't ask for everything."

Then she adds: "I may never get married. It's certainly

not in the cards for me right now. The idea of marriage truly frightens me. I'm not being phony about it. All a person my age has to do is look around and see how destructive marriage can be. Besides, I've got my work, and despite it all I kind of look upon Washington as my town. I found it all by myself, and that makes me feel good."

One of her favorite books, as it is for many an independent and free-spirited and intelligent Southern girl, is William Styron's *Lie Down in Darkness*, and although the heroine, Peyton Loftis, is star-crossed and tragic, she wishes desperately before her fall to make life an adventure, to live it without compromise. "If the crazy sideroads beguile you," as Styron's words come to Virginia boys and girls, "take a long backward look at Monticello."

Nancy may need that advice someday, but now, bless her, is not especially the time.

2.

FOR THE LAST two months I have lived in the most curious house you ever saw. It belongs to Jeremiah O'Leary, a much beloved reporter for this publication for many years, and is adjacent to Jerry's fine townhouse on Prince Street in Old Town Alexandria, on what surely must be one of the most gracious blocks of dwellings in America.

It is a solid 18th century structure with two floors and a loft with a skylight added at the top with a ladder to get to it. In the back, beyond a patio, there is an ancient well which once had been filled in and which began collapsing after I arrived. Jerry plans to excavate when the springtime comes, and God knows what he will find down there, but rumor has it there will be the skeletons of several Yankee collaborators.

I have not been in my house too much, having spent a good deal of time in the Washington Star newsroom, which the Smithsonian should one day ask for, that and skittering about the surfaces of this city. My work here as the "writer-in-residence" has meant getting to know, in the voyeuristic sort of way, a diverse collection of the human fauna now flourishing here: defrocked priests who sleep in firehouses, pundits who curry no political label, moderate revolutionaries (or makers of middle-sized firebombs), congressmen and senators who likely have not changed all that much in the last several decades, Marxist cheeseburger chefs, both varieties of AAs, housewives drifting in ennui, blacks who want to go back to Dixie, Xerox peddlers, young ladies who should have stayed in Colorado Springs, parking attendants who have been mugged eleven times, bookies from the James River in double-knits, liberationists who say a woman's place is in the House and the Senate, drunk linemen for the Redskins, and politicians, politicians, politicians. Almost in an existential mist I have observed this blend, which reaffirms my intuition that human life has its nobilities but is essentially inchoate. It has also led me to sense, rightly or wrongly, that Washington is not the town it was even as recently as eight or ten years ago, but is steadily becoming an amalgam of such places as New York and Atlanta, although if it had to carry the unbegrudging ideological commitments of the former it would not survive past next Tuesday.

This being more or less my life here, however, the only time I stayed in my house on Prince Street during the day was Saturdays and Sundays. That was when the difficulties started, because my house is only eight feet wide.

You would not believe it if you saw it. It is one of the narrowest houses in the whole town. The front of it has a patina of time, a deep gray facade with an old door; it will break your heart to consider who might have once lived in it, and what happened to their lives; and when you look at it from the sidewalk which comes right up to it, or from the street where cars must stop for a sign, there it is: an apparition, an afterthought, squeezed between Jerry's big house and a larger one on the other side, and I have heard people walk by without the guidebooks and say of it, "My God!"

I discovered later that it is listed in one of the Bicentennial guides to the walking tour of Old Alexandria. The tourists, reading their guidebooks, are instructed to turn right off Royal, and the book says: "Take a close look at 40 Prince. How wide do you think this house is?"

My first Saturday here after the icy January weather I was lying in the rollaway bed I had put just inside the front door. All of a sudden a male Midwestern voice boomed through the wall: "Take a close look at 40 Prince. How wide do you think this house is?" I sat straight up, because the voice was so close the man could have been posing the question to me. Then: "Jimmy, count it off with your shoes!" A woman laughed while a small boy began counting: "One . . . two . . . three . . . it's seven feet wide!"

About ten minutes later, this time an accent from the canebrakes or the darkest deltas: "How wide do you think this house is?" "It's so skinny," the wife said, and then two children did the measuring and eventually came up with the figure of seven and a half feet. Shortly on their heels, a teacher with what must have been her kindergarten class deliberated before my door. "Now, children, how wide is it?" and fifteen brats of all sizes and colors and faiths began assaying its puny dimensions. I sank into an uneasy afternoon's nap, and all that day, as if from the nearest surfaces of the psyche, strangers were asking that horrendous question and measuring my house.

This continued through the following afternoon, at intervals regular as a metronome, people sometimes staring in through the half-shuttered windows as I tried to read a book, faces out of Walker Evans and social registers, hands holding ice-cream cones or popsicles: "Take a look inside. The rooms sure are long." Sometimes small bets were made, and I heard their commerce in coins from right outside my wall.

Finally I knew I must fight back. I stood next to the front window. A vociferous couple came by with their offspring, female twins with red hair. I was waiting for them. I flung open the shutters and shouted: "It's eight god damned feet!" They stared at me briefly, then scampered off in a hurry.

Next, with the shutters open, I put my elbows on the window sill, adopting the pose of one of those relatives they never mentioned, but used to keep in their attics in the South of a generation ago and not even let out on nights of wisteria, looking stolidly out across Prince Street like a figure in a Hopper painting. A family turned right and strolled in my direction, an angular couple trailed by three mischievous boys. Then, all at once, the five of them caught a glimpse of me, drooling in a white T-shirt, twitching a little with the face and arms. They paused for an instant, wordlessly, looking at me out of the corners of their eyes. Then the wife said, "Come on, children."

After that, like a squirrel, gleaning and gathering, I went to the hardware store for the utensils and made a big sign on white cardboard. In large block letters it said: "Danger! Quarantine! The People of This House Have Diphtheria!" I sneaked looks from the shutters out toward the sidewalk, and soon another family arrived with their guidebook. They stopped abruptly, the parents leaning at a slight list to read the sign. "It's some kind of joke," the woman whispered. "The very nerve!" Momentarily another group came along, and as they

107

stopped before the sign I swung open the shutters, gripped my neck in my hands, and said: "I've got a sore throat." They laughed a little unsurely, gazed at one another, and they too were quickly on their way.

Finally, I bought six sets of imitation dog droppings at Al's Magic Shop and late one afternoon I darted outside, making sure no one was coming, and placed them in front of my house. Soon people came by, stepping gingerly, children or women saying "Eeeewh!" One man said, "It must be a stable."

But it became too much for me, this town and its histories, and the temerity of our Bicentennial explorations. I posted one final sign: "What is real? This question has plagued all philosophers. This house is as damned well wide as you want it to be." Then I put on my suit and tie, got my notebook and pen, and went out to find some people.

3.

NOSTALGIA isn't what it used to be, Peter De-Vries said. They have restored Old Alexandria, and done it with taste and grace, but I hope you do not mind my saying that with all its charm it is ever so ersatz at the edges, an exercise in honorable caprice.

The other day, a moody winter afternoon following snow and slush, the streets of the town where I have taken residence were crowded with outlanders, mainly from the District four or five miles away, and the suburbs and the shops along King Street with the Bicentennial flags astir were geared up for the dollar.

This revival of one of America's authentic villages has brought in a crop of newcomers from way down in real Old Dominion boondocks country, not unlike the Mexicanos who migrate toward the border to be close to Texas towns and the dollar flow. These old white country boys are all over the place, bless them; Alexandria may not be a one-industry town, but it is becoming a city of transients. I was in a rush that day to meet an appointment in the District. I have not lived in Washington for more than two years, and even then was perpetually getting lost in the inextricable maze of L'Enfant's hubs, wheels and circles around circles. They tried to build a Versailles from the swamps and ended up with a paradise for haphazard thieves, who roam in numbers and catch you alone at the circles. Even a dim-witted Anglo-Saxon would have followed the example of the Christian cross, or the Mormons when they laid out Salt Lake City, or Jefferson himself when he designed Jackson, Mississippi, without having seen it and before anything was there. Since this was not the case, I left my car in Alexandria to look for a cab. I found one next to the new Holiday Inn.

"Hi, there," the driver said. "Whereabouts?"

He was in his middle twenties, thin and wiry, with short-cropped hair and a sunburnt nose, a seed-store, feed-store, courthouse-square down-home boy if ever there was one. He was spare as hardtack. I knew from my own inheritance he would have been one of them with Stonewall when we outflanked Hooker at Chancellorsville.

I told him the Mayflower.

"Uh-huh. What's that, a street?"

"It's a hotel in the District."

"Lord, no!" He groaned, then turned around and looked at me. "Do we have to go there?"

"I can get another cab."

"Don't do it! I can stand a little visit." He started the motor and drove toward Washington Street. The dispatch radio crackled, and he spoke into his microphone: "Cab E-8, to Washington, D.C."

Just beyond the airport he said, "Mind if I smoke?"

"Not at all."

"I enjoy a little smoke sometimes. Some people I drive don't like me to."

"Go right ahead."

"What's the best way to get over there, anyway?"

"I'm sorry?"

"What's the best way to Washington?"

"I'd take the Fourteenth Street Bridge. We want the Eleven hundred block of Connecticut."

"Uh-huh. What in your opinion is the best way to get to the Fourteenth Street Bridge?"

"I'd just follow these signs and bear right."

"We'll do that. What's that building ahead?"

"That's the Lincoln Memorial."

"Pretty."

Somewhere across the bridge, however, we were already lost, and foundering in terrible traffic.

"These one-way streets weren't never good," he said. "I'll just ask the dispatcher where we are."

He spoke again into the microphone, tried and failed. "They don't never answer me. I been trying to get him all day. I don't think they like to talk to me."

Finally, after several fruitless efforts, he succeeded, "Where's the Mayflower?"

A staccato blast: "Eleven-0-two Connecticut."

"Where's Connecticut?" But already his advisor was irretrievably gone.

A black parking-lot attendant was standing on a curb on New York Avenue; I suggested we ask him for instructions.

We pulled to a halt. "Say, where's Connecticut Avenue?"

The parking attendant pointed in the very direction from which we had come, out over the Potomac and the purple horizon. We started again.

"That ain't right. That fellow's lyin'. He's foolin' around with us. One thing I know, Connecticut ain't

110

that way. They think they're smart doin' that, but they're just common. Ain't that common? They don't even know no better. Wise-asses! Here's Pennsylvania. We're on the right track."

We cruised the streets, now heavy with the rush-hour traffic. Sirens whipped the air. The subway construction gave this terrain a feel of destruction, like the bombed-out sections of London in the early 'Fifties. Moving objects caught me in my lethargy: a woebegone Chevy with a squirrel-tail on the aerial, a pink Volkswagen with "Virginia Is for Lovers" on the bumper, a Cadillac limousine double-parked, from which two large women emerged.

As we moved bumper-to-bumper in directions uncharted, he turned off his meter. "This ain't no way to live. Fredericksburg's got too big for me."

"Is that where you're from?"

"I'm from Charlotte Courthouse, Va., down toward the Carolina line. But I live in Goldvein, out by Fredericksburg, and drive to Alexandria to work. Say, it's startin' to snow!"

Sure enough, the uncertain day had turned to gloom, and I was badly late for my appointment.

"Yeah, I'm glad it's snowin'. It means I'll get some rabbits and squirrels. I bring in twelve, fifteen every weekend in bad weather. A lot of people here used to do that. A lot of people come from right down there."

"Let's ask this cop for directions."

He stopped near a Texaco station, got out, and in the gathering dark I watched the cop gesture here and there, drawing a map with his hands.

"We got it," he said. "Up Seventeenth on the service road, right on Connecticut. You ain't too upset, are you?"

"I'm just late."

"We'll make it. I wish we could pick her up." We

111

gazed out at a lovely Indian girl in a sari, standing near the Statler. "I've seen a few of them with red dots. They're not all white, they say. There sure are a lot of foreigners in this town, do you notice? Foreigners and coloreds, that's about all. Now look at him." An exceedingly tall African in native garb stood waiting for the light. "He's all dressed up and ready for somethin', ain't he now? And look at all these single girls—a lot of girls over here, and always, you know, gettin' *assaulted*. Hit over the head with their own purses."

Miraculously, right in front of us, was Connecticut Avenue, and then with a whoop, the shout of a warrior, an old bosky yelp of triumph and retribution, of old misappropriated instincts straight from the blood of the whipped-down South, arousing me from my bleak despair not over being lost again in the city I should know, but merely in being in the city I really knew too well: "That's it! Here it is! Here's the hot-damned Mayflower Hotel!"

His exultation was contagious. It gripped me also, this joy of discovery. As I opened the door and got out, I gave him a two dollar tip.

He thrust his head out the window, and for an instant his craggy, young-old face seemed ineffably sad. "That's too much," he said. "I got us lost. I don't deserve it."

"Yes you do. I enjoyed it."

"Well, we'd have found it on our own sooner or later, wouldn't we?"

"You're damned right we would have."

He waved goodbye, made a U-turn against the traffic, and in the twilight's snow of our capital headed the wrong way down a one-way street.

4.

I WENT down to Union Station the other day to meet a friend on the Metroliner, and the inside looked

112

as if it had just been hit by one of Hitler's buzz-bombs. The tourist center they are working on there, under the graceful old hall resonant with echoes which has been the first sight of Washington for many thousands who came here, is a gaping hole, and settling over everything is a fine swirling dust. You will get no information about Washington here.

Just coincidentally, on the advice of friends, I went the next day to the National Heritage Theater, which is at the site of the old Warner at 13th and E, to see a presentation which people have begun to talk about. It is called "The American Adventure," a multi-media show, and it is a little difficult to describe; but the skeins of it all run to Washington as a place, and as a concept.

I attended it with skepticism, because the idea of a curved eight-panel screen seventy feet wide and twelve feet high showing all sorts of slides and movies all at once seemed on the face of it eclectic. But it is overwhelming to the senses and surprisingly good, and if it has a bias about the civilization and the things Washington represents it is one of optimism, which is fine with me these days. I can recommend it not only to the tourists who are here this weekend to watch Carolina basketball boys, some of them white, perform mayhem on one another at the Capital Centre and need a stopping-off point, but also to the natives who might come with their children and have a good Bicentennial cry.

I happened to see it on a quiet late afternoon with a group of about twenty black college students from this area, who came as a class with their professor, and I watched it a little through their eyes. During the Revolution there were a few yawns, reminding me in that moment of the two Jewish friends I once took to the Bloody Angle who had to fight hard to stifle their boredom. But I can say that things picked up among the students around the 1850s, a subtle wave of human curiosity which seemed to go through them as the show entered the 1860s, and from then on they were riveted. However, I did not fully comprehend the remark of one of the young black men to his companion when we later left the theater: "Let's go start a war." I was tempted to ask him what he meant, but it was one of those questions you let lapse from time to time in Washington.

The narration is by William Conrad and the music is by the National Symphony. What you get is a panoramic dip into American history through the words and music, movie footage, still photography, and a whole stunning range of special effects. All this touches on such qualities as the courage of simple survival, those three hundred or so years ago, and the idea that tolerance, the toughest part of the experience, may be the very purpose of it. It goes along with Jefferson's notion that the earth belongs to the living, not the dead, and it explores quite realistically not merely the genesis of this compromise city built out of its swamps but the way Washington itself has encompassed the sorrows and triumphs of the imperfect experiment.

This latter is an intriguing subject, and despite the fact that we have all been exposed to a lot of trite words about it, the real meaning of Washington as our fortuitous political focus goes deeply into the wellsprings of our history. It is, of course, only one of a bare handful of political capitals that is not the cultural and business nexus of its nation, along with such places as Berne, Canberra and The Hague among others. Would this country have been any different, in matters of mood and tempo, if New York had been the choice? Or Germantown, which Adams advocated at one point, or Shepherdstown, which Washington himself momentarily favored? Probably not, although I am not too sure. People more knowledgeable than I about governance here tell me the same two or three thousand souls who congre-

114

gate to run things would do so no matter what city they were in, so that if the place were Manhattan they still would not get lost in a miasma of hucksters, money-changers, media moguls, writers and ex-Existentialists, but would probably long ago have taken over P. J. Clarke's all for themselves. But one can say with some assurance that if the site had been elsewhere there would be no Watergate having risen out of Foggy Bottom, nor would there be a Cellar Door or a Sans Souci or hippies on M Street, but mainly a preternatural quiet overlaid by Federal Expressway 95 to Richmond.

"An American Adventure" is obliquely suggestive of all this when it treats of this original hamlet free of ties to the past, unfinished, underfinanced, surrounded by mud, and the struggling town of the Civil War with its five or six federal buildings where Lincoln wandered alone and unguarded in the nighttime with the Rebels twenty miles away, and where Julia Ward Howe looked out her window and saw, stretching into the eternal darkness, the campfires of a hundred thousand men.

5.

LEON HINKLE as we shall call him, is a bookie who lives out in Prince Georges County and works the whole terrain around the District. I met up with him through a friend named Joe Bob Duggett, a buoyant and generous Chapel Hill man, class of '62, who deals in real estate in Georgetown and gives Leon a large amount of business. The three of us had a rendezvous in a shady place over on the Hill this week, a place with enough shadows to make Leon feel anonymous and comfortable, where middle-aged people from the offices hold hands at lunchtime in dark booths.

"He lives from ledge to ledge, and that's the best view," Joe Bob said of Leon one night. We were talking with about fifty other Chapel Hill people, who sometimes seem the only people I meet in Washington, about the techniques of bookmaking in the District and the suburbs. "He's smart and honorable and talks good. And what a head for figures! He's just as professional as a New York bookie, and that's unusual for Washington. He'll even work through his country sources in South Carolina to get a point or two shaved off the spread. With Leon it's more social, a friendship thing. You're doing business with a good Tidewater boy as opposed to a big-time urban operator who's really just a runner for a clearinghouse. Wait and see. He ain't a Damon Runyan."

Leon is forty years old and sells insurance in the daytime; he grew up on the banks of the James River and talks in the Tidewater accent, dipthongs and all. He is the only bookie I ever met who likes to fish for trout, shoot squirrels, and knows about the growing season for peanuts. Also, he keeps a boat in English Harbor, Antigua, a Morgan Outlander 41 called the "Tidewater Wildcard." Because of him I have learned as much about bookmaking down here as an outlander probably needs to know.

"They're bustin' everybody over there in Prince Georges," Leon complained. He was dressed immaculately in a tweed jacket, and on his blond hair he has a cowlick. "Of course, the FBI wouldn't be looking for me because I'm not organized. I'm free private enterprise. The locals haven't bothered me much, but I guess they could knock my door down if they wanted to. There aren't any organized pros around here." There was a fellow here named Billy Martin who had the biggest book in town. "Back then, about twelve years ago, it was damned well organized. Bobby Kennedy broke that up, so Billy went legit and took all his knowledge to Vegas."

There is no Mafia in the area that he knows of. "I've

probably known about fifteen different bookies all around the Beltway. I understand that Beltway. I'd know. I don't think there's that much money in it here for the Mob."

Bookmaking is tougher for the bookies, or "holes," as they are called in the vernacular of the trade, in Maryland than in Virginia or the District because the bookies there have to compete with the horses and the lottery. Right now Leon's business comes mainly from basketball games (called "baskets" or "roundballs"), and he uses the line put out by the Weekly Sports Journal from North Hollywood, California. He'll take up to $2,000 on one game and $25,000 on one night's piece of action. He works at home on the telephone beginning in late afternoons during the basketball season.

His clients here are doctors, lawyers, businessmen, "a little bit of everybody." But no politicians. "The pols go through a second person, such as a friendly bartender. They're being careful. I don't know of any pols who place their own bets." One of his steady clients is a Justice Department lawyer; another is an undersecretary in a Cabinet department, but he has no elected people. The worst bettor he's ever known is an executive in national television sports who once lost on eighteen straight baskets at roughly a nickel a shot ($500), and Leon says this unfortunate man telephoned after his eighteenth setback and wanted to lay a dime ($1,000) on another basket. "I told him there weren't any games that night but we had some hockey action, and he said, 'I don't know anything about hockey.' You'd think he'd have inside information, but he's awful. As we say, he couldn't pick his nose."

When Leon moved to Washington he lived for a while in Southern Towers off Interstate 95 in the direction of Alexandria, the swinging place of the 1960s with considerable and diverse activity of all kinds after dark. He

117

was gambling a lot and people kept asking him to place their bets. "Rather than laying the bets I'd start sitting on them," and that's how he got started in the business. "I'm usually paying up front. People who lose are notoriously late. You need about ten or fifteen grand at all times. You keep it in a safe-deposit box, and it may be gone in three hours. I'm extending more credit than the Riggs National Bank." He has debts outstanding to him right now of about $25,000. "Another bookie stiffed me for $19,000, and he's only paid off four.

"Not too many people in this area make a living betting, unlike New York. People aren't that aware here. It's more a transient place, a prestigious place. Hell, the whole government's here." Most of the bettors are city people between the ages of twenty and forty. He says people who came through the Depression don't want to take any risks.

There are probably about twenty bookies in the District area, large and small. "Most of them are uneducated, unorganized. They're just amateurs compared to the New York boys. The ones who've been around a long time are consistently in trouble, always owing money. That's on sports. I'm not talking about horses and the lottery." There are several big entrenched colleagues who deal only with serious bettors—five or ten thou a night people." Bettors like our friend Joe Bob Duggett are called "squares," 100 or 200 a night types.

There are quite a few fly-by-nighters and a lot of Italians in the trade. But all of them drive Cadillacs, dress well and live in the suburbs. Leon sees them to pay and collect. Either them or bagmen. They meet in prearranged places outdoors such as street corners. Last week he met a bag man in front of the old Episcopal Church in Alexandria, and once, on a big job, near the Tomb of the Unknown Soldier.

One of the most successful bookies in the District is

a black who deals in the numbers with blacks and in sports with whites. "I don't know of any Jews. They may be backing with money, but they don't come out front. But I'll tell you one little ol' thing. The Jews here are the best gamblers I've ever known. They research it here like they do everything else. They're very professional. I've never known a Jewish loser."

It is a difficult business, full of wrong turns, and Leon knows its hazards. Sometimes during our lunch in the shady place he looked toward the doorway, and he stopped talking when strangers came by. Every time a suspicious person drifted through, this would prompt him to complain about his work.

"Bookies are at a real disadvantage," he said. "If the client doesn't pay off, you're in trouble. But if the bookie doesn't pay, all the sucker has to do is call the FBI down the street and say, here's this guy's name, here's his home number . . ." He shook his head morosely and gave us a melancholy Tidewater look, as if his honor were in jeopardy.

He knows one bookie here who made a little money one year and became overconfident, and then lost $100,000 in six months. "The big bettors who study sports, and research it carefully, can beat your brains out. There's so much information now. A smart fellow can do a lot better at this racket than he can in the stock market."

Leon is certain about one thing: he has dealt with more dishonest souls than he has honest ones around here. It has nothing to do with the job a man has, he says, or his position in civic life or the church. A man is either honest or dishonest, and that's that.

"I don't want to sound stuck up, but it's the last gentleman thing in this town, what I do. You've got to come off dependable because there's tremendous suspicion on both sides. I look at it this way—sports betting is very fair to the bettor. You're only bucking five percent odds. Any other betting—craps, horses, you're going up to twenty percent. We're at a disadvantage. You get a couple of people who don't pay, and that blows your five percent. And you have to worry about the law. I don't know why they want to bust 'em in Prince Georges. They should sympathize. Right at this very minute, while we're talking here, a lot worse things are going on in that big white building with the round top on the Hill."

It is also an involved profession, and you have to know what you're doing. "For instance, you get the basketball line here at 6:30 in the afternoon. It closes down absolutely at 7:30, Eastern Standard. That gives you an hour to make all your decisions, to know precisely what you've got on each game, on Maryland, say, or Georgetown or Carolina when those crazy guys from Chapel Hill phone in to bet the Tarheels with all the party noises in the background. The phone rings constantly. You've got to plot some very sophisticated charts. You've got to know how much you want to sit on and how much you want to get rid of. This can involve thirty grand in one sitting. I've got to be writing down one guy's bet and talking with another. It's hairy as a rattler. All you have to do is get something backwards and it'll cost you two grand in five seconds."

But gambling is in the blood of the human species, in the Nation's Capital and everywhere else, Leon feels, and because of that he perceives he is performing a public service, more valuable than any number of government agencies and departmental buildings on Constitution Avenue. "Ol' Sigmund Freud said gamblers want to lose deep down," he snorted. "I heard about a fellow from Bethesda in Vegas who blew ten grand at the roulette, and he jumped up on the table and shouted, 'To hell with Sigmund Freud. I wanted to win!' Freud probably never bet a dime in his life."

There was one sensitive question I had to get out of the way with Leon. Our rendezvous had thinned out, and Joe Bob Duggett, who had brought us together, had to go back to his real estate office to study the lines on the baskets that night, and Leon had to meet a bag man in front of the Commerce Building. The question was, how does he collect his debts, a problem around which there is of course a great corpus of myths.

"Well," Leon drawled. "I've never threatened anybody. I just keep calling him. I stay in touch. I appeal to his honor."

And he added, our gentleman bookie from the banks of the James, with one last glance at the doorway: "I don't know what they do in the Bronx. But from here on south we don't break legs."

6.

WHEN I was growing up in a small delta town in Mississippi, one of our friends made a trip all the way to Washington to visit relatives. I remember the consternation which gripped everyone in town when we found out that our friend's vacation did not turn out well. He had been attacked and badly mauled in one of the parks up there while doing little more devious than picking a handful of flowers.

For a long time people in town discussed how Jack DeCell had been jumped by a roving black gang, as if what were happening in Washington in those muted days in the Deep South was a threat and an affront to the very structures of our life. What was going to become of us if a pleasant white Mississippi boy suffered a gratuitous head-knocking in the capital of the United States?

The talk here today is of violence. I have never quite seen anything like it. In restaurants, bars, buses, I have

121

seen the full extent to which people are obsessed with it, exchanging all those tales about aimless violence to themselves, to their friends. Everyone has his own story, it seems, and this is the Washington prerogative, talking about the sudden panic and defenselessness. There is no reason even to invest this pervasive fear with symbolism, this failure to accommodate to simple human safety in what we are told is the capital of the world, for it is such an everyday thing, mundane almost, enmeshed in the substances of ordinary life. Make no mistake that this is a frightened city, even more than the more beleaguered precincts of New York which can be as miasmal as the next; the fear is more encompassing, and the likely next victims feel they are outnumbered.

Apartment houses now have dial systems to unlock front doors. The new living complexes in Southwest are gaunt and forbidding fortresses, spectres out of Orwell, everything arranged for the illusion of security. I took a wrong turn into an enormous apartment garage the other night and the sign inside the entrance said: "You are under television surveillance." In the Washington Star Building, many people leaving after twilight ask an armed guard to accompany them to their cars. And there are the things I have seen on the streets, the way people look about furtively, at certain times of the day, a heightened awareness simply in the way people walk.

The murder last week of an elderly society matron in Northwest during a mugging by three teen-agers has galvanized this special Washington malaise, much as the injury to Sen. John Stennis three years ago. I once dined with Barry Goldwater in a hotel in Haiti when the Haitian government dispatched six bodyguards with sten guns to follow him everywhere. "I'm safer here than back home," he said.

There is nothing like casual violence against someone who presumably makes the system work to convince your average rider of buses of his own vulnerability. And *The Washington Star* recently noted that in a one-week period a year ago there were fifty muggings in Washington, none of which made the newspapers.

The matron's son was perhaps performing a service when he posed the question: what harm had she done to anyone? Even though she had apparently been warned about the neighborhood, why couldn't she live wherever she chose to? The blow to her head which fractured her skull was done by a soda bottle, surely no easy thing to do, unless the rage and hostility behind that blow was unbelievable.

From my reading of our history, I have always believed the central thread that runs through us as a people is the relationship between the white man and the black man in America. Perhaps it takes a Southerner to know in his heart the extent to which we in the cities, and especially in this one, are paying the terrible price of slavery.

The founding fathers, to whom we now pay homage, and for whom the national television commercials in this Bicentennial year may be wreaking their own peculiar vengeance, were ambiguous at best, most of them, about the horrendous future price of that institution, to the breaking of families, to the crime of it. They were not brought here on the Cunard Line. It took the bloodiest war in the history of mankind up until then to so much as partially delineate that relationship. As we have sown, so shall we reap.

The mass migration of the black people of the South to the cities of the North in the 1930s and 1940s was an exodus out of the settled folk culture of the Southland which the novelist Ralph Ellison explored so vividly in his book *Invisible Man*. There was nothing like it before, this wholesale uprooting, producing a life in city streets that was more often than not hostile and root-

123

less, with little at all to fall back on. It is a phenomenon that the whole society and the institutions of that society have not confronted in its full human dimensions. The irony is that it is in the small to middle-sized cities of the South, precisely those places which as recently as fifteen years ago were condemned by the North for an impregnable racism, where workaday racial tolerance is working more effectively than anywhere in America. Yet hopeful as this may be in a broader context, there is little value for the cities in dwelling on it.

But it is from all of this, and one's own impressions as an outsider, which makes me feel the most important thing in Washington is not the detente with the Chinese and Russians, or whom the Democrats might or might not bundle off to the White House, or whether it will be Ford or Reagan in New Hampshire, but the relationship between the races in this town. It is a thing of high and brutal torment, and it is killing us.

7.

THE WRITER James Jones and I and our teenage sons were doing the battle country. We saw the car parked outside the Civil War Museum in Chancellorsville, an undistinguished sedan of some years' vintage with District of Columbia plates and a faded George Washington University decal on the window. On the doors and the back were the faint contours of the words someone had tried to scrub away—"Just Married"— and inside, on the front seat, a few scattered grains of rice.

We sighted them for the first time several minutes later, gazing in the reverential semi-darkness at a museum exhibit which outlined the casualty figures between the Rapidan and the Rappahannock in the spring and summer of 1864. They were both in their middle twenties—he a tall, gangling boy with a reddish beard wearing corduroys and a pullover sweater, she a small, pale figure with rather pretty features, wearing a blue dress which somehow seemed out of place in those circumstances, as if she were trying to please him beyond the measure of the moment and the surroundings.

She reached for his hand two or three times, and he would comply for a few seconds and then disengage himself and move on ahead of her to the next window. He seemed unhappy. Perhaps the catastrophic new arrangement bothered him and made him insecure in the secret places of his heart and he wanted a little time to sort it out. Or perhaps it was that these old mementos of death convinced him that he had made an error so cataclysmic that nothing less than his manhood could be at stake, and that he should have borrowed the money and taken the honeymoon in Miami, or even New Orleans, or somewhere a long way from Washington.

We drifted outside at the same time, to the back of the building to visit the monument where Jackson fell to the volleys of his own men. They stood there wordlessly, examining the words carved in the stone, then briefly studied their maps and went back to their car. Soon they disappeared around a bend in the direction of Spotsylvania.

An hour or so later, we were at the Bloody Angle, walking over that ground where the forlorn shape of the trenches remains, and we saw the car turn and come toward us on Bloody Angle Drive, stopping just behind our pickup truck. The two of them emerged and paused before the enormous painting on the plaque there, at what had been the apex of that salient on the precise spot where we stood, showing in close detail the hundreds of men who had killed each other there with bayonets, knives, rifle butts, and pistols. The birds sang all around us; the warm Virginia afternoon could have been springtime if the trees bordering these fields had not been bare of leaves.

He stood with his hands in his pockets, absorbing the details of the painting, then looked up at a jetliner slowly descending toward Dulles or National with immaculate puffs of smoke in its wake, a gesture on his part so casual and mindless and yet so private that it seemed to evoke in the girl, who was standing to the side of him and had been observing him there, an emotion of sorrow and bewilderment.

Now it was our turn to depart, leaving them to that haunted place, but I sensed that we would see them yet again, and more than once, much as I sensed such things in those years I was a student in Europe when the dollar lasted a long time and the green passport rode high—when you might see the same couple from Pennsylvania in a tour group on the Left Bank one day and at Versailles the next, then Avignon or Nimes, and never really speak, out of mutual embarrassment, that or the ennui of being with too many other Americans in Europe in 1959.

So it was no surprise that after we stopped for a while in the Wilderness, then ascended into the Blue Ridge to lose the taste of destruction, dipped into the Shenandoah and made a loop around the Massanutten before going north, we found ourselves at an adjacent table in the motel restaurant on the mountainside in Harpers Ferry the next morning. That was when I discovered, eavesdropping as hard as I could on the strained, sparse fragments the honeymoon couple exchanged, that he works for one of the agencies, that he comes and goes in a carpool in the farthest of the suburbs and that they had best be getting back tomorrow. When she asked him why they should go back now, he said it was just the time, that was all.

Harpers Ferry is not the ghost town I once loved, not

126

since the federal government more or less took it over, but it was quiet and lustrous on this day and with so few visitors about and the rippling of the Potomac and the Shenandoah from their lonely banks was the evanescence of every lazy childhood. The couple had come there too, of course, to view the sight where Brevet-Colonel Lee and Lieutenant Stuart of the United States Marines had been dispatched to find John Brown, and in the small cluster of tourists the couple had noticed, as we had, the presence of a celebrity, a figure to be reckoned with on the national talk shows, a singer of masculine eminence who also acts and plays the guitar and who at this moment was in the company of a lovely brunette whose silhouette bedazzled us. As we looked at the ruined outlines of John Brown's last stand, we heard the singer, whose name was Glen Campbell, ask his companion if she had brought along their map of the village.

It was the most astonishingly perfect *deja vu* from literature I have ever experienced. It was straight from Walker Percy's *The Moviegoer* when the young groom in the French Quarter of New Orleans gives Bill Holden the light for his cigarette, so close to it that at first I watched as if it were a dream I had had a long time ago, or an old prescience of truth unfolding, as if Percy were a prophet of the human heart. Here, in Harpers Ferry, the boy was at first more apprehensive. He withdrew his map and approached the celebrity, tapping him gently on the shoulder.

The man turned about, with that irritation of all such souls with well-known faces who have had their flesh touched too many times by strangers. But when he saw the boy was offering him what he had asked for, he smiled generously, and the two of them walked away a few steps to confer on the locale. And when the boy finally gave him the map, he smiled again and thanked him warmly, then with a gesture of farewell, left down

127

the street with his companion.

The boy went back to his bride, and he too was smiling, the first we had seen in two days from him. The aura of recognition had seized on him. In his casual brush with greatness, in this village of blood and lost causes, of pillage and rapine, perhaps he felt he had performed well before her. Or he had a story to tell in the office. Or he had retrieved something in himself which profoundly mattered to him.

Who knows the true reason for such human things? Surely it is enough that the two of them walked away benignly now, leaving us all the happier also as we turned once more to the ground where Brown, Lee, and Jeb Stuart's lives had briefly converged. Then we left in our pickup truck for Antietam.

8.

I CAN thank the CIA, moiling now in the revelations we are given of it, for my first true introduction to this town, to the responsibility and thrall of its theatrics. I hold the CIA culpable also for my first glimpse of your precinct of Georgetown, which claimed me, as it does many of us, in a nearly trance-like vise. This was 1965, and Arthur Schlesinger, Jr. and Ted Sorensen had just published, in two reputable mass-circulation magazines which are no longer with us, the chapters on the Bay of Pigs from their forthcoming books on John Kennedy. I had not yet turned thirty, a very junior editor on *Harper*'s magazine, hoping most of all, as I recall, to find my way in the tangle of Manhattan literary politics, from which Capitol Hill—if it ever acknowledges a master in its own game—might one day acquire valuable insights into logrolling. Allen Dulles, the former director of the CIA who had been out of power since late 1961, had told my boss at *Harper*'s, John Fischer, that he wished to write a rebuttal to Schlesinger and Sorensen, a defense of the CIA in the Bay of Pigs. Fischer sent me down to Washington to help Dulles put his piece together.

I arrived on an Indian summer afternoon, one of those elusive late-September days when the white facades of the official town seem to swim in the sadness of its memories. The old man who greeted me at the door of his mansion on Q Street in Georgetown was legendary long before, surely not at all an ordinary mortal. "It's hard to operate with legendary figures," Kennedy had said of him, when the consequences of the Bay of Pigs were finally in, and I was fearful that he might be as cold and rigorous as his brother John Foster had been— a Calvinistic figure to me when he was Secretary of State, with his unbending rhetoric on massive retaliation and brink-of-war—or as forbidding as his own occasional photographs on the front page of the *Times*. But from the moment we sat down to our twelve-hour work days in a study overlooking a sedate walled-in terrace I knew I was in the company of a courtly and civilized man, a little precise at first on the arcane calling which had obsessed him since his OSS days in Bern, but still an easy man to be with, curious and feeling about his fellow creatures, a casual and entertaining host, and—best of all—an engrossing raconteur, especially with stories about spies.

We worked hard, he with his sleeves rolled up at the table where we met each morning, I with a small pile of notes gleaned from much of what had been published up to then on the Bay of Pigs. He relied on me to pose the right questions for his answers to Schlesinger and Sorensen. I came across a few of those questions not too long ago in a yellowed notepad. Why did he and the other planners overestimate the strength of the Cuban resistance organizations? Why did they believe a successful beachhead could be established so easily? Why did they not see the impossibility of an escape into the Escambray? Were they wise in envisioning a continuous enlargement of the perimeter around the beachhead for a long period? And there were many more.

In this heady exercise, my attention was drawn to a sizeable collection of bound Joint Chiefs of Staff and CIA documents which he had brought with him when he left office, all stamped in red: "Top Secret—For Eyes Only." He referred to them constantly, keeping them in front of him on the table as if they reassured him by merely being there, quoting and paraphrasing them as I took notes, mulling over them in long silences. His mind wandered as the day waned.

His family was at the Dulles compound in Watertown, New York, on Lake Ontario, and in the summer twilights, after my questions and his soliloquies, the two of us took walks around Georgetown. The first lamps flickered above the rusty brick sidewalks and I looked into the enormous lower rooms of those mysterious dwellings and saw the bookcases lined with books and impeccable furnishings. I never saw real people stirring around inside, although I felt there had to be people about somewhere. Here the two of us were, the old gray eminence and the ambitious young editor, chattering about the Cuban Brigade or those early meetings with Kennedy and his new men in the Cabinet Room. Then back to the terrace behind his house for two or three scotches before our lonely dinner, where I asked him what Europe was like during the War.

Suddenly one afternoon he said:

"Well, Morris, I've been telling you my secrets, but I don't know anything about you. For all I know you've been sent here by the Soviets"—the last word said crisply, bitten off at the end.

Emboldened by the scotch, or the strange camaraderie I felt we had established, I remember replying: "Mr.

Dulles, I was your man in Budapest for five years."

A widening of eyes, a gesture of the brows: "Yes, I can imagine."

His rebuttal was going badly, and we arranged to meet a few days later in Watertown. This time I flew in from New York with a highly unsatisfactory draft of what we had discussed, along with a dexterious young secretary named Millie Matasia who had scored the best in shorthand among the entire publishing corporation of Harper & Row. Our deadline was approaching, but the difficulties now became insurmountable. Dulles' daughter and his sister, the latter a living image of their brother John Foster, gave every indication that they suspected me of having been dispatched to compromise him, to damage his most esoteric defenses, and to embarrass him before the judgment of history.

In that sylvan mileau—a large house on the water and a cottage hidden in pines where Allen Dulles and Millie Matasia and I went about our labors—I was reminded of Henry James' *The Aspern Papers*, in which an impecunious Englishman comes prowling around the villa in Venice where the aging mistress of a long-deceased heroic poet, presumably Lord Byron, is ensconced, the Englishman plotting to make off with the poet's dog-eared love letters to the old crone, to offer to such literary fences as to this day do commerce in the melancholias of tormented artists.

Not that any of this bore the faintest resemblance to my own innocent motives. My mission was much that of the young lawyer sent to assist an illustrious client. But the mistrust among the client's blood-kin was tangible, as if the two of them, daughter and sister, feared the alien world of Manhattan publishing as much as they feared the world of Kennedys and Washington politicians and other dissemblers just as John Foster had. Working in the cottage in the woods on his dictation, I would hear the rustlings of leaves from outside the window, and then have a quick glimpse of Allen Dulles' tall daughter peering in suspiciously at Miss Matasia and me, her hand over her eyes to shield sun from shadow; or overhear the muted whisperings of sister and daughter in the big house; or catch the swift wisp of a warning to him to be very careful.

In the end none of this distrust, understandable as it might have been, mattered at all. I knew up there on the Great Lakes that my magazine would never get this rebuttal, much as I would still work hard with his words, not because those dearest to him were wary he might be hurt, or that in their solicitude of him they knew he was vulnerable—but because I had come to realize he was old and weary, that something had been lost to him forever from those days of derring-do and adventure with Nazis and Italians that could never now be retrieved, that men other than he had really planned the Bay of Pigs, and that somehow this had less to do with a failure of honor as an inability to perceive true dimensions. Or was that the whole of it?

Near the end of our last day he had a pinched nerve in his back, from leaning down to pull in a boat, and he walked about bent over and in pain. "Well now," he said to us, "what haven't we addressed ourselves to?"

I suggested that he had yet to confront what would have been the minimum adequate air cover on the day of the landings—the strikes which had been cancelled at the last moment by Kennedy.

"Yes." He turned to his documents, paused for an instant, gazed into the woods touched now with the nip of early winter. "Miss Matasia. Take this down!" Momentarily he spoke of four or five Navy jets, no more than that number and then gradually of other things, until out of his memory he was dwelling on something else entirely.

I saw him again the next morning, for the last time, out in the cabin. I looked again at the documents marked "Top Secret—For Eyes Only."

"Mr. Dulles, it certainly would help if I could take these back to the city and work with them."

"Well . . ." It was only a whisper. Then, from a closet in the cabin, he brought out a large shopping bag. The two of us packed the documents inside. "But don't on your life get caught with these," he said. "If you do my name is mud."

That was almost twelve years ago. The client is dead, and the junior editor is not so junior anymore. The Bay of Pigs, for all the regrets and acrimony, has receded into a footnote to the Kennedy years. What I remember most from those days is not the complexities of adequate air cover, but the tales over scotch whiskey of spying against Hitler in the 1940s, and Georgetown unfolding sensually for me in a September sunset.

And the top-secret documents in the shopping bag? They are there today, somewhere, in some boxes I have in an attic in a house on eastern Long Island, among the old debris and paraphernalia of those days.

9.

I FOUND the place, a most unlikely one, quite by accident in Old Alexandria. It is called the Independence Tavern, in the brand-new Holiday Inn on King Street. I walked into the lobby to get a newspaper, and from far down a hallway I heard a girl singing.

I'm not half the girl I used to be,
There's a shadow hanging over me,
Yesterday
Came suddenly.

I went down there out of curiosity, through a corridor, to be greeted by a unique blend of human beings. At the bar was a group of couples in black tie and evening dress, and on the dance floor, as I later surmised it from their talk, quite a few people from Culpeper and Mount Vernon and Woodbridge, the men in pullovers or jackets, the women in gaily-colored pants suits. The ones in formal dress turned out to be members of a fancy Alexandria cotillion called The Assembly, if not old families then close enough, stopping in for a drink on the way to their semi-annual celebration on the fifth floor. It was one of those Washington juxtapositions, which you won't find at Elaine's or P.J. Clark's, or for that matter at the bars of Holiday Inns in White Plains, Babylon, or The Pelhams.

Whenever I go into a new town, and it is something I learned a long time ago in the newspaper racket, I try to get to know the bartenders and the cops first. The bartender here was a good old boy named Bill Esham from Occoquan, who sells real estate in the daytime. This is the first bartending job he has ever had in the suburbs.

"These are people looking for another place to go," Bill said, "a nightclub in old Alex. Middle-income, basically, with very confused tastes. They're a mixed bag. They like the Top Forty, they like country." He surveyed the dance floor, like a hunter squinting out from the brush, the tables with flickering candles, the walls glowing in lavender light, the waitresses, in short black dresses with ruffles from Quito, Ecuador, and Paris, France, who send money back home.

My attention was drawn to the figure on the podium, a strikingly lovely dark-haired girl, tall and lithe in a red and green and black floor length gown, who at this moment was singing and playing a guitar.

Think of all that we've been through
Breaking up is hard to do.

134

I asked Bill her name.

"She's Martha Sandefer."

"She's awfully good."

"She sure is."

The number ended, and then she said into the microphone, in a lilting and altogether child-like voice: "Have yourself a few more drinks. After all, it's Friday night in Virginia, and you'll have tomorrow to recuperate. Moving on with great speed and accuracy, here's a disco tune, just when disco was flowering. Now it's a full-grown tree."

I started coming in there occasionally, after long days with various eminent souls in the District. Martha's songs, her lyrics of loss and lament, of old loves betrayed or forgotten, were something I looked forward to after I came in off the icy, deserted streets, and I began talking with her a little during her breaks. She would order hot tea, and we would talk about each other, and we became friends, in the manner of late-night people in populated places. Sometimes the bar would be crowded, with people shouting requests from all over the room. At other times almost no one was there, when that peculiar languor of loneliness had set in, the loneliness of single men in dark places, when songs elicit a mood of solitude.

She is twenty-three years old, and she grew up in Silver Spring, where she taught herself the guitar and started singing in the coffee houses in junior high school. Now she lives with her parents, who are both retired.

"They like me living there," she says. "I think it gives them a sense of movement, and I believe they're kind of proud I'm a singer."

Her mother was a minister in the Unity Church, one of those offshoots into "humanistic religion," she says, which held its services in the downtown "Y" in the District, and her father worked for years in various Peoples

Drug Stores around the area. She was religious as a child, "a very obedient kid," but she left the Unity Church when she was around fifteen. "I was trying to define those nice, high philosophical thoughts, but people weren't talking about those things, much less living by them." She went to Kalamazoo College in Michigan for a year or so after she graduated from high school. "I wanted to get away from the East Coast, to find some small college with a sense of community. Then I came back. It was too small, you know. You get used to Washington, to hanging out everywhere." She went on to the University of Maryland for three years, working on a degree in education, and she still wants to go back there someday and become a teacher, unless she makes it at singing.

She has been singing in places like this for money for a year and a half. Usually she thinks of herself as a hippie college type, and she likes going around any old way, "but I wear nice dresses and do up my hair to sing and make a salary." She makes $180 a week on this job, and there have been times when she has made as much as $250. It's the first time she ever had a little money of her own, and she finds herself spending it all.

"The District is strange," she says. "It's very heavy on current disco. In this club, I was expecting more people wanted country music, like out in Bethesda. But Holiday Inns and Ramada Inns have the same kind of people, business people, transients. This is what we call a commercial 'gig,' a Top Forty. Most of the people who work them had rather be playing their own tunes. But they end up playing the Top Forty rather than their own."

She is an open girl, warm and friendly and almost sweetly innocent. Some men misinterpret this, she says, and try to make a play for her when she is working, so she relies on one of the young men in her trio—Steve, the drummer from Culpeper, or Mike, the organist from Alexandria.

"Most of the girls around here in music are kind of in a sad state. They play a certain role, a woman's role, a victim. But I feel lucky and special. Every year I get older I find how much younger I am. Sometimes it gets frustrating, doing the same old thing, the same tunes all the time, night after night. Sometimes I just sing for myself. But you can make of it what you want. I'd hate to stagnate. It's a challenge to make a song different, no matter how simple and predictable they are. When someone likes what I do, feels the warmth of what I'm trying to put across, I'm very happy. I mean, really happy."

And, of course, there have been people who have put her on by saying they can give her a big break. "A lot of men come up in this business and say, listen, I used to work for Columbia, and I know this great guy who'd like your stuff. It happens all the time. The first time— wow!—but then you learn, you realize it doesn't work that way, you have to do it on your own. But I'm not sure it'd really be nice to be famous. It seems like such a liability."

Then she pondered this, laughing a little and looking out over the mostly deserted surroundings one night, the Muzak blaring during one of her breaks: "Maybe it'd be great to be playing in big places before big crowds who love what you're doing."

One night last week I dropped in there, to meet an old friend who is in politics from Missouri. He is in the midst of a divorce, having lived in Georgetown until his marriage split up, and now he reads more books than he ever did and likes out-of-the-way places. He has moved to Mount Vernon and taken to stopping by George Washington's house there in early mornings to let the traffic thin on the Parkway and to dwell on himself and Missouri politics and the intricacies of divorcing and

137

joining the great army of the incompatible, while looking over the mists on the Potomac River beyond Washington's slave quarters.

He had had a few drinks and was waiting for me. Martha was singing "Midnight Blues" and my friend said: "You know, she's great!"

There was merely a smattering of patrons on this rainy weekday evening. The lavender shadows danced on the walls, and the girls from Quito and Paris were lounging around with nothing to do. On the dance floor a large woman in green, bosoms bobbing to the tune at hand, was swaying and gyrating with her partner, and my companion said: "You've got to believe that girl's been in every truck stop in the South."

At the next table, two young men were talking. One of them, from Detroit and stopping over at the hotel, was posing a question to his friend, a local fellow, and we paused for the instant to listen.

"Alexander couldn't be such a Southern town. It's too close to Washington."

"Aw, come on. Sure it was Southern. Ol' Lee grew up here."

"You mean, Confederate flags wavin' in the breeze and all that?"

"Sure, man."

I can't keep from crying
Like a heat wave burnin' my heart . . .

"Goddam!" my friend said. "She really is good. She's got a look about her. I hope she's not like Miss Carrie. You know, in *Sister Carrie* by Dreiser?"

His gaze wandered across the empty facades, and he said, conspiratorially: "What you ought to do is go over there in the corner and interview Sally Quinn." Indeed, the blond girl sitting at a far table looked like my old friend Sally from the opposition press across town, not as good-looking as Sally but a resemblance nonetheless, but the big man in the leather jacket and the red baseball cap with the letters "F.C." (Falls Church?) sitting next to her was probably not an editor, and most assuredly was not Ben Bradlee.

"My name is Martha." Her voice drifts through the microphone. "That's Mike and that's Steve. We'll be here 'til midnight, so stick around 'til we get back. If you've got anything you want to hear, please give us a try."

She dips down from the podium, radiating a friendly hello, and my friend the Missouri politican stands up and asks if she has a favorite song.

"Love Has No Pride."

And why does she like it?

"Well, it's about a victim. Here I am devastated by you, and you left me. I guess one of the things music expresses is the terrible emotions we feel. When I love somebody I feel close to, it's that feeling of wanting him back. That's suffering. That's when you have no pride."

In a moment she returns to her singing; only two or three couples are there on the floor.

I've had bad dreams
Too many times
To think they don't mean much anymore.
Fine times have gone
And left my sad home . . .
Love has no pride
No one's to blame
I'd give anything to see you again.

She sings it with feeling, the best I ever heard her. As we get up to leave, her words follow us out, echoing after us in a midnight gloom, out into the village of ol' Lee—a pretty young girl in a flowing dress, from Silver Spring, singing for herself.

10.

"I DON'T think we'll have any springtime for you down here," the voice on the phone said. "We lost it in about the last forty-eight hours," reminding me of what my mother had predicted on the line from Mississippi that day: "Everything's putting out, but we're in for some more weather."

He was right. Washington the next morning was caught in a sudden snow, and the twin-prop Piedmont plane at National got ice on its wings even before we took off and had to be thawed out. The plane buffeted in the snow and fog, and the pilots were warned not to try to land across the Blue Ridge at the first stop in the Shenandoah Valley.

We finally touched down in a swirling fog at Winston-Salem, and I took the rented car west over icy roads into the mountains. It had the feel of Thomas Wolfe country, the rust-red earth, the Catawba River coming down from the hills, the forsythias and the pear trees nearing full bloom on this dismal day, road signs with the place-names Mocksville, Cooleemee, Cornatzer and Eufola: "Out of the darkness, strange as time." In this lonely drive I felt once again my profound love for this state: Old Catawba! It has given us Chapel Hill and haunting terrain and head-for-head the best newspapers and some of the most civilized people in America, a state that deserves and receives the loyalty and memory of those who have been nourished by the fineness of it.

And then Morganton, a quiet town with a courthouse square surrounded by old stores from the turn of the century and brand-new ones, the South Mountains seeming to come down right into its backyards, and people with the mountains and the country in their faces. I had expected his building to be right on the square, like Gavin Stevens' who practiced the law in Yoknapatawpha County, ancient brick with an outside wooden stair-case; but it, too, was a new one, and a block or so from the courthouse.

I went inside and took an elevator to the second floor and was welcomed with much warmth by a secretary. And there he was, Senator Sam, emerging from an of-fice crammed with books and windows overlooking some open space and a water-tower for a hosiery com-pany—the nervous eyebrows and eyes, the mischievous look that confounded Mr. Erlichman in that classic though unequal American confrontation and played hell with the whole cosmos and confection of Southern Cal-ifornia, the sparse white hair plastered down, and with it all the peace and calm of eighty years on the Lord's good earth. Not as large as I expected him to be from the television, where sometimes he seemed a little bigger than life, but solid, substantial, and in one fine mood, and I told him there wasn't another man in America I'd have come down so far in these elements to see, nearly getting myself impaled on the Blue Ridge in the process.

"Well, come on in and we'll talk about it."

It wasn't just the things we talked about through that long day, I suppose, although we talked about God, war, Shakespeare, Tennyson, Churchill, Kipling, Lincoln, Tom Wolfe who was with him at Chapel Hill and whom he knew in the Sigma Upsilon literary fraternity, Jeffer-son, greased-eels who lie in public, the United States of America and poker-playing Protestants, to an extent that I can only touch the surfaces of it here, as it was the substance and texture of him, the gestures of a brilliant and happy and very funny man, the playfulness and then the intensity on some of the old verities, and the pleasure of two men of different ages so spontaneously getting along, and laughing so much that at one point Miss McBride stuck her head around the door to see what was going on, or to see if we had opened the corn gourd, as if we had known one another for years.

Perhaps in a way we had. I wrote once, back during the Watergate days, that he reminds me of my grandfathers and my uncles. He makes me miss them in their graves. He talks in the accents and phrases of my boyhood. He helps me remember.

He lives about half a mile from his office these days, and he gets in about ten, goes home for lunch, and comes back and stays til about six or seven. No, he doesn't miss Washington, he honestly doesn't, he says, because he's formed the habit of not looking back with regret after he's made up his mind. He enjoys being back home, having his books in just two places, the office and the house. When he was in the Senate his books were scattered all over four places, his Senate office, his apartment in Washington, and his office and house down here. Of course Morganton's grown bigger. "When I was growing up it was a town of about 2,000, including the cats and dogs, and I knew where all the cats and dogs belonged. Now it's extended out, and a lot of people have come in from the country."

He doesn't stay in touch with any of the other senators on the committee nowadays either. He talks with Sam Dash on the telephone sometimes, most recently about a column or two Roscoe Drummond had written based on the book by Fred Thompson, the minority counsel, called *At This Point in Time*, which he deems an appropriate title "in view of the fact that they were always saying it." But he considers the Thompson book generous and fair, and feels it doesn't support Drummond's view that it was a corrupt investigation.

Right now he's re-reading all the Watergate books. He just wants to get a different slant on it, he says. He thinks Clark Mollenhoff's recent book is the best and most complete, not only on Watergate but on Nixon, but he also has a high opinion of Bernstein and Wood-ward's.

"Bernstein and Woodward are the men who did so much to unearth it. They were of great help to me. I'd read Xerox copies of everything they'd written in the Post long before the hearings. I called them into my of-fice and said, 'I don't want your sources, I know the journalistic ethics, but I need to know the people you suspect and why.' They gave me a good idea of the peo-ple they suspected but couldn't prove as the ringleaders of the thing, and it was all corroborated by the tapes."

He's been reading other things too, right now for in-stance Fred Friendly's book on free speech in broadcast-ing and the new biography of John Wilkes. "One of Wilkes' critics said he'd either die on the scaffold or of venereal disease. And old Wilkes said, 'Which of these fates awaits me will depend on whether I embrace your principles or your mistress.'" And he's lecturing around the country. The next day he was flying out to Pittsburg, Kansas, to speak to college students, and as soon as he finished he'd take a Lear jet to Pittsburgh, Pennsylvania, to address a business group. He's received very fine, he says, and mainly talks about the Bicentennial and not Watergate, but nine-tenths of the questions are on that. "Many of the students seem to have more of an under-standing on Watergate than some of their elders. They understood it went to the vitals of the system." Lately he has written a long essay on the Bicentennial for the 1976 edition of the "Brittanica," from which he reads a para-graph to me: "The Constitution, which consists of words on a piece of parchment, is not self-executing. It de-pends for its vitality on the love which men and women nourish for it in their hearts, and the fidelity with which public officers chosen by them manifest it. Strange as it may seem, the Constitution has covert enemies who appear to be unaware of their enmity for it. They do not seek to destroy it in one fell swoop. They undertake to nibble it away bit by bit."

The talk moves to other things now, such as the Civil War, and he leans forward in his chair, sometimes with his elbows on his desk, moving the eyebrows as he summons up things. He had a great uncle killed at Second Manassas, another outside Richmond, and a third who was the youngest brother of President Polk had his left leg amputated at Shiloh. He's been to most of the battlefields over the years, and is a student of them. He and one of his Senate assistants used to get in a car on weekends and go to Antietam, Gettysburg, Fredericksburg, the Wilderness.

"I have a grandson, Jimmy, who's nineteen now and a sophomore at Davidson, and once was a page in the Senate. Jimmy and I went over to Gettysburg when he was younger, and a retired general took us on the battle tour, and after a while the general said to Jimmy, 'You know more about this battlefield than I do.' Jimmy knows more than I do about the Tennessee campaigns, but Tennessee's a long way off."

Well, would he have fought for the South? "I'm pretty much of a Southerner," he says, "My grandmother used to say she had this first cousin in the Confederate navy, and when it was all over he wouldn't go back to the Episcopal Church because it had a prayer for the President of the United States.

"Dick Russell liked to tell about Bob Toombs of Georgia, who told his constituents when the states were seceding, 'The Yankees can't do anything about it. If they do we'll whip 'em with cornstalks.' Long after the war down there a man with a patch over his eye and one leg came up to Toombs and reminded him of what he'd said, and Toombs replied, 'The trouble is, you can't ever count on the Yankees to do the right thing. They didn't

144

want to fight with cornstalks.'" And what if the South
had won? "Well," he says, chuckling mightily, "some of
the Northern states would be trying to secede right
now." And it wouldn't have surprised him if the Russians back in the 1950s had confounded John Foster
Dulles by coming into the South to offer foreign aid, and
maybe more.

Once, a few years ago, he met General Ulysses S.
Grant III at a meeting and offered to buy him a drink.
Grant said, a little facetiously, that he didn't know
whether he should or not. "I told him that after Appomattox the Confederates hadn't eaten in days, I had uncles there who hadn't eaten, and your grandfather ordered his officers to share their rations with them. And
General Grant III said, "'Well, under those circumstances, Senator, you can buy me a drink.'"

And now we are talking about Rupert Brooke, one of
his favorites, whom he began reading at Chapel Hill in
1916 before he went off to become a much-decorated
hero. He studied Brooke's poems under Dr. Edwin A.
Greenlaw, who also passed along to him the advice of
Sir Walter Scott, a Scottish lawyer: "A lawyer without
history or literature is a mechanic, a mere working ma-
son; if he possesses some knowledge of these, he may
venture to call himself an architect." Moving a little behind the desk, he recites his best-loved of Brooke:

These laid the world away
Gave up the years to be of work and joy
And that unhoped serene which men call age
And those that would have been their sons
They gave their immortality.

Suddenly he leans to the side of the desk and fetches a
copy of Paul R. Clancy's book, *Just a Country Lawyer*,
which he wishes to sign for my son. He considers this
for a moment or so, then writes in it: "With the hope
that you will study history, which is a light to our future

145

as well as a record of our past. Sam J. Ervin Jr., just a country lawyer."

That gets us on the subject of education, and I remind him that Lyndon Johnson used to boast he had never finished a book.

"I just don't undersand people who don't read, even if for amusement and not edification. Make books your friends. You can summon them to your fireside in times of loneliness. Take Jefferson. A most versatile man. A widely read man. If those people who wrote the Constitution had never read a book, we'd be in a lot of trouble."

What would his advice be to young people trying to get a good education? What is the mark of a civilized human being?

"I think the best thing a person can do to get educated is a desire to keep on learning, long after school. There's an Indian phrase, 'When man attains a hundred years he should cease to learn.' The best education a person can get is a thirst for learning. And I think the true mark of the civilized man is intellectual integrity. I mean facing reality and then coming to conclusions about things in an honest fashion. Being willing to accept the truth, often when it's not pleasant to you." That reminds him of the Dirksen Prayer Amendment. "People didn't quite understand my being against it down here in the Bible Belt. It was hard. My wife said I ran as far away as I could and stepped right in the middle of it. I prayed very fervently the Prayer Amendment would go away.

"I reckon I believe in an orthodox God, except my God is a sort of merciful God." Lincoln often manifested his disbelief in stern and eternal punishment, he says, by quoting the epitaph:

Here lies poor Johnny Kongapod;
Have mercy on him, gracious God,
As he would do if he was God,
And you were Johnny Kongapod.

146

Now as for the Presbyterians, of whom he is one, "They believe in predestination, in the ordered structure of things unfolding. You Methodists have many beliefs, and then when something unusual happens, the Lord is just surprised."

And as for some people's notion of sin, a group of Carolina Protestants got together to play several rounds of poker, under the righteous gaze of the woman of the household. Certain cards floated out to the husband, as the husband's son George stood behind him and watched: the ace of spades, the king, queen, jack and ten. "From across the room the mother said, 'George, look at your father. He's going to hell,' and George said, 'Mama, if he loses with a hand like that he ought to.'"

The day has waned, the shadows come into the office overlookiing the water tower, and we talk a little about the survival of the country. "I think the United States is going to have to change its ways, act more wisely economically. Also, I don't like the kind of diplomacy now with the Secretary of State whispering in the ears of heads of state when the American people don't know what's he's promising. I think we're going to have to realize we live in a very difficult, pressurized world, and take to heart what Cromwell said to his men when they crossed the river near Edgehill: "'Have trust in the Lord but keep your powder dry.'"

It is dark now, and we take the elevator down and stand for an instant outside the new Ervin Building. There is a touch of cold in the Catawba mountain air, and the courthouse up the way is a darkened outline against the sky, and the rustlings of Tom Wolfe are too much to bear. At any moment W. O. Gant will drift by, with stonedust on his hands, and a little tall boy coming in search of him. "I hope our lives will cross again someday," he says.

There is a passage at the conclusion of Kenneth

Clark's *Civilization* which says something about Mr. Sam for me.

"I hold a number of beliefs that have been repudiated by the liveliest intellects of our time. I believe that order is better than chaos, creation better than destruction. I prefer gentleness to violence, forgiveness to vendetta. On the whole I think that knowledge is preferable to ignorance, and I am sure that human sympathy is more valuable than ideology. I believe that in spite of the recent triumphs of science, men haven't changed all that much in the last two thousand years, and in consequence we must still try to learn from history. History is ourselves. I also hold one or two beliefs that are more difficult to put shortly. For example, I believe in courtesy, the ritual by which we avoid hurting other people's feelings by satisfying our own egos. And I think we should remember that we are all part of a great whole, which for convenience we call nature. All living things are our brothers and sisters. Above all, I believe in the God-given genius of certain individuals, and I value a society which makes their existence possible."

11.

DO YOU remember La Belle Aurore in *Casablanca*, where Bogart and Bergman used to hang out and drink champagne and listen to Sam play the song, back in those fine days before the Germans came to Paris? The world always welcomed lovers then, until the Nazis arrived, and Bergman left Bogart standing in the rain at the Gare du Nord.

I've found my La Belle Aurore, which by circumstance is just down Pennsylvania Avenue from the White House, a joyous little place with Impressionists on the walls and food and wine good enough to bring your favorite girl and say to her, "Here's looking at you, kid," or if you're in a mood of introspection to tell her you've been around long enough to know that the problems of three people don't amount to a hill of beans in this crazy world.

Its called Dominique's, and it's also fitting that Dominique D'Ermo, a generous and buoyant owner, was in the French Resistance when he was a boy and says that if a German in one of those green uniforms which haunt him from his boyhood came in the door he would tell him the place was sold out. He left France after the war because he was tired of all the Frenchmen fighting each other.

One of the cliches about Washington is that people go to restaurants to be seen, much as people do in Manhattan when they go to 21 or Elaine's or the old Sardi's, but my friend Dominique says that the same people who go to Rive Gauche or the Sans Souci to look and be looked at come to his place just to enjoy themselves. He has sat down at my table of an evening with a bottle of Dom Perignon and told me the story of his life, which in some ways is a peculiarly indigenous Washington story even if it doesn't seem so on the surfaces, and I think if we heard the rumble of big guns from twenty miles away as they did in La Belle Aurore that day in 1940, Dominique would get word to the Germans, or the Russkies, as Bogart warned the Gestapo major concerning New York, that they would take certain sections of this town at their own risk.

Dominique gets a lot of lawyers, doctors, politicians, O.A.S. and State Department people, secretaries and their bosses. One night recently Mr. Levi, the Attorney General, and Mr. Justice Powell were in earnest conversation at a table. A big shot from the State Department comes in three nights a week, with different girls each time, and Dominique says all three are in love with the man. He bought his restaurant about a year ago when it was called Jacqueline's, and then it was known as a

149

place where State Department people always brought their mistresses. Romances are made here at lunch, he says, and broken at dinner. A couple came in here for lunch a couple of days ago and were very cozy and happy, and they came back for dinner and got in an awful fight. A man named Martin made a late-night reservation and came in on time with a lady. "Mr. Martin?" Dominique asked, and the man said yes, then "Mrs. Martin?" and the lady said, "I'm not Mrs. Martin, I'm Mrs. Johnson," and Dominique said, "Right this way, Mrs. Johnson."

He came to Washington in 1962 at the age of 35. He had attained, he says, the zenith of the pastry business, and had written the Bible of all the pastry chefs in America, *The Pastry Chef's Guide to Modern Baking*, which Harper & Row put into a second printing this year. Prior to that he was an executive in the Shoreham, and the Caribbean director for the Billy Butlin enterprises, and before he took out his American citizenship papers in 1952 he worked in some of the best spots in Europe, including the Savoy in London. He worked for a while in Miami Beach, where he got in a crowd of mad French gamblers who played the horses and dogs in the afternoons and shot craps by night, but the only things the patrons of the hotel where he worked wanted were apple pie and cheese-cake. Sometimes they wanted swans and elephants made out of ice cream. This was a letdown after the Savoy, and that was when he decided he would have his own restaurant someday.

Dominique knows a great deal about life, all its swirls and dervishes, and that includes the French community in Washington. When he talks about them, and about his days in France during the Occupation, his accent is a little like Chevalier's, and you have to lean down over the champagne glass to listen more closely, or else you will lose the drift. "Let me tell you about the French

150

colony here. Most of the French in Washington outside of the Embassy are hairdressers, waiters, kitchen employees, restaurateurs. The French people like to be organized. It's the only similarity they have with the Germans. The French must have someone to tell them what to do. Since nobody's telling them what to do here, the French community you have here is very chaotic."

He was standing on the street corner on the Champs Elysee one afternoon after the war. "I'd just come back from all the blood and scenes of horror with the Maqui. I heard guns." All around him Frenchmen were beating each other up. The veterans of Free France were clashing with the Communists. A man came toward him and punched him with a pair of brass-knuckles. He was in the hospital 10 days, and when he got out he told his mother and father, "I can't stay here any more. I'm scared."

He was a teenage boy in the Occupation, living in the woods arounds Lyon. He and his friends robbed drugstores for cigarettes to give to the resistance fighters, and then he got in deeper with them. In 1943 the instructions from the Liberation were to liberate three cities: Nantua, Oyonnax and Savoie. They ran up the Cross of Lorraine in these places and were the heroes of France. These were the only three cities occupied by the Free French during the war.

About then the Germans brought a whole Panzer division into southern France. While you're on your way there, they were told, you might just as well destroy those towns. "They came in with planes, tanks, they had the help of the French collaborators, and let me tell you there was no pity. We had bazookas, sten guns, and grenades, and that was as far as we went.

"We were scared because we were so young. All of us were between 16 and 20 years old. I was in a truck on a road when one of those Messerschmidt 110's dove down.

151

I saw the German pilot, I saw the flame coming out of the guns. I was hypnotized. I thought of my aunt who died in a monastery and told me we'd meet someday in paradise. I couldn't move. My friends were in a ditch shouting, 'Dominique, Dominique. Hide!' I thought, if I move my blood will run out. Then we ran away from the Germans. We ran and ran and starved to death." They begged bread and butter from people who gave it to them and then told them to leave. They arrived at a railroad track about three miles from Nantua and saw eight or 10 German soldiers. They had a conference among themselves about whether they should starve to death, or surrender, or be killed. "We were tired, beat, hungry, and we gave up."

They were taken to Gestapo headquarters and saw a German SS man beating a little kid with a whip. Fifty people were put in a cell half the size of his restaurant. They were interrogated two or three times a day about where they had gotten their bread. Later they were taken to the courthouse in Nantua, 10 of them chained together. "The same people who greeted us a week before were spitting on us, jeering at us. I was crying so much, I was so afraid. They didn't kill us. They kept us in jail. I remember those terrible days, sitting here five blocks from the White House, entertaining senators and diplomats. How strange it seems now. We could've been transported to the hills and killed." The Germans shot 20 from the Resistance in Lyons. They took five boys, about 16 years old, and hanged them on butcher-hooks in a public place. They had their hands tied behind them, and they were bleeding to death. The German soldiers were standing around laughing, smoking cigarettes, taking photographs of the boys. People begged the soldiers to take them down, or to shoot them because they were dying so slowly.

Dominique sits now at his favorite table, orders some

more champagne. The waiters bustle by with the fine camaraderie of the place. People know each other here, and send over greetings to him and to other tables. Dominique and I are still talking about the war, about suffering, and about America. "The Germans were murderers by profession. The Maqui became murderers by chance. Germans killing French. French killing French. You get people to die, people to suffer, people to survive, and that's what it's all about."

And then he laughs a little. "From all the blood and tears, I even feel relaxed now. Relaxed and happy. I have a house, a nice family, two kids in college. I own my own little business and it's five blocks from the White House. I walk around a lot. This afternoon was a beautiful day. I walked from here to Lafayette Square. While I was walking I met about 10 people I knew—lawyers, people in government who come here, and they all said hello to me. From all the chaos and blood of that time I thought: I really am proud of this civilization. It's a great feeling, just to have this freedom here. I'm Dominique D'Ermo, nobody's going to tell me what to do. I'm an American. This is a refuge from the barbarians, because civilization is protected here. This country will protect civilization. And the people will die for it if they have to, whether they like it or not."

And then he adds: "And on top of that, my friend, I'm interested in what's on your plate and what's in your glass." At which point, if one is the romantic I am, you would expect to hear a little something from the original score, the brass and violins, slipping from *The Marseilles* into Sam's piano, the love songs and laughter, the hearts full of passion, the jealousy and hate.

I am not Resigned

I WAS SITTING in Rick's, a bar on Main Street in Bridgehampton, talking with Rick and a couple of the potato farmers about baseball. From outside the big window I saw him park his car behind mine and cross the street in our direction, a pale figure in blue jeans, and a sweater, a green-and-yellow baseball cap, and the leather satchel with the strap flung over his shoulder in which he carried his cigars and a few of his knives.

He walked in and came up to me. "Your mom just died," he said. "I'm sorry."

She had gone into the hospital that week in my hometown in Mississippi. Nothing very serious, the doctors said, but I had made reservations on the plane for the next day. She had died suddenly that morning. Some friends there had tried to telephone me at home, then called his house down the road from mine in Sagaponack.

"I been looking all over for you," he said. "The cops had it out on the radio. Come on home with me for a while. You shouldn't be alone."

Grief comes first as in a trance. Physical things stand out sharply. It is as if you are someone else, being observed from afar by yourself. Yet even in this moment, or perhaps because of it, driving through the countryside with his car following mine, I acknowledged for

The Atlantic Monthly, March, 1978.

the first time that the two great presences in my whole life were my mother, who had just died, and this man, my friend Jim Jones; I did not know that he, too, would be dead within the month.

We drove the mile or so to his house. I had two hours before leaving for La Guardia. I telephoned the undertaker in Yazoo, and the preacher and some friends, and my son David in school in New York. I sat alone in the front room of the old farmhouse, among the hundreds of books lining the shelves. The big dog named Wade Hampton Jones lay asleep close to me, and two cats who only understood French darted here and there. I looked around at the antiques Gloria and he had brought back from their years in Paris. Outside the potato fields stretched away in a somber haze. When they moved into this house two years before I had christened it "Chateau Spud."

Jim was in the next room, writing in a notebook at the ancient wooden pulpit which they had found in the flea market and turned into a bar, then brought back to America. Near him were more shelves, dominated by the leather-bound copies of each of his ten books which he had signed for his children Kaylie and Jamie on their various birthdays—*From Here to Eternity* first, then *Some Came Running*, *The Pistol*, *The Thin Red Line*, and the others. I watched him for a while as he wrote in his notebook. He looked gaunt and tired.

He had almost died three months before. His son Jamie had come to fetch me. It was during a blizzard on a night in January. He had had another serious attack of his illness—congestive heart failure—and the men from the volunteer ambulance unit could not get the ambulance up the driveway. We had to carry him down a slippery embankment to take him to the hospital in Southampton. He had been working harder than any

155

writer I had ever known, sometimes twelve or fourteen hours a day in the cluttered attic in this house, trying to finish the novel which had obsessed him for years, the one he considered his life's work. He called it *Whistle*, the third book in his trilogy of World War II. I had known for months he had a premonition he was fighting against time.

Now, in the next room, he turned around facing me.

"Are you okay?"

I was thinking about grief, I said, how strange it is.

He emitted a characteristic sound, half sigh, half defiant growl. "There's a poem," he said. "It's one of my favorites." He went to the bookshelf and pulled out a first edition of Edna St. Vincent Millay. He thumbed the pages, then sat down and read the poem to himself.

"Do you know this one?"

I read it for a long time.

"I'll go upstairs and type it out for you. Maybe you'll want somebody to read it at your mom's funeral."

It was time to go. He came down the stairs in the chair-lift he had rigged up after his last attack to take him to and from the attic. We stood for a moment in the airy sunshine. The first touch of spring, always late to eastern Long Island, was all around us. We shook hands, in that shy, casual way old comrades do. "You know I'd go with you if I could," he said. "I have to finish *Whistle*."

On the plane to Mississippi, somewhere high over the Blue Ridge, I read the poem again before handing it to my son David.

> I am not resigned to the shutting away of loving hearts in the hard ground.
> So it is, and so it will be, for so it has been, time out of mind:
>
> Into the darkness they go, the wise and the lovely. Crowned With lilies and with laurel they go; but I am not resigned.

Lovers and thinkers, into the earth with you.
Be one with the dull, the indiscriminate dust.
A fragment of what you felt, of what you knew,
A formula, a phrase remains,—but the best is lost.

The answers quick and keen, the honest look, the laughter,
the love—
They are gone. They are gone to feed the roses. Elegant and
curled
Is the blossom. Fragrant is the blossom. I know. But I do
not approve.
More precious was the light in your eyes than all the roses
of the world.

A month later, when Gloria and I were going through
the concluding pages of *Whistle* on his worktable in the
attic, two or three dozen pages before that one final
page which ended abruptly in the middle, there was a
scribbled note in the margin: "April 15, 1977—Willie's
mom died today."

Her friend Hannah Kelly played "Abide with Me" at
the funeral. We buried her in the radiant Mississippi
springtime in the Yazoo cemetery next to my father.

For more than thirty years she had been the organist
in the Methodist church. I remember as if it were yesterday the night Miss Lizzie Hoover, the indomitable old
organist, died and she had to take over. She had taught
piano to four generations of Yazoo's children, on a
Steinway baby grand in the parlor of our house. When I
was a child I would sit in my room, on late afternoons
when it began to get dark, and listen to the music from
the front. I can sometimes hear her music now, after all
the years, and remember the leaves falling in some
smoky autumn twilight, the air crisp and the sounds of
dogs barking and train whistles far away.

Once, not too long ago, she said to me, "I could hear
the typewriter in your room when you were twelve years
old—always scribbling on the typewriter. I knew you

157

were going to be a writer even then. I was that way with a piano. My mother said to me when I was a little girl, 'Well, I guess you better stick with it.'" When my first book came out, I know some things I wrote about the town were hard on her, but she did not complain. When I was the editor of a magazine in New York, she bought more than a few subscriptions and gave them to public libraries way out in the countryside.

The old houses still go by the family names of people long dead. In the schoolyards there are interracial games at recess now, and white and black children arm in arm on the boulevard we call Grand Avenue. I roam the cemetery under its elms and oaks and magnolias to see who has died since my last trip home, and touch with my hand the burial stones I knew by heart as a boy:

"My husband with thee departed all my hopes."
"Asleep in Jesus, Blessed Thought."
"God's finger touched him, and he slept."
"Remembered in Life, Lamented in Death."

The death of the last of one's parents is one of life's great divides. It brings back one's past in a rush of tenderness, guilt, regret, and old forgotten moments, tortures one with the mystery of living. What did all those moments mean? Was there any meaning to them at all? I had the most acute awareness that my son and I were the last of our line.

I was there almost a month. I had to close down the house where I grew up and put it up for sale. No brothers or sisters to share that trial of finding family things in the back corners of closets—a program for my mother's piano recital in 1916, a faded photograph of my father in a baseball uniform in 1920, another of my great-grandmother holding a parasol in 1885, yellowed clippings, trinkets from high school. The movers came to take away the furniture. The last item to leave was the baby grand, which would go to the church.

I telephoned Long Island my last day there. The familiar gruff voice came on, weak and breathless now. He wasn't feeling too good, Jim said. I was driving back East in the morning, and I told him I was going to stop by the battlefield at Shiloh.

"I wish I was going too," he said. "Shiloh's one place I never got to. If you have time, check what western Tennessee looks like to see if I have the physical description right in that chapter." He paused. "Oh, shit. You had to close down your house, didn't you?"

The moment came that I stood alone in the empty house. Did I know then how it would grow to haunt my dreams and nightmares? In the gloom of it that day I strained to hear the music again, my father's footsteps on the porch, the echoes of boys playing basketball in the backyard, the barks and whines of Tony, Sam, Jimbo, Sonny, Duke, and Old Skip. I locked the front door and did not look behind me.

Late the next night, from the motel in the Pickwick Dam State Park just across the Mississippi line in Tennessee and only a few miles down the road from Shiloh, I telephoned again. Gloria had taken him that afternoon to the hospital. He was very sick. "I think it's time for you to get on back," she said.

Just west of Nashville I hit the big expressways, a world to themselves, keeping the speedometer precisely at seventy. The great landmarks of America drifted past: Knoxville and the Smokies, the mountain villages of Bristol and Abingdon, the Shenandoah Valley, the mists of the Blue Ridge and the Massanutten, Lexington, and Winchester and Harpers Ferry, where Jim and I had brought our sons only a year before, on into Pennsylvania and New Jersey.

It seems I am forever traveling out of the South and

into the North, the magnetic points on the compass of my existence, and this was now to me, in retrospect, one of the cataclysmic journeys of my life. Caught there in the serenity of a fast-moving car, using the big diesels to run interference, stopping only for coffee or gas or to sleep or to empty my bladder, I felt the South recede as an element of nature recedes. Ever since my boyhood, driving through the South had never failed to suffuse me with a bittersweet sadness, the sadness of love and belonging, and now something there had ended for me, something irretrievably lost in the land I knew in my heart, some connecting vein with one's own mortality. In the trunk of the car, sealed in a cardboard box, was the family silver, which I had not entrusted to the movers—the same family silver which my great-grandmother had hidden from the Northern troops when they took the town in 1863. On these interminable stretches of freeway, in a drive I managed to make in slightly more than two days, I thought of my friend who lay dying in a hospital out at the easternmost littoral of America. His fate, and the solitary farewell in Mississippi, became enmeshed for me on this drive, one of those junctures which, once passed, becomes symbolic almost, and makes a man ask: What now?

The eastern end of Long Island, when one lives here year round, bears little resemblance to the Hamptons of the summer society columns of our day. The summer influx distorts its true character. In the off-season it is still a rural place with a quiet village life—anything but a "writers' colony," thank God for that. When the summer ends friends fall back upon themselves and people seem relevant again. It is the beauty of the land which helps hold us together. There are hauntingly beautiful days in the autumn when you feel you do not want to be anywhere else. Little wonder some of America's finest painters chose to settle here years ago. You do not have to go to the ocean every day to remember it is there; the roar of it is never far away. Wherever you first came from, when you leave for a while and then return, and finally cross the Shinnecock Canal, you feel you are coming home.

I discovered the area by accident, from the back of a chartered bus years before, with people from *Harper's* going to Montauk for a meeting. In a half-sleep that day, I glanced out my window; things coming obliquely before my eyes brought me awake: lush potato fields on the flat land, village greens, old graveyards drowsing in the sun, shingled houses, ancient elms along the streets, and far in the distance the blue Atlantic breakers. It was the unfolding of one's profoundest dreams, and I knew then I would come back someday for a long time.

It is likely the most lovely terrain in America, and because of that, and its proximity to Manhattan one hundred miles down the road, I feared it would become a parking lot. In summertime the New Jersey plates grew more and more abundant, and this is always a fearsome sign. From an airplane flying into the city, one saw the higher civilization coming out this way: earth ripped raw, shopping centers, developments, all that immense apparatus at the edge of America.

It is a land that enlists loneliness, and also love. It reminds me a little of the Mississippi delta, without the delta blood and guilt—no violence to this land, and it demands little. The village itself, among the oldest in America, remains part of the land which encompasses it. It is a place of bleak winters, of long nights and silences. When my son, as a young boy, came out from the city he walked all over town talking with the farmers and the merchants. One day I noticed from my car this simple tableau: my son on the lawn next to Bobby Van's, having sandwiches for lunch with Spindley, Bobby's ubiquitous golden retriever. The boy and the dog sat there on the grass, motionless almost, in the sunshine of a crisp December noon; the sight of them as I spied on them in their unaffected pose evoked my own small-town childhood, and overcame me with a sadness for mortality.

It is a very small town in the winter, numbering just over a thousand people. The names of the oldest families reflect the Anglo-Saxon blood source. Just as the potato fields bring back the Mississippi delta, the village reminds me of Yazoo, because along the streets, in daylight and in darkness, there are the sounds of Negro voices, all the vanished echoes of one's youth. It is nearly thirty percent black, mostly Southerners brought up a generation or more ago by the farmers, and one of the sadnesses of the town is that it does not have the despair and cruelty and tragedy of remembrance—the shared past, the common inheritance of the land. There is an old Negro man whom we all know, who perambulates around town at all hours, drinking Thunderbird behind hedges and trees, talking incessantly to himself, head aslant in his aimless journey. No one knows where he sleeps, if he does at all. Eight or ten times a day I see him, one moment down by the tracks, five minutes later in the graveyard, then near the church, and I have even sighted him as far away as Sag Pond. Being a Southern boy, I must believe he is a reminder to the town of something it does not truly understand of itself, but then that is a fragile thing. When Jim Jones first saw the old man on one of his endless walks, he said, "I think I knew him in Robinson, Illinois."

There is a fine countermelody of sophisticates and good local people. Once in a restaurant around Christmastime I saw Woody Allen and Diane Keaton dining alone, surrounded by dozens of Rotarians and their wives singing "God Bless America." It is an area abundant in characters—characters of the American species.

162

The radio station encourages telephone calls on all matters from local people, everything from the state of the tides to the rude manners of the New Yorkers, and puts these calls live on the air. Merchants are invited to telephone in their commercials. Once a nursery owner was phoning in his commercial. In the middle of it the announcer interrupted to report he had just received word that a Coast Guard rescue helicopter was on its way to get a sick sailor off a Russian trawler eighty miles south of Long Island. "Go ahead with the commercial, Bill," the announcer said:

> We got hyacinth bulbs, that good Ortho fertilizer, we got spaghetti squash seeds—no, somebody came in and bought the squash seeds. Say, how come the Russians are only eighty miles away? They're not supposed to come within two hundred. What's going on? Maybe we'd better get some machine guns out there. I don't like squash myself, but we'll have more seeds next week.

I was driving down the road with Jim and Kaylie late one September afternoon three years before, right after the Joneses had bought their farmhouse. The sunlight caught the seared brown of the fields. A flock of Canada geese flew overhead. "God, how I love it here!" he said. With all his appetite for his native land and his native language, he embraced this community and made it his own. His taste for "simple" people, for country ways and country accents, found flourish again. When he first came up from Miami, looking for a house, I introduced him to "Squeak" Lambrecht, owner of the Vogue Beauty Salon. He asked if she would give him a haircut. It was late afternoon, and she opened the shop for him. They talked while Squeak cut his hair. "I'm sick of traveling around," he said to her that day. "I'm through with that fancy French life. I'm coming home."

In the old farmhouse there forever seemed to be laughter, voices of children, wisps of music, something good in the kitchen—and always the presence of literature. Perched there on its hill, it was, he said, "like a ship riding the waves," and it was rumored to be haunted by the ghost of a Mrs. Halsey, who hummed old folk ballads on still nights. Inside there was a poker room, bedecked with Paul Jenkins and Delaney paintings and equipped with chess pieces, Monopoly, Risk, backgammon, and a sinister game of wits called Southwest Conference Football. In a downstairs bathroom was the framed drawing he had done for Burt Brittain's book of writers' self-portraits, and underneath the likeness was his inscription: "Old soldiers never die. They write novels."

Outside the house, a Southern-style gallery with a porch swing overlooked the lawn and the fields beyond. Immense elms, cedars, and flowering bushes dotted the landscape. Off to the side was a set of shrubs and fir trees with an open place in the middle. One day Jim and Jamie and I were exploring these shrubs. "Were you a loner when you were growing up down in Yazoo?" he asked. He was smoking a cigar, and he spat on the ground, apropos of nothing in particular. "I was. I used to hide in shrubs like this and watch the girls go by and think dirty." Just down the road from the house, beyond other farmhouses, were a red one-room schoolhouse and a post office-general store right out of turn-of-the-century America.

Dominating this good old house was a large country kitchen with cupboards and cabinets and kitchen equipment on the walls, and in it the dinner table—a long medieval French piece around which there were many meals lasting into the night, and much conversation. Surely it was not unlike the kitchen Dave Hirsch—the returning soldier, survivor of the Battle of the Bulge—saw in *Some Came Running*, in Gwen and Bob French's house in Israel, Illinois:

It was like a haven, like a haven on a snowy blowing freezing night. Like in one of those old-fashioned Christmas card pictures you always loved to look at but didn't much believe in places like that anymore . . .

He could not escape a sudden feeling that here suddenly for the first time in his life of thirty-seven years he had walked into a place that was safe. And the more he looked at it, the stronger the feeling became. Just safe. That was the only word. Safe from what? He tried to analyze from what, but he could come up with only the vaguest of generalities. Safe from the savageries of frightened men. Safe from the witch burnings and destructions of people determined by their guilts to prove themselves unguilty. Safe from the frightful insanities of reason and honor and justice and happiness . . .

The book he was working hard to finish was full of blood, suffering, and meanness—the walking dead, the ruined and the maimed—fistfights in bars, all-night parties in the suites of the best hotel, brief and savage sexual encounters, drinking and coupling with the newly liberated town girls just as he and his buddies had done in Memphis in 1943, the altered relationship between men and women resulting from war, the cynical affluence of this country in wartime. Perhaps it is paradoxical that he was trying to finish this life's work in a time when he had at last found the small-town America he wanted so much. There were good moments in this little town, which must have seemed so different from the years in Europe, and what follows here is just a simple litany of some of them.

In the summertime he went to some of the big social parties at first, parties given by rich women, but then he pretty much stopped going to them. He never cared much for the inherited rich anyway—as if, for him, they had not really faced the music. "Those damned parties will make a Communist of me," he said. "You have to have a built-in shit-detector to go." He once said to me,

165

of a certain breed of urban intellectuals who attended such parties, "They're city hicks." Everything in his nature rebelled against being an "in group" man. So more often than not he would stay home with Jamie and watch the ball games on television, or you would see him at Bobby Van's at lunchtime, talking with potato farmers or truck drivers or fishermen or carpenters or veterinarians or tree surgeons.

I am a late sleeper, not prone to answer a telephone, and I remember all the countless late mornings he would come round to the back of my house and knock on the window. "Willie Morris! Get your ass out of the sack. Let's go get a hamburger"—or go meet a friend, or take his dog to the vet. One morning, quite early, he got me up to watch Richard Nixon's farewell from the White House the day Nixon resigned. While we were drinking coffee and watching the television in my front room, he went to the door and peered outside. "What are you doing?" I asked. "In damned near any other country there'd be blood running in the streets now," he said. "I don't see none out on Church Lane."

In the bitter days of winter, there was an odd inclination towards tricks. I will never reveal the secret, but we devised an elaborate scheme by which someone picks a card from the deck and telephones The Wizard at a local number, and The Wizard tells him the card. We won $9.00 one evening from Adolph Green, who went home cross and dejected. I must confess to being an inveterate telephone prankster, a man of many voices. When the Jones family moved here, they were a great untapped resource for such things: construction crews coming to build a new access road through their backyard, mysterious power failures on the eve of a birthday party, elm trees to be cut down because of the bark blight, friends of friends from Europe arriving to stay for the weekend with six small brats. Once Jim found in his fortune cookie after a Chinese dinner: "You made your wad on human suffering."

One afternoon the honest-to-God genuine cultural attaché to the Soviet Embassy in Washington telephoned Jim. "On behalf of the Union of Soviet Socialist Republics," the attaché said, "we wish to invite you to our country to speak to our college students about American writing."

"Oh, go fuck off, Willie."

There was a long pause. "I beg your pardon?"

"I'm up here in the attic trying to work. Just go fuck off."

The next day the Soviet official telephoned again. "I talked with some strange person on the phone yesterday by mistake," he said. Realizing the man was who he said he was, Jim tried to explain to him that he had a friend who sometimes talked in a Russian accent, but when this was greeted with silence he had to apologize, undoubtedly against his better nature, since he never especially liked Communists.

We have a softball team here in the summers called the Golden Nematodes, named after the microscopic potato bugs which attack the young potato plants without succor or mercy—an amalgam of bartenders, potato farmers, writers, and teen-agers, a team of unusual ethnic diversity held together by Jeffersonian democracy and the double steal. We play on Sunday afternoons in gold-colored shirts and caps behind the Bridgehampton school, to galleries of village dogs, children, and softball groupies, on the same field where Carl Yastrzemski once hit his memorable line drives as a boy. These languid Sunday afternoons might have made a perfect scene for Norman Rockwell were it not for the violence and profanity that were customary. For a while, before he grew more ill, Jim played first base; he was held in high affection by his teammates. On one of these afternoons we were playing a benefit game against a Sag Harbor team for the animal shelter fund. A crowd of about two hundred people turned up, and there was even a public-address system. The game was going in our favor, and in the late innings Jim and I decided to insert a diminutive black kid into center field. We got one of the young white local boys to write down our substitute's name and take it to the public-address announcer. Momentarily the announcer left his post and came up to Jim and me, trailed by the local white boy. "I can't announce *this*," the man said. He showed us the piece of paper, on which was written "Coon Gamble—center field."

"We got a problem," Jim said. "Ain't he got a real name?"

The white boy said, "Yeah, but Coon's the nickname he calls himself."

"Any other names?" Jim asked.

"Well sometimes we call him 'Jew-Baby.'"

"Jew-Baby?"

"His real name's Julian, so Jew-Baby's for short."

"I think you better call him Julian," Jim said to the announcer.

"This is my last game," he said to me one day. "My legs have give out. Besides, my adrenaline gets flowing, and I want to win so bad I can't get back to work the next day." Early on, a batter for the opposing team, safe on a close play at first base, ran him down. Jim held onto the ball, and did not complain, but he got up limping badly. The next batter hit a grounder close to second base. Adam Shaw, the sturdy second baseman, put his foot on the bag and then proceeded to knock the base runner into short right field. After the Sunday games we would go with our opponents to Rick's Bar on Main Street, all of us, and have frosty mugs of beer and discuss the events of that day's game. The two songs which people always seemed to play on Rick's jukebox on

168

those late days of summer were "The Way We Were" and "The Whiffenpoof Song," the latter with its words: "Gentlemen songsters off on a spree, doomed from here to eternity."

On the cable television at my house on Church Lane one evening there was a showing of *Gone With the Wind*. I invited a few friends over. Gloria and the children were in the city, and he came alone. "I haven't seen the fuckin' thing in twenty years," he said, "but mainly I want to see it at the same time that damned Willie Morris from Mississippi does." He liked my story about my grandmother, who told me she had seen *Gone With the Wind* eighteen times, and the last time she saw it she went just to look at the furniture. He sat on the sofa that night with my dog Pete next to him and took off his shoes and socks, chewing on his cigar and watching closely, spitting every now and again into a brass spittoon. In Atlanta when the camera moved away from the railroad station with its dead and dying and the tattered Confederate flag in the foreground and the sound track breaking into a mournful "Dixie," he turned around to us and said, "I think I better go put into the backyard with Pete before I embarrass myself."

In the summers or early fall we would organize cookouts down at Peter's Pond beach, just a few of us with our children and dogs. We would all get there an hour before sunset, and Jim and I would dig two holes, one for the fire and one for the cooking, and cook a mound of hot dogs and hamburgers. Then we would sit around the fire and listen to the tides and watch the sun disappear into the darkening Atlantic; and, if we were lucky, wait for a full moon to ascend and make what Jim called a "moon's path" on the waters. Someone would have brought a radio, and he was one of the few people I ever knew who loved as much as I to listen to the college football scores on Saturdays in the early fall drifting in from everywhere—first the little Eastern schools, like Bowdoin or Colby, or Allegheny and Gettysburg and Susquehanna, on down to the Southern and Midwestern ones which really mattered, then slowly westward—a roll call of America. "There's a poetry of its own in that, ain't it?" he said, while all around the fire the children would be singing songs or telling stories. He never tired of my giving whatever children were on hand the call words of the radio station I worked for as a boy: "This is WAZF, 1230 on your dial, in downtown Yazoo, with studios high atop the Taylor-Roberts Feed and Seed Store." Until he began having attacks of breathlessness, he would help organize one of these cookouts on a moment's notice.

It is an area dominated by the wind. Since eastern Long Island is a sliver of land, divided into two forks and surrounded by two great bodies of water, the wind plays curious tricks, bringing on a quick rainfall without warning, or fogs so thick one has trouble driving. The farmers talk constantly of the wind. The winter grass in the open fields will be creased in the wind just as the ocean will be. One day I watched a monarch butterfly fighting against the wind until it was gradually wafted far out to sea.

There can be much worse than that. One late summer the eye of a major hurricane, one of the most dangerous in years, was predicted to come close to the village. That afternoon the main street was deserted and ghostly still and an eerie orange glow had set in as Jim and I and our sons drove toward his farmhouse with provisions: canned food, water, flashlights, candles, hurricane lamps. He was a good man in an emergency, and stored some of the things down in the cellar just in case. Then we all sat down around the kitchen table, everything battened down and even the cats strapped to something secure,

170

and listened to the screaming wind and the roar of the ocean from afar and watched the trees swaying into contorted silhouettes. Huge branches crashed on the lawn and small objects flew by outside and the big dog began to howl, and then all the lights went out. As we sat there at the mercy of all God's elements in that unholy mutual whine, Jim made a giggle of nearly atavistic joy, as a man who had seen and heard much worse would, and said: "Well, kiss my ass if *this* ain't a show!"

Jim's eternal search, as he once wrote, was for "some nice quiet dimly lit old-infantryman's dream of a bar somewhere." That place for him was a saloon named Bobby Van's, an angular structure on Main Street with dark paneling, Tiffany lamps and old fans suspended from an undistinguished ceiling, a long mahogany bar, and from the back the flickering of candles on small booths and tables covered with red tablecloths—then, too, a covered porch outside named "Nematode Hall" after our softball team, or perhaps named after the potato bugs themselves. It is a village of dogs, big country dogs with friendly faces who roam about unencumbered—all honored local personalities—and it is indicative of the notability of Bobby Van's that they hang around outside, led by my own dog Pete.

I first met Bobby Van one night several years before. He was standing guard over a corpse, a drunk man run over on the road outside, and while we waited in this deathwatch for the coroner, I learned that Bobby was a dropout from the Juilliard School, a pianist since the age of five who decided somewhere along the way that he wanted his own baby grand in his own bar.

He is a native Long Islander, a short dark young man in his thirties—loyal to all, full of good graces, well-brought-up as we would have said in the South. He wears a white chef's suit when he is cooking in the kitchen, and he comes most to life when he is playing his piano—at home with Rachmaninoff or Cole Porter—sometimes in the summers to a packed house of New Yorkers who have frightened the locals away, but in the winters to a handful of us who come in out of the cold.

Bobby knows the tempos and cadences of his native place—a place that, being a resort in summer, changes character more drastically with the seasons than any stretch of earth I have ever known. Only once had I seen him embarrassed by the treacheries of nature here, when the Coast Guard hauled him in after he was lost while fishing in Gardiners Bay for eight hours. (Several of us waited anxiously in the saloon for word of him, meanwhile helping ourselves to free drinks.) He knows the flight of the geese and the next change of the wind. People come there to find out where the bluefish are running or for the baseball scores, they wander in with ducks they have shot to be dressed and eaten, and like our predecessors who sought out deep caves and built fires in them, we came to Bobby's to huddle together during storms. Like the land, there is not much violence in Bobby's either—only occasionally. Once a gentleman threw a coffee cup across the room at me, for reasons not to be disclosed, and with an aim so erratic it clipped Bobby Van on the ear in the middle of *Rhapsody in Blue*. One night very late Bob Dylan wandered in alone and began composing a song on the piano about Catfish Hunter. The local Lions Club meets there; some patrons have been known to go unshaven; and my black Labrador Pete, the official mayor of Bridgehampton, who does his rounds regular as can be to check on his constituents, makes Bobby's his last and most significant stop. Pete, once described by a friend as the only black Labrador on Long Island with a Southern accent, opens Bobby's door with his nose, and the men at the bar turn and say, as Jim Jones did: "Here comes the mayor. Good afternoon, your honor."

Bobby Van, who also served in the 25th Infantry, in Vietnam, became a subject for a certain levity because of his hypochondria. He always had pains somewhere. Sometimes he carried in his pocket X rays of his sinus condition to show his friends, or of his damaged wrist which he broke one celebrative night climbing a tree outside the saloon. Jim would walk up to Bobby and ask, "How are you today, Bobby?" and without giving him time to reply, add: "That's too bad." Then he would turn to somebody and say, "All's right with the world. Bobby looks awful today."

On New Year's Day Bobby Van would have open house for the college football games and invite the regular local clientele to bring dishes to supplement the ones he and the kitchen had prepared. We arrived in a good mood that day, since Jim and I were well on our way to winning $400 apiece on four bowl games in a row. We greeted the mingling regulars and then gazed at the long rows of food on the buffet tables. "It sure don't make me miss the Deux Magots much," he said.

The Day the President Left Yazoo

IT WAS A Friday afternoon of 1977, hot only as the Mississippi Delta can be in the middle of July, and I was about half asleep in my room in the Yazoo Motel. The President of the United States had been in Yazoo the night before for one of his town meetings, but had left in a helicopter at six a.m.

Everyone else had left too. The thrall of the Presidency is extraordinary. The reporters and the researchers and the television personalities and the camera crews and the tourists and the White House staff and the communications technicians and the state troopers and the Secret Servicemen who had swarmed into town for several days had simply vanished overnight, as if they had never really been there at all. I had stayed up all night doing an essay for *Time Magazine* on the President's visit, and now I was exhausted and rather sad.

The White House had taken over the entire hotel, and my old junior high English teacher, Mrs. Olive Love, who worked at the front desk, had to use all her influence to get this native son his customary room Number 74. Mrs. Olive and the other ladies at the desk had been calling the Yazoo Motel the Yazoo White House. "I've got a line right here on this switchboard that goes straight to you-know-where," one of them had said. An

Time Magazine, August 1, 1977, and *Mississippi Magazine*, March 1979.

old Negro man had wandered in a few days before and they got him to push in that line and listen, and he damned near fell over. Near the swimming pool there had been a huge truck which held some of the communications equipment. It too was gone. That morning I had driven around town, only now under the ominous sun it reminded me of the empty fairgrounds after the Clyde Beatty Circus departed in 1947. The only remotely active precinct was around Owen Cooper's residence on Grand Avenue near Billy Goat Hill. Mr. and Mrs. Cooper were getting ready to have an open house so that people could see the room where the President had slept and the bowl out of which he had had peaches for breakfast, along with his dishes and a glass. They planned to give the bowl, dishes, and glass to a museum later.

For the last few days, I had never seen so many lawns being cut at the same time. The smell of newly mown grass drifted out of the hills and overpowered the senses. There were American flags on the houses of the meanest and most ageless old recluses of my boyhood.

I must admit that the Yazoo of my truest reality is a languid village on a summer's day of thirty years ago, when one big car whipping through with out-of-state plates was diversion enough. I know what Mark Twain meant when he returned to Hannibal: "I had a sort of realizing sense of what the Bastille prisoners must have felt when they used to come out and look upon Paris after years of captivity and note how curiously the familiar and the strange were mixed together before them."

I had brought Jamie Jones down from our village on eastern Long Island on this visit. He was sixteen that summer, the son of my late friend James Jones, the novelist. Jamie was born and raised in France and was anxious to see what the Deep South was like. He had heard my stories, but I suspected did not believe many of

175

them. I think he felt he could get a report out of this trip for his civics class in the fall. My son David, then seventeen, wanted to come with Jamie and me, but he was in charge of special effects for a production of *Blithe Spirit* out in Bridgehampton and could not make it. However, David knows Yazoo well—in fact he and some of the young Yazoo boys had almost burned down a levee on the river some years back by shooting too many firecrackers at the same time—and he had been telephoning us long distance three times a day to hear us describe what was going on for the President's visit. Now that everyone had left, even David up on Long Island had more or less lost interest and he had not phoned in twelve hours.

My friend Jamie Jones had been spending considerable time with Tarpley Mott, the son of the publisher of the Yazoo paper and a resourceful student of this piece of earth, and Causey DeCell, the daughter of the state senator Herman and one of the finest teachers in the South, Harriet, and Causey's big brother Brister, all exceptional offspring of exceptional parents and, as a dividend, touched with mischief for as long as I can remember them. "They have funny names down here," Jamie said. They had shown Jamie everything in town: the Yazoo River, the jailhouse, the composing room of the Yazoo *Herald*, the baseball field where we had won our state championships years ago and where I had once hit a curve ball over the same green fence off a toothless pitcher named Eckert with the bases loaded, the country club, the Negro neighborhoods, the chemical plant, Goose Egg Park, a couple of plantations, the sawmill, Brickyard Hill, and of course the cemetery. Jamie's companions took him to the grave of the man who owned the funeral home and went askew in 1938 and shot several people on Main Street, then returned to his establishment, climbed into an empty coffin, and shot himself in the temple. Then they showed him the unidentified Confederate dead. Naturally they also took him to the grave of the witch who broke out of her grave in 1904 and burned down the whole town. The evidence for that is right there, because she broke a link of chain to get out and the link is still missing. We had all bet Jamie five dollars that on a midnight during our trip he would not walk alone from the back of this most awesome of cemeteries to the front gate, stopping en route to tap five times on the witch's grave in that anguished glade of trees. He had taken us up on this wager, and now all we had to do was appoint a night. Everything had been so hectic because of the President, however, that we had not gotten around to putting Jamie through this lonely test.

I had gotten Jamie some official press credentials for the President's meeting in the new schoolhouse. We had sat there in the bleachers of the gymnasium and watched the people fanning themselves with the paper fans from the Gregory Funeral Home and heard the band play my old high school alma mater, which concludes with the words:

> Yazoo, Yazoo, in closing let us say,
> That forever and a day,
> We'll be thinking of you,
> Yazoo, Yazoo.

Then we had heard the President speak about Vietnam, the neutron bomb, the South, and other matters. The townspeople were immensely excited and happy. In the heat that night I was drowsing and not listening too well. Toward the end Jamie Jones nudged me and said, "Hey, the President's talking about you," and so indeed he was.

Now, on this Friday afternoon, Jamie and Tarpley were drifting around town somewhere. At breakfast in Stub's Restaurant they seemed to have been suffering the most acute symptoms of withdrawal, along with just about everyone else. As I said, I was half-asleep on the bed in the motel. In a kind of nether consciousness I heard the two boys come into the room and sit in the air-conditioning and start talking.

It was at this moment that I was struck by the most monstrous *déjà vu*. I felt that I was not really 42 years old, but that I had merely been dreaming for thirty-odd years that I was growing older and that I had gone up north to do so, but that in truth I was still Jamie and Tarpley's age on a somnolent July day of '47 and that it was my old comrade Bubba Barrier and I talking.

"What are we going to do this afternoon, Tarpley?" Jamie asked. "I'm getting tired of riding up and down Grand Avenue."

"Then let's go to the petrified forest in Flora."

"It's too hot."

"I guess we could go to see the battlefield in Vicksburg, but I was there twice last month."

"Well, let's do something."

"Let's go down to the Coca-Cola Bottling Company and watch them bottle Cokes."

By now this exchange had brought me fully awake. I sat up in bed and told Jamie and Tarpley that if they would leave and let me sleep, we would go to the cemetery that night and see if Jamie could win the bet.

They agreed. Since Jamie and I were departing the next morning, the trip to the cemetery had to be in a few hours, else I ran the risk of bringing Jamie down there again when he might be too old to be walking around in a cemetery at midnight. Jamie and Tarpley went fishing in the pond behind Causey's house, played a few rounds of Risk, ate some catfish for supper, then met me at a friend's house on Madison Street at 11:45 p.m.

You will have to take me on faith that it was an alarming night, even by Delta standards. The pall of nature was heavy. The town was ghostly silent. Absolutely no one was about.

"They're all inside watching the last TV shows about themselves," Tarpley surmised.

The sky was dark purple, touched ever so often by bolts of lightning which illuminated the grotesque shapes of the oaks and elms in the old section of town. Thunder rumbled down out of the hills. It was a good night to have company. In my rented Avis were myself, Jamie, Tarpley, Causey, Causey's brother Brister, and Causey and Brister's young cousins Charles and John.

It was a long drive through town to the cemetery, past the bayou covered with creeping vines and the big houses that looked haunted on this night. "I'm glad it's not me who's going to walk all the way through," Causey said.

At last, near midnight, we got to the entrance. As we drove through, all around us were the spooky graves of my childhood, the familiar names on the tarnished stone, the magnolias which seemed to hover like specters there, and in the inky darkness the rows of dead so etched on my memory.

"Oh, wow!" Tarpley said. It was a cry, not of astonishment, but of primal dread. Jamie said nothing, but his wrinkled brow suggested ambivalent emotions. Young Charles DeCell sank lower into his seat, and so would I, had I not been the leader of the arcane expedition.

I drove the car slowly up the long road toward the secluded place where we would deposit Jamie, and where under the terms of our arrangement he must wait five minutes until after we had departed before launching his journey.

Then we saw a terrible thing.

From far across the cemetery in the quiet there was another car, and there was a spotlight on it, and the spotlight was directed at us! The light bounced off the gravestones and made an eery glow that would have terrified the most intrepid heart.

"What is it?" someone asked.

"It's the Yazoo cops!" Tarpley shouted. "Let's get out of here."

It was indeed the cops. In my many nights in this cemetery, going back more than a quarter of a century, I had never once seen them in there at such an hour.

I did not want a chase. I drove the car at normal speed, to the back of the cemetery, left through the Catholic section, left again at the Negro section, past the Jewish enclave, and eased on down the incline to the front gate.

But our pursuer would not allow escape. From a hundred yards away we could still see the gleaming spotlight, inexorable as time. Finally the car was up with us, and its lone occupant motioned me to get out.

I was confronted there among the graves by a large black policeman. I immediately recognized him from a photograph that had appeared on the front page of Tarpley's father's newspaper only a few days before the President arrived. A whimsical little piece had accompanied the photograph, because the black policeman's name was Jimmy Carter.

"You're breaking the trespass laws," Officer Carter said.

There were several things I could have said in that moment: that I had made this cemetery famous, that people came from miles around, sometimes from as far away as Belzoni to see the witch's grave because of my written accounts of it, that I was writing up the President's visit for a magazine, or that we had a five dollar bet with Jamie Jones of Sagaponack, Long Island, New York as to whether he would walk through the tombstones alone at this hour, stopping at the witch's grave as part of the bargain. None under the circumstances seemed appropriate.

"I was just driving the kids through, officer."

He looked at my driver's license, then said: "We've had some vandalism in here lately." During the distraction of the President's visit, someone apparently had been trying to dig up graves. For an instant, I think he suspected us of this calling.

"It was an innocent trip on our part," I said.

"Well, okay, it's all right," he replied and returned to his car. "That's *our* Jimmy Carter," Tarpley affirmed. "It really is," Brister said. As we drove out of the cemetery, we turned and watched as Jimmy Carter circled through the graves again, searching for graverobbers. There was lightning out on the Delta horizon, and it began to rain again, a warm, unhurried Mississippi rain.

"I didn't want to do it anyway," Jamie said.

The Lending
Library of Love

WE ARE NOW living in a time in America, and I
am writing especially of those of us in our thirties and
forties who have absorbed the brunt of all this, where
there seem no ground rules to sexual love. The old essential things of the blood, the structures, principles, inhibitions, are swept away, and few of us truly know
where we are.

All about me among these men and women of my
generation there is an immense pain and desperation
about abiding sexual relationships. We search our friends
for some answer, but they know nothing we do not
know; they have lived in the crucible of it, too. So the
blame goes to the partner. Everyone is too highly keyed;
we seethe with introspection and self-aggrandizement;
we want someone to save us from ourselves; nothing
seems to last.

What I am describing involves not just the destruction
of marriage, although among this generation in eastern
America almost three marriages in four end in divorce.
It derives from something infinitely more subtle and
basic about sex, and it is hurting us where all our impulses and fears conjoin with the revolution that has
taken root in our society.

It *is* a revolution, and individual people, lovers together, are convoluted in its current. Relationships among

people are at best very difficult; I suspect they grow more so as one gets older, robbed as we are of the blinding faiths of youth, and nowhere must this be more true than of love. In earlier times, not too distant, people were locked in by all the social contracts of love, and although this did not make things any better, incurring among other traumas the worst hypocrisy, the rhythms and expectations of love now have entered a wholly uncharted terrain, far out at another extreme.

Toward this common bafflement I sense the smallest beginnings of a reaching out across the sexes. A young Canadian woman named Merle Shain has written a warm-hearted and warm-blooded memoir, *Some Men Are More Perfect Than Others*, which has touched me with its perception and maturity about men who are attempting in these times to encourage the women they love to be themselves, to engage themselves in their best talents, to reaffirm the things they want and need in life—and still the failures abound. I would very much like to meet this Canadian girl, and I wish an equally good man would write a similar revelation about the women who are trying to deal with men through love, against the chaos which engulfs it.

Most of us have been through a marriage once (some, poor souls, a few times more) and when we feel the gradual deepenings of love we become wary and afraid, and then distrustful, for we remember too much. Yet this terrible lending library of love in which we are indulging ourselves now—this shuttling from one affair to the next, always seeking the unattainable, replacing in a matter of days some long, sustaining relationship that fell on strange times with a newer and perhaps more treacherous one, with scant concern or respect for the one who still loves—is bound by the nature of it to cause the greatest unhappiness. It usually diminishes both lovers, leaving each more vulnerable than before.

But what are we to expect? *As ye sow, so shall ye reap.* All of us have done it—some with guilt, which can be a most civilizing virtue, some without.

Recently a vivacious young California woman, well-known for her observations on men and "sexual mores," said to me after a drink at a party on the West Coast (confessing to me that she had never expressed this before to her public, who admire her apparently for her image of unbounded sexuality): "I want love, but only on my own terms. Sometimes I want sex, but most of the time I don't, but when I do, I want it on my own terms, too. I want men, but only to use them precisely for my own pleasure when I feel like it." A perfectly understandable sentiment, one might suppose, especially if she sees herself as the public sham she is, and if any man who is drawn to her is forewarned of it. But let there be no misjudging its implications, which are nothing if not contemporary. For if this feeling is acquiring any significant hold, as my intuitions tell me it is, as the flowering of our liberation, then it will ultimately begin to destroy that fragile skein of mutuality that binds men and women together, and will be the first sure tremor of death to mature sexual love itself.

But in the heart of me I know the delicacy of this question I have been the fool to raise. Perhaps I am being too much a creature of my day and ignore the immemorial perspective that should tell me there is nothing new under the sun. With this self-doubt I gently demur. In our country and our age, perhaps more than at any time in any advanced mass society, there has grown between lovers of my generation a fearful reluctance of any enduring mutual trust, an obsessive dwelling on the failings of the other, an urge to hurt and to tantalize—and all this buttressed and encouraged by strong and unprecedented social forces.

In those inevitable moments of despoiling ill temper, as we damage what we cherish, we know that we can go elsewhere, and soon. All the time we may have thought we were growing from the sinews of our own past experience—for what is intelligence if not coping with the recurrences of one's existence?—learning somehow to give more of ourselves and to expect less, until one day we awaken in a cold dawn to see there are turbulent things in ourselves and in those we love that we did not really comprehend at all, and that we are unable to conduct ourselves compassionately.

We pray to reach out, then, for one of the most ennobling truths of all: at the base of sexual love, as with all good things we have created, lies the generosity of the spirit. But we expect as our modern inheritance our swift next chance, waiting for the passing of the days which alone heals all wounds, not choosing to acknowledge that as mortals we have not quite evolved enough yet.

Good Friends . . .
Dogs, Sons and Others

IN RECENT WEEKS, no fewer than three books have been published on getting and keeping friends. Have we reached the point of needing books on how to have friendships?

This is not written by one who believes in the "art" of friendship, for in the anomie of the late 20th century this suggests too much of Dale Carnegie or group therapy. You can train someone to kick a football or to take out an appendix, but some things cannot be learned. If there is an esthetic to friendship, it exists in the reality and not in the effort. As with most of the complex achievements of life—sexual love, or tranquility, or the sensibility to comprehend that which is beautiful and passionate and true—friendship may even be God-given, and in this sense it is also a creature of accident and hence a rare blessing. It is an emotion of esteem and affection, undergirded by shared remembrance and the evocation of time. In these transient years—when most Americans travel their land seeking new roots and fresh beginnings, often finding more than they bargained for—friendship may be as difficult to retain as a good marriage.

We are all terribly alone in this life, I fear. This is part of our mortality, and there is not really much we can do about it. The awful armor of our isolation is pierced

Parade Magazine, September 7, 1980

only by those fragile loyalties which we pray will abide—
children, or a lover, or friends. All of these ask for tenderness and care.

I am not just talking here about male friendships and
female ones, but also about friendships of a nonsexual
nature between men and women. One of the dividends
of the women's movement of this generation, perhaps,
has been the enhanced freedom of American women to
choose affectionate relationships with men whom they
trust outside the bedroom. Some of my own closest
friends are women; I can count four whom I believe I
would go to the brink for. Two are married to men I
admire, one is a widow, one is divorced, and they are as
important to me as anything in my existence, including
my male friends, who are also only a few. I suspect a
person can only have a handful of steadfast friends, if
that. Be wary of those who claim to count their friendships by the dozens, unless they are politicians up for
reelection.

Parenthetically, I must also go so far as to confess that
one of my best friends is a big black dog of acute
warmth and intelligence. He and I are huckleberry
friends who ride the river together. By my personal measure, another of my finest friends is my twenty-year-old
son. We have lived through too many moments as a two-
some to be forgetful of them. Among genuine friendships, never discount the possibility of good dogs and
good sons.

At the core of friendship, I feel, is fidelity. We all make
fools of ourselves now and again, and do things which
cause us guilt—or worse, shame—and there are our
times of ineluctable grief and sorrow. A trusting friend
can call us back to earth and remind us of the universal
failures and sufferings. Laughter is no less an ingredient
of friendship than loyalty, or charity, or forgiveness.
Conversely, in the lexicon of human cruelty, I rank the

betrayal of a friend—even a friend from an earlier part of one's life—as dastardly almost as child-abuse or manslaughter. I am reminded of the New York editor and writer who recently published a memoir belittling old friends, ferreting out their faults in retrospect as finely as a sculptor chiseling at a bust, all in the spirit of his own aggrandizement. Gratuitous betrayal often exacts its own special price.

I am reminded too of a worthier example, one that remains with me as vividly as the moment I first heard of it as a boy, so that it has become a kind of symbol for me. In his rookie season with the Brooklyn Dodgers, Jackie Robinson, the first black man to play Major League baseball, faced venom wherever he traveled—fastballs at his head, spikings on the bases, brutal epithets from the opposing dugouts and from the crowds. During one game on a hot day in St. Louis, the taunts and racial slurs seemed to reach a crescendo. In the midst of all this, the Dodger who was Jackie Robinson's particular friend, a Southern white named Peewee Reese, called time out. He walked from his position at shortstop toward Robinson at second base, put his arm around Robinson's shoulder, and stood there with him for a long time. The gesture spoke more eloquently than the words: this man is my friend.

Even across the divide of death, friendship remains, an echo forever in the heart. The writer James Jones has been gone for more than three years, yet so alive was he for me that I have never quite admitted he is dead. He and his family lived down the road from me on eastern Long Island, and he struggled against death in his last months to finish his fictional trilogy of World War II. He was a connoisseur of cigars, a believer in the written word, and an enemy of meanness and pretense. He was courageous without ever talking much about courage; he appreciated mirth and he understood sorrow. I am not sure why we were closer than brothers, for he was older than I and more inured of the siftings and winnowings of this world. Yet we were. Two years ago, as I began a book which means much to me—struggling with the very first sentences with a radio somewhere in the background—the song that came on was the theme to the movie of Jim's big novel, *From Here to Eternity*. "Keep the faith," he might have said.

When I see an honored friend again after years of separation, it is like reassuming the words of an old conversation which had been halted momentarily by time. Surely as one gets older, friendship becomes more precious to us, for it affirms the contours of our existence. It is a reservoir of shared experience, of having lived through many things in our brief and mutual moment on earth. To paraphrase another writer from Mississippi, it is a prop, a pillar, to help us not merely endure, but prevail.

A Girl I Once Knew

I SHOULD have married Annie. She wanted to. I was forty and she was twenty-four. She was a Tennessee girl of good lineage. She had studied English at Vanderbilt, a Chi Omega who knew about the Fugitives and whose favorite book was Agee's *A Death in the Family* and whose second was *Let Us Now Praise Famous Men*. Her father was a lawyer in a Civil War town south of Nashville, of the progressive type, who had played halfback for the Vandy Commodores in the middle 1940s and once scored two touchdowns against General Neyland's Tennessee Volunteers.

There she was, thrust suddenly into a Long Island winter. She had come up to work as a reporter for the big Long Island daily. We huddled together in her first wintertime out there. As in the song, we fell in love because it was cold outside. She covered murders, rapes, the courthouse—a little of everything, as I remember. One afternoon she came to me in tears from the ocean. Forewarned, she had been there with the authorities to observe a headless corpse which had been washed in by the waves after drifting around for two or three weeks. At other times she would come into my house and use my telephone on her stories, and from my workroom I eavesdropped on her conversations with the small-town lawyers or the police or the oceanographers or the men who were experts on Dutch Elm disease. She had a high-pitched voice, but very soft and Southern, and I suspect

190

that is one of the reasons she always got her story.

She was a beautiful girl, a tall blond, full-breasted, a warm girl too, passionate as an earlier generation might have said of her. She had a cottage ten miles down the road from me near the ocean and got off work at seven in the evening. Many days at six, putting up work, I would go to the I.G.A. and buy things, then drive to her house and start cooking; as my strange concoctions simmered in the kitchen, I would sit by the fire I had built and think about the day. I would hear her steps on the porch, and I would surprise myself by how much I wanted to see her, and in she would come, wrapped in her sweaters, rain or snowflakes in her swirl of golden hair, and we would hover by the fire and talk of the violence or injustice she had reported on that day, or of the words I had put down.

Annie missed the South a little, as did I. It was her first time away. Neither of us could really stand the snow and the cold, and the howling February wind from the Atlantic, which came to us as a grotesque whine with a life all its own, drove us insane. Sometime it got down to twenty below zero. Some nights we would sit on the sofa holding each other and listening to this ungodly ocean wind. "What are we doing here?" she would laugh. "We'd better kiss some."

Our best days were Saturdays, when she was not working on her deadlines. We would get in my car and drive the roads of eastern Long Island, Montauk to Riverhead, Sag Harbor to Bridgehampton—take the ferries to Shelter Island and the North Fork, tarrying in the antique stores, lunching on lobster and oysters and clams and white wine in the fish places, later stopping along the way by an inlet to watch the gulls and the play of the frosty sunlight on the water. Then home to my house, and after that dinner with our friends. One afternoon just before Christmas, we went into the Episcopal

Church in Southampton where the recorded Christmas carols came out of the speaker near the chimes for all the people to hear. She bumped into the record-player which fed the chimes, so that "O Little Town of Bethlehem" played twenty straight times for the citizens of Southampton, Long Island, New York, and we got away from there fast. It was sleeting outside, of course, a fine icy mist which obscured the decorations of the old town. I gave her a tea-set that afternoon for the holidays, and a book of the correspondence between James Agee and Father Flye, and drove her to the airport down the Island for her plane to Nashville, and she kissed me and said, "We should have Christmas together."

One day of early April, a harsh day of threatening snow and the infernal wind, I took her to a wedding in the ancient Presbyterian Church in Bridgehampton where I was the best man, and to the reception afterward in a pitched tent which almost blew away. She wore a red spring Tennessee dress and watched the Yankee girls in their wools and flannels. During the reception she said, "I need to go off and be alone with you. Weddings do something to me."

She would say, "You're not too old and I'm not too young." But she was the marrying age, and she wanted a baby. The love we had was never destroyed; it was merely the dwindling of circumstance. How does one give up Annie? Only through loneliness and fear, fear of old loves lost and of love renewed—only those things, that's all. The last departure came on a windswept October noon of the kind we had known. We stood on the porch of my house and embraced. "Oh—*you!*" she said. She lingered for the briefest moment. Then she was gone, a Tennessee girl with snow in her hair again. She married a local boy and now has two little daughters, I hear on good authority from Long Island. The years are passing, and don't think I haven't thought about it.

192

Legacies

"THE PAST IS never dead. It's not even past," our fellow Mississippian Mr. Faulkner, whose work is so crucial to an understanding of the complexities of our heritage, wrote in *Intruder in the Dust*. I put these words at the beginning of *North Toward Home*, which was my own young man's attempt to make a boyhood in Yazoo live on for a while, and I feel them even more profoundly as I read this history of a place which has touched all of us who have known, at one time, or another, its pull.

Because this book is not just for those of us now living, as we happen to be, in the latter years of the twentieth-century. Even more I believe it is for those of you who will turn to it many years from now—perhaps a young boy or girl sitting in a corner of the old Ricks library on main street, as I once did, discovering on its shelves as if by accident the lost voices, the feel of time which envelops this ground of half hills and delta, the shades of darkness and light which have encompassed our common humanity here, the sense of soil and of memory.

I hope that the very name itself, *Yazoo*, will still exert its strange, bittersweet spell on you who will dwell here then. Surely place-names create their own unique aura,

Introduction to *Yazoo: Legends and Legacies* by Harriet DeCell and Jo Ann Pritchard, 1976 and ours always seemed to have shaped our land and its realities—a brooding land to me when I was a boy, a land of slow and opaque seasons, rich in one's own conjurings of the Indians, the first Anglo-Saxon settlers and their black slaves who cleared its forests and swamps with what unimaginable labors, the life along the river, the Civil War with Pemberton and Grant and Sherman and those thousands of boys engaged in the miasmal flatlands around Yazoo and down the road in Vicksburg in one of the single most monumental battles of our nation and of Western civilization. And then the Reconstruction time, the Great Fire of 1904 and the legends of the escaped witch which haunted the imagination of Yazoo children over the generations, the Depression years and that driftless moment of World War II when we seemed forever to be walking down the lonesome streets collecting our friends from house to house in the journey to the Dixie Theater for a war movie, the band marches through town and the football games and the hot summers of baseball and the funerals for the Korean dead in the 1950s, and the integration of the public schools one dramatic morning in 1970—that moment which came to symbolize almost quintessentially the deep human changes in the soul of a town and a region.

And through all this, if one loves this place as I have, the perception of the venerable continuities of time— the births and the deaths, natural and violent, the forgotten tragedies and triumphs, the sadnesses and joys of man's existence in one small stretch of this planet. From the old photographs of its people one saw the likenesses of the boys and girls my age when we were growing up in the 1940s. From the close proximity with its black people one learned much of the truth and struggle of our national experience. I among many was nourished in these legacies of Yazoo's past, and as I grew older they taught me, as they did others, something tangible in what it was to be both a Southerner and an American.

The Yazoo of my youth was more closely akin, physically and in spirit, to the 1920s and 1930s than to the 1970s. In its isolation and vanity it was a pause, a halfway point, between older and lingering things and something new which stirred in the blood of a different South. In the very textures of boyhood then lay something poignant and fragile.

This was merely my experience, and my contemporaries'. They are scattered about now, those boys and girls, yet across the years I see them in my mind's eye. And even as I write these words, I have before me something which touches me: dozens of letters from children now living in Yazoo, responding to a book I once wrote for children set there in that vanished time. The recognizable landmarks obsess them, the memories and legends, the violence and mischief and the echoes of old laughter. They are our inheritors in the human comedy; they are reaching for their past; they are Yazoo people.

Different Terrains

ONCE, SEVERAL years ago out here on eastern Long Island, within the circulation area of this very journal, I was in love with two women at the same time. It was terrible. No sooner was I with one that I started missing the other. I dissected their characters piece by piece, taking them apart bit by bit for my perfervid scrutiny, casting aside a faulty coil here and a cantankerous bolt there for the sake of a finer amalgam, reassembling their disparate elements out of the mortal puzzle. I began comparing their children and dogs. My friends suspected me of self-indulgence, failing to comprehend my prickly guilt. As such things often happen, I took to spending a great deal of time alone with my dog Pete, usually in cemeteries. The one behind the schoolhouse in Wainscott was my favorite, mainly because of the inscription on a tombstone which says "No Comment" rather than "Rest in Peace." This dead man's mood caught mine perfectly.

There is a classic of Chinese literature, the 18th century novel "Hong lou meng." The protagonist is an adolescent aesthete who lives his youth in a mansion in Peking, passionately in love at the same time with both his beautiful cousins. The two girls are quite different, yet they possess qualities which could be merged in a single ideal woman whom the poor protagonist never meets.

Bridgehampton Sun, July 1, 1980

Instead he is torn between Black Jade, a brilliant, brooding, petulant, narcissistic beauty on the one hand; and Precious Clasp, a girl of "grown-up beauty and aplomb" and a "sophisticated, generous, accommodating disposition" on the other.

Ah, Black Jade! Precious Clasp! For any sins against you, both of you have returned to bedevil me now, in the two places I love above all others. The same emotions are engendered for a place as for a woman: belonging, serenity, fulfillment, remembrance, torment, fed by buried anguish that is sexual, almost, in its intensity. So it is for me, with my Mississippi and my Long Island.

No two places of modern America could be more different. My Mississippi is poor and isolated, slow-moving and inward, proud and communal, quick to anger and quicker yet to forgive, obsessed until recent days by race, tormented by the burden of its memory. Beneath its older layers of violence and xenophobia lies an honor and civility. It is home.

And my Long Island, the eastern end of it: rich, sophisticated, cosmopolitan in the recent years, up, up, and onward, suffused with triumph and glitter, ineradicably linked to the most restless and powerful metropolis in the history of the race. There is little blood and guilt in tourism and potatoes—art galleries and summer lawn parties, where grown men have been seen wearing red suede shoes without socks. Svelte ladies in tennis shorts perusing The Village Voice. Swarming summer crowds. Stockbroker talk. The older culture—the Anglo-Saxons and the Poles and the Irish—commingling reluctantly but inevitably now with the world of the arts and the big Eastern wealth, giving to the summers the heady excitement and also the rootlessness of the Upper East Side. Given its marvelous distractions, there is almost too much to do: its titillation carries all before it. Sometimes, in its summers, it strikes one that the New

Yorkers are doing little and care less for the other, older life: of local baseball and the volunteer fire brigades and the blacks out of the Carolinas, as if the worlds of de Kooning and the young Yazstremski are irredeemably apart, separated by America's profoundest chasms.

But my Long Island is the other one, its autumns and winters and early springs, when tranquility comes with the wind, and loyal friendships come together again. This, too, is home.

And there are similarities, too, in these different terrains of the heart. Both are acutely beautiful. Mississippi has its hills and delta, the lingering woodsmoke of autumn, the crossroads hamlets where time has stood still, Long Island its fields and dunes and shingled houses and manicured lawns and great Atlantic tides— my wild and serene beauties.

My friend Pete the Mayor is no stranger to their loveliness. He greets the students in the magnolia grove on their way to classes, and sometimes he goes into their classes with them. He swims in the catfish ponds with his Southern Lab cousins. His eyes sparkle as his friend's do when he crosses the Shinnecock Canal after the long ride north, and in Bridgehampton he strolls along Main Street greeting his constituents, and nudges open the door of Bobby's or George's or Billy's or Stefan's to see who's there today. "*Mr. Mayor! Where the hell you been?*"—yet Pete knows he soon must be heading down the Shenandoah and through the Smokies and into our other place.

In the heart of a man, and a dog, there must be a reason for this. The dualities of deepest belonging can never be merged. We will not compromise on Wilkes-Barre. In this mortal world, two loves are better, surely, than none at all.

Stingo and Bilbo in the Mansion

I CAME DOWN from Long Island to the University of Mississippi in Oxford to be the writer-in-residence. Mississippi is likely the most *communal* of all the fifty states, and so it was no great surprise to me when my telephone rang one recent Sunday afternoon to find that it was the Governor dialing me himself.

The Governor is William Winter, who had just been inaugurated. On that Sunday he wanted to welcome me home where he said I belonged. Then he said: "I hear Plimpton and Styron are coming to see you."

He was referring, of course, to my friends the writers, George Plimpton and William Styron. I confirmed that Plimpton was arriving on a quick visit to Ole Miss in two weeks and that Styron would be here shortly after that. With Plimpton we forthwith devised a plan. Since Plimpton's great-grandfather was Adelbert P. Ames, the Radical Reconstructionist Governor of Mississippi after the Civil War against whom impeachment papers were eventually brought, the Governor would issue a pardon to Ames and grant Plimpton a twelve-hour safe conduct through Mississippi. His pardon, however, would not include George's other great-grandfather, Benjamin Butler of Massachusetts, the occupying general of New Orleans, better known in the South as "Beast," so reviled in those days that the citizens of New Orleans later manufactured "Beast Butler Chamber Pots" with

199

the likeness of Plimpton's great-grandfather on the bottom.*

As for Styron, the Governor during our telephone conversation invited him and his wife Rose, my son David—a student at Hampshire College, Amherst, who makes frequent forays into Dixie—and myself to stay as guests in the Governor's Mansion in Jackson. He and I also thought it would be a good idea to have a three-man panel, the Governor and Styron and I, before an appropriate audience to discuss the Southern past and present.

I thought it fitting that Random House brought out Styron's extraordinary novel *Sophie's Choice* on his 54th birthday. The timing was appropriate not only because this was his most powerful and ambitious book in a succession of distinguished contributions to our literature—*Lie Down in Darkness, The Long March, Set This House on Fire, The Confessions of Nat Turner*—but also because, perhaps more than most great novels, it springs in its profoundest impulse from recognizable autobiographical sources.

His previous book, *The Confessions of Nat Turner*, had been published in 1967; it was number one on the best-seller list for many weeks and subsequently won the Pulitzer Prize. After this, he began another novel, *The Way of the Warrior*, set largely in Camp Lejeune, North Carolina, and in Japan during the Korean War, its protagonist a U.S. Marine colonel of much complexity and brilliance. After months of hard work, Styron felt the novel was not going especially well. "Not that I was ashamed of it," he says. "I wasn't. But I'd been floundering with it for several weeks." One spring morning in 1974, in his house in Roxbury, Connecticut,

---

* *Author's note:* The details of Plimpton's subsequent arrest are described later in this volume.

200

he awoke to the awareness of a vivid dream he had had—"almost as if the dream had given me an urgent message, a mandate. I don't want this to sound too metaphysical, or dramatic, or spooky, but the dream was a return in my memory to a girl I had known in Brooklyn many years before."

The time was the late 1940s. He had moved into a boardinghouse on Caton Avenue facing Prospect Park to begin writing what would become his first novel, *Lie Down in Darkness*. One day he met a beautiful blond Polish girl who rented a room on the second floor. Her beauty stunned him, and then he noticed the tattooed numbers on her arm. She was a survivor of Auschwitz, and her name was Sophie. Her English was poor, and at first they communicated in broken French. She served elaborate delicatessen lunches in her room, as if she were trying to elude starvation itself. To the fledgling writer from Tidewater, Virginia she seemed desperate for companionship. Yet she had a rather attractive Jewish boyfriend from Brooklyn, and Styron grew to know them. The sounds of their strenuous lovemaking reverberated through the house, sometimes rattling the chandelier in the reclusive young writer's room on the first floor.

The morning of his dream, and over the next several days, he sat down in a high pitch of energy. Calling himself "Stingo," he wrote the opening section of *Sophie's Choice*, a hilarious autobiographical sequence about his first lonely days as a Southerner in New York City. When he had finished these introductory pages, he resolved almost immediately to go to Poland; he felt he had to see Auschwitz. On his return, the novel unfolded for him slowly but steadily. He had always been a deliberate, painstaking writer, and *Sophie's Choice* would take him more than four years, his imagination moving inexorably from the real Sophie and those summer days of the 1940s in Flatbush into a narrative of compelling and tragic magnitude, so that the actual choice Sophie had been forced to make at Auschwitz, undisclosed until nearly the end of the tale, becomes the ultimate expression of modern despair, dreadful to the heart, the final anguish of our being human. *Lie Down in Darkness*, published in 1951, had touched me strongly in my youth, and when I came up from the South in the early 1960s, as callow and provincial as Stingo, to work for *Harper's* magazine, Bill Styron was one of the people I wanted to know. My Mississippi and his Virginia are different places, having produced quite different strains of the Southern-American personality, but writing is a mutual thing, and so too beneath the surface disparities there is finally a tenacious bedrock bond between our two native states, having to do with many old nuances of the greater American fiber. The best way to get to know Styron, I sensed, was to persuade him to do a magazine piece. The piece would be about his fascination as a young man growing up on the banks of the James River with the black slave Nat Turner, that legendary, heroic presence of Styron's neighborhood of lower Virginia. I drove up to Connecticut to confer with Bill and met him for the first time in C. Vann Woodward's office at Yale.

It was the beginning of a comradeship that over the years would span many miles, literally and figuratively, on the American landscape; an interest in one another's families and work; a common regard for the written word; evenings of conviviality in the house in Roxbury and in the farmhouse my wife and I had across the ridge in New York; the lofty plateaus and dismal swamps of two writers' lives; the growing up of our children; the gradual formalizing of an occasionally boisterous but, one hoped, not unedifying intellectual partnership called by common consent "The Bill and Willie Show" on college campuses from Carolina to Texas; the

202

rhythms and continuities of getting older.

From these many years of knowing Bill in numerous moods and moments, from the antiseptic lounges of Los Angeles and the oyster bars of the French Quarter to the watering spas of Manhattan and the faculty suites of Ivy League universities, I believe I grew to recognize in him the sources of his genius as one of America's foremost novelists. Writing fiction is a hard and draining calling, and at the core of his talent, both protectively and toward the fruition of high creativity, lay always an abiding humane intelligence—that humane intuitiveness which outlasts mere brilliance and cannot be taught in a man—this undergirded by his own especial obsession with the haunted land of the Old Dominion and the dark resonances of its past. This, and more: a passionate belief in the better instincts of our nature against the insufferable odds of existence, if only the best in men might fight unfettered against those odds.

Abetting these impulses of the spirit, two people more than all others contributed to his commitment and accomplishment as an artist. One, his wife Rose—nee Burgunder—a beautiful Jewish girl from Baltimore, whose poetic feel for literature and her talent as an editor and an advocate have supported him beyond measure, and whose boundless giving and buoyancy have provided a milieu for immemorial fellowship, as well as four healthy, intelligent American children.

The other, his father, William Clark Styron, who died in 1978 at age 88. *Sophie's Choice* is dedicated to this splendid man, a Southern gentleman who never spurned his country origins and whose loyalty to Bill never deviated. The expression of joy which washed his features when his son and I came to fetch him from a nursing home in North Carolina to bring him to Connecticut three years before he died will remain with me to my own dying day, and the character of Stingo's father in *Sophie's Choice* is his deserved memorial.

203

It is all such as this, I think, which has helped give Bill the courage in his work to address himself to the great moral themes of life, to "the old verities and universal truths" toward which one of his heroes encouraged those of us who write. In *Lie Down in Darkness* the theme was the disintegration of family and community in a transient age, in *Nat Turner* it was the institution of slavery, and in *Sophie's Choice* it is the 20th-century madness, the totalitarian bestiality which engulfed all humankind. "The literature that has meant the most to me," Bill said recently, "was written by people who concerned themselves with the moral sense, with the meaning to the riddle. They were grappling with the imponderables of life. I always felt I had to try to do the same thing. It's always seemed to me that writers should be ambitious, in the deep artistic sense, that they should strive to climb the highest mountain. Faulkner said we should be measured by the splendor of our failures. I'd rather come a cropper on something which mattered than succeed at something precious, something merely to be cuddled and fondled. Auschwitz, all that it represents, is one of the staggering events in the history of the human race. I wanted to confront it."

Bill had only been to Mississippi once, and that was the briefest of visits. He came down one oppressively hot July day in 1962 for Faulkner's funeral in Oxford, on assignment from *Life Magazine*. He flew in with Bennett Cerf, Faulkner's publisher at Random House. As I was told it years later by Oxford people who were there that day, Bennett Cerf and Styron entered Faulkner's large antebellum house called Rowan Oak, where they were sighted by Faulkner's sister-in-law Aunt Dot. Aunt Dot rushed upstairs to Miss Estelle, Faulkner's widow, and said: "There are two suspicious-looking Yankees down there." Faulkner's niece Dean rejoined that one of the new arrivals was a brilliant young Southern novelist whom Pappy admired and the other was Pappy's New York publisher. "Well, the writer looks all right," Aunt Dot persisted, "but I don't trust the other one. He's got shifty eyes. He's going to walk off with a book or an ashtray, just wait and see." Later, however, when Aunt Dot discovered that Bennett Cerf was the star of *What's My Line*, she became the perfect hostess, even under the funereal mood. Styron himself told me of a footnote to this. Waiting for the plane in the Memphis airport to return to New York, they were besieged by Bennett Cerf's television admirers. As he signed autographs, a woman asked him what he was doing down South. "I've just been to William Faulkner's funeral," he replied. "Who's he?" the lady asked.

This time Bill's trip to Mississippi was a happier one. He came to address the Ole Miss students, who derive from the rich literary tradition of their state, and he did so with his usual distinction. Bill, I have learned through the years, can be one of the world's funniest people when he is in the mood for it, and this high comic sense emerges in his novels, which are more generally noted for their themes of sorrow, tragedy, and mayhem. Like many artists who are imbibed with the sadness of the human adventure, he appreciates the possibilities of wit, and he had his Ole Miss audience poised between tears and laughter which, given the circumstances of things, is not a bad condition to be in at all.

On our rides through the mad, magic delta, flooded now after its torrential rains, and through the backroads of Yoknapatawpha, Bill was struck by the similarities between his precinct of rural Virginia—the peanut land around the James River and Nat Turner country—and rural Mississippi. He has frequently been to the Soviet Union, where he once lost his temper and walked out of a luncheon with the ranking Soviet literary bureaucrat who had been berating American writing, saying to the bureaucrat as he rose to leave, "At least we don't throw our writers in jail." On these drives through the state he was impressed, too, by these similarities between Russia and Mississippi—the brooding landscape, the obsession with the past, the sense of isolation, the sweep of the sky over rustic hamlets. "And the pride!" he said. "The pride of the people." He kept being reminded, he claimed, of scenes in Georgia, and not Jimmy Carter's Georgia either.

It was time to play another trick on Styron, because for reasons that would make another essay, hoaxes and Mississippi go in tandem and are inherent to this place. Once, several years before, on one of my annual visits to Rose and Bill on Martha's Vineyard, Bill and I were sitting at twilight on his lawn overlooking a broad, serene inlet, drinks in hand, watching the demise of that splendid August day. It was appropriate in that instant for Bill to begin quoting, in a kind of desultory way, those words at the end of *The Great Gatsby*.

> And as I sat there brooding on the old, unknown world, I thought of Gatsby's wonder when he first picked out the green light at the end of Daisy's dock. He had come a long way to this blue lawn, and his dream must have seemed so close that he could hardly fail to grasp it. He did not know that it was already behind him, somewhere back in that vast obscurity beyond the city, where the dark fields of the republic rolled on under the night.

The next day I sought out Herman Gollob, my colleague and book editor at *Harper's* who, despite being a Texas Aggie, owned a house directly across the inlet from Styron's with a dock in back. We went to a hardware store in Vineyard Haven and purchased a large outdoor lamp, and then to a hippie art shop for some green filter paper. We synchronized our watches, then went our separate ways. Late that afternoon Styron and I were again sitting on his lawn in the twilight. I looked down at my watch. "Bill," I said, "will you recite that passage from

Gatsby again?" He proceeded to do so. As he got to the green light, from across the inlet a light greener yet than Gatsby's began tossing and bobbing in the faint darkness; the reliable Herman Gollob, obscured to us from our distance, was running up and down his dock with the lamp.

"Bill, I think I see that elusive green light out yonder." Bill squinted across the waters. "By God, I see it too." He paused to look some more. "That's it, all right." And he shook his head in greater wonder than Gatsby ever did, and poured out his drink.

Now, on this day in the Snopes country of Yoknapatawpha, Styron, my son David, my big black labrador Pete, and I were heading toward a faraway country cemetery which I had discovered quite by accident on a dreary afternoon of February. My wont is to take long drives with my dog into remote places not in the travel guides, and on that February afternoon, lost for an hour or so on dirt roads, I had come across this cemetery. When Pete and I had gotten out to explore, I discovered something eerie about this graveyard. On about one tombstone in three was a photograph of the dead person, imbedded in the stone and covered with glass—photographs of young country boys who must have died racing their pickup trucks on Saturday nights or when their tractors fell over on them, of ancient married couples in bonnets and blue jeans, of an infant or two, some of these photographs fifty years old or more. It had been a day of somber purple clouds and a touch of thunder and lightning, a sudden bitter wind had sprung up from the hills, and from out in the woods the backwoods dogs who must have sniffed out my university dog joined in a chorus of ungodly howls. My dog, who usually is fearless, had tucked his tail between his legs and beseeched me to leave that dreadful place with its unnatural photographs of dead people tormenting us, and I had needed no urging in the departure.

Now, as Styron and I wandered among the graves examining the photographs, speculating on the circumstances of Fairy Jumper's death, or Idella and Ezra Conkle's, or Christopher Columbus Burchfield's, my son David whisked himself away to a far end of the graveyard with a paperback of Styron's novel *Lie Down in Darkness*. As prearranged, he placed the book on the grave of one James Dillard, who had died on February 9, 1909, and whose likeness blazed out for all to see, a John Brown visage, wild beard and fiercesome eyes. On the flyleaf of the novel my son had written: *"To William Styron . . . Come lie down in darkness with us. It is not as bad as it has been made out to be. From James Dillard and the Bethel dead."*

Eventually Styron and I, joined now by David, reached the farthest section of the cemetery. At James Dillard's grave Styron casually looked down and saw the book. In much the same tone as the evening on the Vineyard, he said: "What do we have here?" He picked up the book and read the inscription, shaking his head again at the enigma of it. Then, in a voice that might be heard across the gullies and hollows of that impoverished acre of the Mississippi earth, he read the haunted words from Sir Thomas Browne's *Urn Burial* that he had put at the beginning of *Lie Down in Darkness*, about old mortality and death and diurnity being a dream and folly of expectation. Across the way a farmer walking through a brown field of soybeans gazed across at the mysterious silhouette we must have made, and my dog seemed ready to get on back to Faculty Row again.

A few days later we met Rose at the airport in Jackson and made our way to the Governor's Mansion.

Jackson, like Washington, D.C., before it, was a planned city, and lies near the geographical center of the state. Thomas Jefferson himself, though having never been here, provided some of the earliest plans for its streets and parks. The city of my birth and of my childhood visits to my grandparents on North Jefferson has undergone two distinct destructions. The first came at Sherman's hand in 1863, months before the burning of Atlanta and the March to the Sea. After his and Grant's successful landing on the east bank of the Mississippi south of Vicksburg, he moved toward Jackson to destroy the railroad junction and make the city useless for General Joseph E. Johnston. His job was so thorough that for years afterward Jackson was known as "Chimneyville." The State Capitol and the Governor's Mansion were among the few substantial structures he chose to spare.

The second destruction came from ostensibly friendlier hands, in the form of the New South of recent years. The lovely and somnolent little city of my boyhood is no more—old neighborhoods and whole city blocks ripped raw, and the emergence of the giant shopping malls and suburbias. Remembering Jackson as it once was, I am left only with a broken heart.

But here, suddenly, on Capitol Street, the Governor's Mansion loomed before us, a cherished and familiar place amidst the dwindling of dreams. As Rose and Bill and David and I sighted it from our car in a soft dusk of springtime, it had a touch of lost moments for me when I walked barefoot on the sidewalk and looked upward toward its curtained windows and wondered what monumental events might be transpiring in there. We stopped in our car for a moment to absorb its antebellum Greek Revival dignity, the gazebos and fountains and gardens outside and the oaks my Uncle Henry Foote's wife planted there, and the semi-circular front portico with its four Corinthian columns and delicate capitals which so resembles the south portico of the White House. The

209

Mansion itself is not as large or imposing as the White House, but possesses a splendid grace all its own, the grace of character gained through suffering and loss. At the portico we were greeted by several servants in white jackets (I later learned they were trusties from Parchman, the state penal farm) and waiting for us inside the door were the Governor, his handsome wife Elise and their two daughters, and Charlotte Capers of the state archives. It was an ebullient Southern welcome, followed by a tour of the grand parlors and foyers of the main floor, all dominated by a magnificent curved staircase. This Mansion is, in fact, the second oldest official executive residence in continuous use in the country behind the White House, and once more it reminded me of the interior of the White House with its fine spaciousness and chandeliers and period pieces. I remembered the description I recently had read by a gentleman from Natchez to this small frontier town in the 1840s: "Much is anticipated by the elite here. When the Executive Mansion shall be ready, levees, re-unions, routs, conversations, dejeuners, and soirees will be the order of the day, and our political metropolis will become more gay, fashionable, and attractive. I have serious ideas of moving thither."

Our hosts escorted us upstairs to our rooms, then left us to get ready for dinner. William Winter is a tall, slender man of fifty-eight who talks and listens with an intensity that is by no means grave, and there is, God bless him, a touch of mischief in his gentle patrician chemistry, as when he assigned Rose and Bill Styron the Bilbo Bedroom.

The four of us wandered these splendid rooms in the spirit of children freshly awakened on Christmas morning. We felt adventurous on this night. David showed us his hand-carved four-poster bed in a pineapple design and the view from his room of a lush green garden. Rose

Styron, whose legendary Baltimore beauty has always been in full flush at such moments (she was remarkably beautiful on a midnight visit we once made to Appomattox, and her husband says she was equally radiant at the Parthenon) pointed out the old Boston looking glass and the red antique fabric and the gas chandeliers and the etagere between the windows. I took them into my enormous room and told them, as I had been advised, that General Sherman had slept here after the Fall of Vicksburg, not to mention the fabulous Mississippian Leontyne Price when she was a guest during the Winters' Inaugural.

"Wait til I tell my friends in New York!" Styron interrupted. I noticed he had been ruminating. "Sleeping in Bilbo's bed! Come on in here." He tried the mattress on the tester bed, then stood back to take it all in. "I'll bet a lot of mischief took place in *this* bed."

As with most Southern boys of a certain generation, Styron was not unacquainted with the follies and complexities of Theodore G. Bilbo. In his *Sophie's Choice* there is a painfully comic exchange between the young Southern protagonist-narrator "Stingo" and the brilliant, mad boyfriend of Sophie, the ill-fated Nathan Landau. It was a summer's day of 1947, and Bilbo, then U.S. Senator, was reported in the New York *Post* to be dying of throat cancer. "I read the article just a while ago on the subway," Nathan said. "I propose a toast to the slow, protracted, agonizing death of the Senator from Mississippi, Mushmouth Bilbo. To the death of Bilbo, to the sounds of the screams of his last agony."

I sensed the blood flashing scarlet somewhere behind my eyes . . . "Nathan," I said, "not long ago at one point I paid you a slight compliment. I said that despite your profound animosity toward the South, you at least retained a little sense of humor about it, unlike many people. Unlike the standard New York liberal jackass . . . I've got no use for

211

Bilbo and never did, but if you think there's any comedy in this *ham-handed* bit about his death, you're wrong. I refuse to toast the death of *any* man—"

"You would not toast the death of Hitler?" he put in quickly, with a mean glint in his eye.

It brought me up short. "*Of course* I would toast the death of Hitler. But that's a f------ different matter! Bilbo's not Hitler!"

In debate, especially when the issue is hot and super-charged and freighted with ill will, I have always been the flabbiest of contenders . . . "You've read *Faulkner*, Nathan, and you still have this assy and intolerable attitude of superiority toward the place, and are unable to see how Bilbo is less a villain than a wretched offshoot of the whole benighted system. . . . Besides," I persisted, "you totally fail to realize what a man of real achievement Theodore Bilbo was." Echoes of my college dissertation rattled about in my head with the filing-card rhythm of scholarly blank verse. "When he was governor, Bilbo brought Mississippi a series of important reforms," I intoned, "including the creation of a highway commission and a board of pardons. He established the first tuberculosis sanatorium. He added mutual training and farm mechanics to the curriculum of the schools. And finally he introduced a program to combat ticks . . ." My voice trailed off.

"He introduced a program to combat ticks," Nathan said.

Startled, I realized that Nathan's gifted voice was in perfect mockery of my own—pedantic, pompous, insufferable. "There was a widespread outbreak of something called Texas fever among the Mississippi cows," I persisted uncontrollably. "Bilbo was instrumental—"

"You fool," Nathan interrupted, "you silly klutz. Texas fever! You *clown*! You want me to point out that the glory of the Third Reich was a highway system unsurpassed in the world and that Mussolini made the trains run on time?"

He had me cold—I must have known it as soon as I heard myself utter the word "ticks" . . .

After a pleasant dinner for twelve in the State Dining Room, we four guests retired to the Bilbo Room for a nightcap. David was perusing a guide to the Mansion and passed along the information that Mississippi was so poor after the Civil War that many of the leaders wanted to sell the old house to private interests. But the sentimental attachment to it, towering as it did over "Chimneyville," carried the day. Later, in 1904, Governor James K. Vardaman also proposed to sell the Mansion, David said. But the United Daughters of the Confederacy, the Daughters of 1812, the United Confederate Veterans, the Women's Christian Temperance Union, and the Old Ladies Home Association successfully petitioned the legislature not to "destroy what Sherman would not burn." David had taken to calling Styron "Uncle Stingo." He said: "Listen to this, Uncle Stingo," and proceeded to read from a section about George Plimpton's great-grandfather Ames. In 1868 General Ames, a proper New Englander, could not find suitable quarters in Jackson, so he sent over some soldiers with bayonets and had Governor Humphreys and his family vacate the Mansion. "The prediction that Old Ben Humphreys will long live in the memory of the people," David read, "while Ames would only be remembered for his infamy has been fulfilled." David showed us the guide with a portrait of General Ames. "He looks just like old George," Styron observed.

Sitting around Bilbo's bed, the four of us talked of many things—of Styron's great-uncle Clark, who had been the Mississippi state treasurer under my great-uncle Foote, and of how they must have sat up late talking like us in this very house in the 1850s; of how we wished Plimpton were with us so we could evict him into the stormy night; of whether Bilbo's ghost roamed these halls.

As I lay in my bed (and Sherman's, and Leontyne Price's) before sleep came that night, listening to the rain falling steadily on the new Chimneyville, and the thunder rumbling in from the delta, and the gentle nocturnal echoes of the Capitol Street of my childhood, I dwelled upon the arguments that must have taken place under this ancient roof on national allegiance and sectional interest before that long-ago war, of the strains of music and the laughter of the Mississippi belles lost now to dust, of Bilbo walking the room across the foyer in the witching hours planning his campaign against ticks.

Quite early the next morning I was awakened by a rude shaking. It was Bill Styron. "Get up!" he said. "I've got something to tell you." At first I thought the Mansion might be on fire, such was the look in his eye. "I had the most extraordinary dream," he said. "I'm sure it's because I was sleeping in Bilbo's bed. Listen to this——." He had an appointment with Henry Kissinger, it was hazy whether he was supposed to meet Kissinger in Washington or New York, but it was on some question of overwhelming national importance, and Kissinger had to see him. Then another figure entered the dream, Kissinger's mulatto secretary, a beautiful and enigmatic figure, who refused to allow him to see Kissinger. "She simply wouldn't let me go into Henry's office," Styron complained. "She kept getting in my way. It was mildly erotic, and very frustrating. Hell. It was the strangest dream I ever had. All that damned Bilbo's doing." He kept talking about it in the tour we made in one of the Mansion's cars that day of Raymond, Port Gibson, and Vicksburg.

That evening a capacity crowd came to the "William and Bill and Willie Show" in the auditorium at Millsaps, a small and distinguished liberal arts college which Big Hodding Carter at the height of the racial crisis called "the most courageous little college in America." The topic was to reflect on our region as a great source and training ground for writers, and to discuss something of the Southern past in the burdens of its history and in the changes now taking place.

Without intending to, the Governor stole the show. He began by introducing several dozen of my friends and neighbors from my native Yazoo whom he had invited to the discussion and to a reception later at the Mansion. It was easy that evening to see why the quality of leadership he was bringing to the state was different from anything Mississippians have gotten out of any Governor they have had in modern history. He is eloquent and scholarly, yet he has not turned his back on the colorful rhetoric of his political tradition. He spoke of Mississippi's writers as the finest part of the heritage of the state, of the communal and historical sense which has contributed to this heritage. He discussed literature in relation to social changes, of the old grievances in the racial climate and the possibilities residing in the new awareness. I do not have notes on that session, but I did write on a scrap of paper which I have before me now: "He is saying things which no Governor of a Deep Southern state has ever said, and with the eloquence of a Stevenson or a John Kennedy. This is a historic moment for Mississippi."

On the way back to the Mansion, the Governor and Styron and I were talking. Writers have terrible things to get over, Bill said—such as destructive reviews when they are getting started. For a politician the equivalent has to be *defeat*. The Governor remembered, he said, his first loss for the governorship. "I never wanted anything more badly. I thought I had it won, that I deserved it. I thought it was the worst thing that could ever happen to me. I didn't want to face myself or anyone else for a long time." We entered the gates of the Mansion, floodlit now against the threatening sky. "Then it dawned on me—you have to keep going. Not feel sorry for yourself, but *keep on going*."

The next morning, as we were preparing to leave, Styron came in to report another dream he had had in Bilbo's bed. This time it was not about Henry Kissinger's mulatto secretary, although she figured in it in a rather obscure way. Rather it was about our mutual friend Robert Penn Warren. "This dream was telling me not to worry about growing old," Bill said. "It was telling me about Red Warren. I had this vivid image of Red—over seventy, strong and vital and having fun and doing wonderful work. It was a message to me. If getting older means to be like Red, then there's nothing to worry myself about." Then he shook his head, as he had on discovering his book in the Bethel cemetery; he was plainly impressed with this fine and unusual dream about keeping going.

The Winters came to say goodbye in the portico. As we departed, the magnificent old Mansion reflected the morning's sparkling sun. We had an appointment, not in Kissinger's office, but in Yazoo, forty miles up the road, beyond the hills toward the delta.

A Cook's Tour

THIS BOOK is an echo. It has evoked for me
many memories of the food of my childhood, and the
fine rituals of cooking as it then existed. I remember my
grandmother's stories of the Sunday suppers in the
1880s at the family house in Raymond when the preacher
came, and since she was the youngest of the seventeen
children, she sat at the farthest end of the table. "By the
time the fried chicken got down to me, all that was left
were the necks and the wings," she would tell me, pausing to add, "But they were still mighty good." I remember her own fried chicken, which she would soak overnight in buttermilk and make for me late at night after
the Jackson Senators baseball games, and we would sit
on the front porch and gorge ourselves on this nocturnal
feast and talk over the events of the ball game.

I remember the political rallies in the woods of Yazoo
County in the 1940s, where Senator Bilbo and the others
were of secondary importance to the barbecue and the
buttered yams and the biscuits dipped in molasses and
the corn-on-the-cob, steamier and richer even than the
perfervid rhetoric. I remember, too, the squirrels my father and I would bring home to Yazoo from an afternoon's hunting in the dark autumnal woods and the in-
comparable squirrel-and-dumplings my mother would
make, inviting the neighbors over for some of it. And

Introduction to *A Cook's Tour of Mississippi*, 1980

217

the covered-dish suppers at the country churches right out of the Nineteenth Century where a young Mississippi boy could be a paragon of religiosity just to sample the venison stews and chicken pies and casseroles of a dozen kinds and cracklin' bread and meringue pies that made the eternal ragings of the Devil himself less contemptuous.

And I remember, as my friends and I got older—the journey-proud college years—our wanderings out into the Delta to Lusco's in Greenwood for pompano and red snapper and to Doe's in Greenville for the best tamales and T-bones in the Western world. It was to this latter establishment that the famous Northern journalist David Halberstam came on the first evening of a long sojourn in Greenville. As told to me years later by Halberstam himself, he looked around the not-so-modish kitchen where the tables were set and almost left forthwith but stayed at the urging of friends and returned every night after that for three months.

One learned early on in Mississippi that the state's truly fine restaurants were very few, and that remains true today. The tradition of Mississippi cuisine in all its variety and eccentricity still largely emanates from the private home or the strange, colorful places like Lusco's and Doe's. In Lafayette County, which some know as Yoknapatawpha, several miles from the Ole Miss campus I have found two such institutions which make me forget the martini business lunches in Manhattan. Both of these Lafayette County establishments are grocery stores. One of them, in Abbeville near the Tallahatchie River, has a long counter in the back and has changing menus written every day on a blackboard—a local meat dish and five or six delectable fresh vegetables straight from the garden. The other is in the hamlet of Taylor, where William Faulkner placed his novel *Sanctuary* and where Temple Drake eventually found herself in serious trouble. At the back of this store are several long tables, and the specialty is catfish, possibly the best I have ever had. On the night before a football game, while the catfish was frying, one reveler among many wrote a graphic synopsis of *Sanctuary* on the wall, which is there to this day. Every county in the state has a place or two like these (Yazoo City has Stub's Restaurant, a couple of miles from where the Delta begins), and they are not to be found in the travel guides. They are continuing the tradition.

In my opinion *The Clarion-Ledger* under its brilliant young executive editor, Rea Hederman, has joined the ranks of that rare handful of truly distinguished Southern papers. It has achieved a flair and an honesty seldom found in American journalism today; it is both entertaining and profoundly civilizing, and it shows its love for Mississippi, for the complexities and the fibers of this most unusual state.

"Publishing a cookbook may seem an odd avocation for a newspaper," Hederman wrote me recently, "but we prefer to think of it as an attempt to preserve something purely Mississippian." He added:

> So many things people reared in this state took for granted only a few years ago have since disappeared—leaving sometimes only exaggerated memories. This book should place some of those things in a permanent form which will not be changed by faulty, though perhaps well-meaning memories. And just maybe by writing of subjects important to Mississippi tradition, some who can will find ways to preserve them. This act of preservation would be an important service by any newspaper and is compatible with *The Clarion-Ledger*'s philosophy of trying to do justice to the past as well as the present.

I applaud these words, and the valuable book which has emerged from this commitment. *The Clarion-Ledger* has covered all the geographical areas of the state seeking not only indigenous Mississippi recipes,

219

but something more—the personal stories and adventures, the social history, which have contributed to them. Most of these 100 or so recipes are from distinctive, out-of-the-way places, and by out I mean *out* from Waynesboro, *out* from Gluckstadt, *out* from Pelahatchie. I am also pleased to see, as I turn these pages, that *A Cook's Tour of Mississippi* deals almost exclusively with authentic Mississippi produce: okra and squash and corn and greens and rooster spur peppers and cushaws (or, for the uninitiated, winter crooknecks); oysters and crabs and shrimp and catfish; venison and quail and squirrel and rabbit; sorghum and watermelons and pecans and blackberries. I doubt if this book could have been compiled in Wilkes Barre, Pennsylvania, or Akron, Ohio, or Newark, New Jersey, not to mention the southern Bronx or the exurbs of Walla Walla.

A Cook's Tour of Mississippi is a reflection of our tenacious heritage. In these pages one will find the old things:

. . . the lady in Natchez who prepares her hot pepper jelly in the makeshift kitchen of a carriage house, where the breezes from the River cool her off even in the summertime.

. . . the sportsman from Clinton whose grandmother's specialty was blackbird dumplings, and who describes fried rattlesnake as "a cross between frogs' legs and fish."

. . . the old black man in Canton who used to walk around the courthouse square selling miniature lemon, pecan and fruit pies to raise money to rebuild his church which had blown down.

. . . the revolving table lunches at the old Mendenhall Hotel with twelve vegetables and four kinds of meat every day.

. . . the biscuit recipe from William Faulkner's mother's handwritten recipe book.

. . . the store-owner who feels he must maintain the illustrious reputation of Hot Coffee, Mississippi.

. . . the recipe for Aunt Beck's chicken pie from the family reunion in Eudora Welty's *Losing Battles*.

. . . the covered dish suppers at the little Gothic church near Gluckstadt and the legends of the ghosts from the graveyard surrounded by its old wrought-iron fence.

. . . the annual watermelon seed spitting contest in Smith County and several mystifying watermelon recipes, which led this reader to believe, as with George Washington Carver and the peanut, that the people of Smith County have found more in the watermelon than was in the watermelon before they started.

Certainly one of the most appealing aspects of Southern and especially Mississippi cooking has always been the people who do it, and this volume is filled with these intriguing personalities. In some homes, of course, the cook has been a beloved servant, helping the lady of the household raise the children—beautiful human beings who brought their own immeasurable love and devotion to the home. That is a time mostly gone by, and is undoubtedly another book, or several, or a library.

Nowadays, in different times, the rituals are changing. The Mississippi cook today is sometimes a woman, or man, or both, with a coterie of children and friends to entertain, often at the same time. I am reminded, for instance, of the lovely young woman from the Delta who serenely marinates and chops and sautes and serves up delightful dishes on the perfect china with the correct liquids in the right glasses for a small tribe of guests and makes it all seem effortless. Much of the work may be done while we ourselves are sitting comfortably in the kitchen during a Delta storm, sour-mash in hand, exchanging stories about people long gone, or events from the past, or the myths handed down. This desultory Mississippi kitchen talk, surrounded by the chatter of children and imbued with the grand oven smells, is inherent to us. In just a few minutes, thirty or sixty—who's counting?—the cook announces dinner in the other room where the perfect table has been appointed. And here it is . . .

A Man for All Seasons

Two of my favorite people in Oxford, Mississippi, are Ed Perry and Jake Gibbs. Ed is the chairman of the appropriations committee of the state House of Representatives, which places him as roughly the third most important public man in the Sovereign State of Mississippi, and Jake is the baseball coach at Ole Miss. They are both around the same age, fortyish, and they have certain things in common. Neither is given much to moods, and both, if I may say so, are men of integrity who choose not to speak of such a quality in themselves. Both are very funny men, too, noted for an occasional flamboyance, and known to tell long stories when the mood is upon them. Both are as Mississippi as the Tallahatchie River. "He's one of the two or three best people at Ole Miss," the chairman says of the coach.

The coach, who goes by "Jakie" to some of us, is soon to open a new baseball season—a game against Livingston here on Thursday, and three conference games against Alabama here this weekend unless it rains, which Mississippi often does in February, March, and April, preparing us for the choking dry summers which are especially bad on our women and our dogs. Then the Fighting Irish of Notre Dame come in for two singles in March, pale-skinned Yankee Catholic boys who have been working out in an overheated basement in South

The Daily Mississippian, February 26, 1981

Bend, Indiana, during the ferocious Midwestern winter, and who last saw the sun in November. These Yankee teams which travel through the South in late February and March are impressed by the Southern curve-ball almost as much as they are by the green grass, the jonquils, and the Dixie co-eds sitting in the bleachers with layers of Royal Hawaiian Coconut Sun Tan Lotion on their untarnished limbs and noses.

This is Jake's tenth season at Ole Miss, and we should pause now to consider whom we have here. He may be the best college baseball coach in America, and he certainly is the best college coach who chews tobacco with dignity. He was the last Ole Miss athlete who was all-American in two sports, football and baseball. This was 1960, two decades ago although it was really yesterday to some of us, and Jakie was the quarterback and co-captain (along with our comrade Warner Alford, the athletic director) of the last Ole Miss team to win the national championship. In the catastrophic Ole Miss-LSU game on Hallowe'en night of '59 in Baton Rouge, the night my son was born in the other Oxford in England, Jakie had the final shot at Billy Cannon on his legendary 87-yard run. He had just punted to Cannon, and he had a chance at him at about the Ole Miss fifteen-yard line. Never mind that he missed. Ole Miss whipped LSU in a repeat engagement in the Sugar Bowl later that season and won it all.

Jakie was a third-baseman for Ole Miss. When he graduated he chose professional baseball over football, and he signed with the New York Yankees. They dispatched him to their Triple-A club in Richmond. Then a curious thing happened. The Yankees were bereft of catchers in their organization; these were the waning days of Elston Howard, the Yankee catcher. The Yanks called on Jakie to make one of the most awesome transformations a human being can ever be asked to make, short of a Swedish sex change, going back to the Old Testament—infielder to catcher. He did so gallantly, as testified by his gnarled fingers. He spent seven years as a catcher for the Yankees. Here are his career major league statistics from the *Encyclopedia of Baseball*—not of mythic dimensions, these stats, but unrelenting nonetheless. There is no copy of this gargantuan *Encyclopedia* in Yoknapatawpha County, and I had to telephone my friend Donald "Cal" Calabrese in Bobby Van's Saloon in Bridgehampton, New York—a distinguished scholar of baseball if ever one existed—for Jakie's lifetime bottom line:

G	AB	H	2B	3B	HR	R	RBI	SB	BA
538	1639	382	53	8	25	157	146	28	.243

"I figured I had two, three more seasons in me in the bigs," Jakie says to me. "But the Ole Miss coaching job opened up. Tom Swayze, my old coach, was retiring. I jumped at the chance to come home. Besides, Trish and I were gettin' tired of livin' in the suburbs of New Jersey. The Mets boys lived on Long Island. The Yankees lived in New Jersey. We could drive to work across the George Washington Bridge in thirty minutes." Trish, of whom he speaks, his delectible wife and high school girl friend from Grenada, Mississippi, remembers the moment. "Whew!" she says. "Was I ready to get on back! Jersey wasn't at all like Mississippi." The first thing Jakie did on his return was to win the conference title and almost the national championship in Omaha, only a nine-run seventh inning by the incorrigible Texas Longhorns denying him that honor, losing 9-8. The polls had him ranked second nationally in '72. He won the SEC again in 1977, and reached the conference playoffs last year.

Jakie and I have a fine mutual friend, Michael Burke, now the President of Madison Square Garden and of the

New York Knicks. Mike Burke is one of America's eminent figures—an all-American halfback for Penn in 1939, a war hero who was parachuted behind Nazi lines and fought with the French Resistance and had a movie made about him called *O.S.S.* with Alan Ladd playing Mike, who still owns five percent of the Yankees and was their president when Jakie was their catcher. Mike was also a close friend of Hemingway, and is of Irwin Shaw and Kurt Vonnegut, among others.

Last spring, Jakie and I got Mike Burke to come to Oxford and speak to my students about his friendship with Hemingway and Shaw and Vonnegut and throw out the first ball at the Ole Miss-Delta State game on "Mike Burke Day." Jakie gave Mike an Ole Miss baseball cap, which barely covered Mike's long and stylish hair, well-known in the Manhattan newspapers; his hair somehow protruded and covered most of the visor. Warner Alford had set up a microphone at home plate. It was one of those dark, windswept March afternoons in Mississippi, purple thunderheads out on the horizon. Boo Ferriss, the Delta State coach who won twenty-three games for the Red Sox in 1946, stood on the Delta State side and applauded as the gentleman he is. Mike Burke went to the microphone:

> We New York Yankees have had our Ruths, our Dimaggios, our Berras, our Mantles. But no Yankee ever wore the pinstripes with more class and distinction and courage than Jakie Gibbs.

Now, as his tenth season opens, you will sight Jakie in the third base coaching box, chewing tobacco and missing no facet of this grand, complex old game, better and more intelligent than all games. Catch him later, in his usual good temper and among friends and with Trish, perhaps with someone playing some Cole Porter on the piano in his "den" on Andrews Circle with all his sports

226

mementoes on the wall, and he will tell you about the umpire in Triple-A who kept talking between pitches about the sexy girls in the grandstand until Jakie had to tell him to be quiet. Or about the time he made his most horrific blunder as the Yankee catcher when he forgot the Detroit Tigers had a runner on third base and ran with the ball from homeplate toward second where the Tigers also had a runner (the Yankee shortstop, named Rueben Amaro, who spoke little English, shouting all the while in his astonishment: "Jakie—the ball to me, Jakie! Is you crazy?" as the runner from third scored) or about the fast-balling Sad Sam McDowell of Cleveland being the meanest pitcher he ever faced, or the afternoon he slipped a curve from McDowell himself into the rightfield bleachers of the Yankee Stadium with two men on base, and knew it was gone, and just stood there for a moment savoring it.

"I love it here and am very much at home," Jakie says, chewing tobacco in his backyard, cold Moosehead in hand, while the steaks sizzle on the barbeque. His words are those of the baseball man long around the league. We got experience comin' back. A good defensive team. Stronger at the bat than last year. Some depth in the pitchin', but not as much as last year. It's a club the fans will like and enjoy. The only thing we don't have is a lighted field."

Yet there is something eminently attractive to me in having Swayze Field remain the Wrigley Field of the SEC—the afternoon doubleheaders stretching across the golden afternoons, the students dropping in after class, the dirt farmers from Beat Two congregating in the left field bleachers, the eternal coeds languidly absorbing the sun and thinking, no doubt, of Kierkegaard, Dostoevski, and Balzac. Three rows down will be Chancellor Fortune, an Old Chapel Hill curve-balling pitcher from the mountains of West Carolina (Thomas Wolfe country), in his shirtsleeves talking with some students about whether Jakie will bunt his man to second. On one such day of a splendid April, against Alabama I believe it was, I was sitting next to Governor Winter when the umpire made an evil call at third base—an Alabama runner out by three feet on a slide, but called safe. Out of ancient impulse I stood up and shouted my unexpurgated opinions to the umpire. Then I realized what I was doing and sheepishly sat down. "I'm sorry about that, Governor," I said. "Don't worry," he replied. "I couldn't get away with it, but you expressed my sentiments perfectly."

I journeyed to Starkville last spring to see Ole Miss play Mississippi State. It was a night game, and the Mississippi State students, four thousand of them, were ill-behaved. It was the last day of their final examinations, and they had been drinking beer all afternoon. I had gone over in a honored vehicle called "The Love Van" with William Lewis, Jr., and several Rebel stalwarts from the Square, an adequate bar having been set up in back. We were a tiny cadre behind the Ole Miss dugout, and the alien fans heckled us without mercy, as they did their regular plate umpire, a large black man, though not without affection: "Go eat some more watermelon, Bobby!" Their taunts toward Jakie in the coaching box were muted, touched with that enigmatic respect even inebriated young Mississippians have for their enemy heroes. "Hey, Jakie, go chase Billy Cannon one more time! . . . Say, Jakie, why don't *you* get on up and take a swing?"

The many conversations I have had with Jakie over the Mississippi days are about baseball, and always tinged with laughter. Several times last spring I would take my students' papers and sit in the bleachers and read them during practice. A few big old football players, guards and tackles, fresh from weight-lifting, would sit in the sunshine too, wondering perhaps if they could bench-press the bleachers. Beyond the outfield fence were the young magnolias, and the football stadium looming there, immense and contained. The sturdy echo of bat on ball brought back in a torrent for me the baseball days of my Yazoo boyhood. Jakie would spot me from down by the dugout and come up for a chat. We would share a tobacco plug, and spit through the seats.

"What you readin' there?" Jakie asks.

"Some papers from my students," I reply. "They're about a book, *Bang the Drum Slowly*. This catcher has a disease, and the closer he comes to death a funny thing happens. He gets to be a better catcher than he ever was."

"Is he hittin' better?"

"That, and better on defense."

"Gettin' better and dyin' too?"

"He really is."

"I think I can believe that, if he was a catcher," Jakie says.

Down on the field the southpaw, throwing seriously to a hitter, is having trouble with his control. Jakie gingerly emits some tobacco juice. Then he cups his hands and shouts, loud enough to be heard in the football stadium: "Keep it low, Jeff!"

The Stable

THERE IS A tradition in the South, as in other parts of America, that a story worth telling places a responsibility on the listener to tell it again, in another place.

These stories link us to our known past. They are best told in the voice of one's oldest living relative, in the dark on a summer evening, the whole family gathered on a screened porch, quiet in their listening so that the thumping of night-flying beetles against the screens and the whine of locusts and cicadas merge with the story-teller's voice to become part of the tale. Such a setting, reaching past into the fiber of childhood, endures as vividly in the memory as the tale itself.

One of the South's greatest storytellers, William Faulkner, was no stranger to this tradition. As a child he listened to stories told by his grandfather, John Wesley Thompson Falkner, of Nathan Bedford Forrest raiding the Gayoso Hotel in Memphis, spurring his horse into the lobby and forcing a Yankee general to escape out a window in his underwear; of J.W.T.'s father, Col. William Clark Falkner, young Bill's namesake, and his adventures as a duelist, railroad builder, lawyer, planter, and writer. And Bill, in turn, passed on his grandfather's stories, and others of his own imaginings, to the next Faulkner generation, including his daughter, Jill, his

American Bookseller, October 1980.

granddaughter, Vicki, and his niece, Dean.

Through the years Faulkner told the stories over and over to the children, sometimes by request, sometimes at his own pleasure. Hallowe'en was a standard occasion for his storytelling, and Mr. Bill created an annual ritual which the Faulkner children and their friends eagerly looked forward to. With all the lights turned off in his big, antebellum home which he called Rowan Oak (after the Scottish legend that a branch of the rowan tree, when nailed to one's door, will keep out evil spirits), and two big jack-o'-lanterns flickering on either side of his front steps, Mr. Bill gathered the children around him for a ghostly tale, usually about Rowan Oak's blithe spirit, the lovely and doomed Judith Sheegog, daughter of the original owner of the house. Judith was said to have committed suicide over an unrequited love affair with a Yankee soldier and was subsequently buried under an ancient magnolia at the end of the front walk. After chilling his young listeners with an account of Judith's demise, her unsanctified burial, and her later hauntings, Mr. Bill would invite the children to approach the ghost's dark grave under the magnolia with a single lit candle as protection against the spirit. "Don't anybody want to visit Judith?" he would ask his young friends.

The children were delighted, however, to be scared out of their wits, and they never hesitated to ask Mr. Bill for a story. To his own children and their friends he was known as "Pappy," and whatever reputation he might possess in the world outside Oxford, the children regarded him as a grownup friend who would entertain them. His stories created for them a magic world of the imagination, and they never tired of hearing the same tales over and over. When Mr. Bill was not at Rowan Oak, they would retell the stories to each other in their best imitations of "Pappy." After they grew up, they

231

continued to tell Pappy's ghost stories to their own children.

Mr. Bill's only niece, Dean Faulkner Wells, has recounted her uncle's ghost stories in her new book, *The Ghosts of Rowan Oak*, published by Yoknapatawpha Press, in Oxford, Mississippi. Mrs. Wells was named after her father, Dean, Mr. Bill's youngest brother, who was killed in an airplane crash at the age of 28. Her book includes three stories Faulkner told—"Judith," "The Werewolf," a tale of the supernatural set in England and "The Hound," a murder story in which the victim's faithful dog gets revenge for its master's death. Dean Wells describes Rowan Oak and the Pappy of her childhood with a rare eye and with the Faulkner care and genius for words, and with the emotion of love. She has recaptured the sorcery of her uncle's story-telling, reviving those moments on the front steps of Rowan Oak in the dark. Here is a sample, in which she addresses her young audience directly to allow them to share the mood and texture of Pappy's Hallowe'en ritual:

> On this night of the supernatural, Pappy would sit on the steps with you and the other costumed children clustered around him, all eyes wide in the flickering candlelight. He seemed to belong outdoors. His skin was weathered, tan, and slightly wrinkled; and he smelled of horses and leather, cedars and sunshine, pipe tobacco and bourbon. His eyes were brown, so dark that they seemed black, and the fine lines around them were traced by smiles and sadness. His hair was gray, cropped close to his head, his small mouth nearly hidden beneath his mustache. Even on the steps he sat very straight, his shoulders squared, his legs crossed. His hands were still, except for the occasional, deliberate movements of his pipe, when he tapped it against the steps. His voice was low and soft, and he spoke rapidly, so that you would strain to catch his words, even though you knew the story almost as well as he. You would be drawn to him by the sound of his voice as much as by the magic of his tale.

Dean Faulkner Wells continues to live in the Oxford of her childhood—a small Southern town yet, full of its lost ghosts and legends. She has three children, two teenaged daughters and a fourteen-year-old son, "Jaybird." (No day is complete for me here without seeing the "Jaybird" ambling about the good old town, seeking his many adventures.) Her husband, Larry, owns the Yoknapatawpha Press, which published *The Ghosts of Rowan Oak*.

After my many years in the publishing world of New York, it touches me to do business with a man with an ancient office and balcony overlooking an authentic Southern courthouse square, and where a publishing contract is a handshake ritualized over a beer in a reconverted cotton gin. There is much fashionable rhetoric about the importance to America of book publishers outside of New York City. Well, here is a functioning one, doing good work and located over the Sneed Ace Hardware Store.

Larry Wells recently brought out a reprint of a children's book I once had published in New York at the same time he published Dean's recounting of the ghost stories. One night in the office above the hardware store (it had been Gavin Stevens' law office in the film *Intruder in the Dust*) I found myself with Dean and Larry putting dust jackets on the books until the late hours, cutting the shrink wrappage, and handling the telephone calls. At Dean's request I telephoned her house to see if "The Jaybird" was doing his homework. (He was watching television.) On a large crate of books Dean scrawled in a felt pen: "Packed and Written by the Author." Judy Trott from Ole Miss and Patty Lewis from The Rose for Emily House dropped in to help. We gave them the shrink-wrappage. I told them I had never had such assignments from my various Eastern publishers. "They don't do it this way at Random House," I said.

Several times that autumn the Yoknapatawpha Press

233

went on the road. We travelled to Memphis, Biloxi, Pass Christian, Tupelo, Yazoo City, Batesville, Clarksdale, Jackson, and Cleveland for book-signing parties. A woman in Belzoni said, "This is the first time an author has ever signed a book in this town. This is the first time," she added, "that a grown man ever held a book in his hand in this town."* In a bookstore in New Orleans I glanced up to see my friend Walker Percy standing in a long line to have our children's books signed. "What's your line of work, sir?" I asked him, as a group of admiring Tulane co-eds gathered about. "I stay in my house across Lake Pontchartrain and drink bourbon," Walker Percy replied.

Invariably, as we departed Oxford in Larry's car, the trunk and back seat would be crammed with posters and boxes of books, so that the rear end sagged precariously with the weight, like the Okies' vehicles on their exodus to California. Our main problem was leaving enough room on the back seat for Dean. Since she is on the small side, as all Faulkners, we usually managed. On these travels, however, we spent a great deal of time at Greyhound bus stations and the offices of the United Parcel Service, picking up more book shipments. We had an impromptu book-signing at the Greyhound station in Gulfport. Larry became known to us as "Boss," which I have never called Cass Canfield, Alfred A. Knopf, or Nelson Doubleday. At book-signings, whenever Dean or I shouted "Quittin' Time!", the Boss damned well knew we were finished. To the Boss, Dean and I were "The Stable," with rights and privileges extending deeply into the Common Law. One table, two chairs, and an ashtray at all bookstores; bourbon on the rocks in the car on lengthy trips, or for that matter short ones; no visits to bus stations after dark. Once, when the Boss stopped in

---

*This is not quite true. A few gentlemen of Belzoni read books, though secretly.

234

a service station between Pass Christian and New Orleans to fetch some ice, Dean looked out the back window and said, "You won't believe this. The Boss is trying to sell his Ole Miss football book to that drunk service-station attendant." Another time, after a strenuous book-signing in Biloxi, in a torrential Gulf Coast rainstorm the Boss pulled in front of a liquor store to get us some Bloody-Mary mix. He opened the door and, just before dashing out into the rain, turned and said: "While I get the Bloody Marys, I want you two to think about your writing."

Not too long ago I read the three-part series in *The New Yorker* about the world of big publishers in this corporate age. No, they don't do things like this up there. I think the Yoknapatawpha Press has a Mississippi way of facing the world.

The Americanization
of Mississippi

WHEN I WAS running *Harper's Magazine*, an irascible friend from New Orleans who had been living in New York City for a long time used to come to the bar on Madison Avenue and 34th Street where we would congregate with our writers after work. One afternoon there were a couple of people there from Mississippi, and we were talking about change in our native state. After listening to a little of this, my friend from New Orleans launched into this tirade: "You fellows are writers, and you have the gall to say you want to change Mississippi? You must be insane. Here you are from a place that's produced the best damned writers in America, that's always had the courage of the most noble fools, and the most tormenting landscape in all the United States, and a spoken word that would make a drunk Irishman envious, and miscegenation that's the envy of Brazil, and a sense of the histrionic that would pale the Old Testament, and a past so contorted that it embarrasses the people of Scarsdale, and you say you want to *change* Mississippi?" He finished with a exultant flourish: "Why if I were you, I'd put up big green signs at every point of entry into Mississippi which said, 'Posted. No Trespassing.'"

I will admit something in the brooding Celtic side of

From a speech at the University of Southern Mississippi, 1978.

me responded to my friend's wild injunction. I described something of this scene in a book I once wrote, and I received two dozen letters from Mississippi people saying my friend was absolutely right. Three of the correspondents said they would put up the signs themselves.

Mississippi, as God help us we all know, has often given itself to extremes, and through the years two of the greatest ones have been the desire, on the one hand, to dwell forever with all the myths and trimmings of a vanished culture which may never have truly existed in the first place, certainly not the way we wished it to, and the frantic compulsion, on the other, to reforge ourselves as an appendage of the capitalistic, go-getting, entrepreneurial North. The quest of the Yankee dollar, in the pejorative meaning, has never been far from the better side of ourselves. Between these two extremes there have been complex lights and shadings, and considerable ambivalence and suffering.

Yet one of the many ironies of our history is that even in dire moments we Mississippians considered ourselves intensely American. All through our early history Mississippians were warriors for nationalistic causes, for continental expansion, for laying to rest the specter of European domination. Even the rhetoric of secession was couched in language that was deeply Americanistic—the constitutional ideals of the founders. In his first inaugural Lincoln was wise in appealing to "the mystic chords of memory" which might hold the Union together. Those chords were strong in Mississippi, but the sound of the distant drummer prevailed, to what staggering costs. L.Q.C. Lamar, a Mississippian, was instrumental in bringing North and South together again after the bloodiest war mankind had ever known. In two world wars Mississippians were noted for their devotion to the flag. In Yazoo City as a boy I played taps over the graves of many Mississippi boys of both races brought home from Korea. The Americanization of Mississippi began before Mississippi was even admitted to the Union. Given our complicated, disparate, ethnic American society, I believe the United States has a reservoir of good will and understanding among ourselves and a tradition of making our system work—the most monumental of our failures being the Civil War—that is unmatched by any other nation in the world. And Mississippi both partakes of this rare human achievement and contributes to it. Few Mississippians can better testify to the importance of being most Mississippian and American than my friend Turner Catledge, who brought to his direction of the greatest newspaper in the world, the *New York Times*, his love for both.

For black Mississippians the urge toward being American was at once more complex and more straightforward. Never have there been more splendid Americans than the black Mississippians who through the decades had the courage to demand justice and equality under the American ideals they shared. The oldest and most incorrigible of all the hyphenate-Americans, C. Vann Woodward wrote in his *Burden of Southern History*, were the white Southerners and their ancient contemporaries, the Southern blacks. America, the finer instincts of it, are in the very soul of Mississippi, and always have been, and that is something not to be forgotten, nor taken lightly.

Now we are witnessing, I think, three peculiar transformations in our life which have surfaced so recently— in a generation or perhaps even less—that, although as Mississippians and Americans we may pay lip service to their presence, we may not yet be wholly aware of their long-range consequences.

One is the patent fact that the North, or the non-South, has become heir to many of the problems of a society such as Mississippi. The tormenting social problems of school integration, inadequate living conditions, and all the rest which the North might have prepared itself for—it certainly preached to Mississippi about them long enough—seemed to rise full born there in the acute urban context. The collapse of civil order in one Northern city after another, continuing now in the violence of the streets, is no cause for rejoicing among Mississippians; it should be a source of the deepest human sorrow.

Second, in these years we are seeing a Mississippi that is trying to live up to the older values.

My third point is that we are also seeing a Mississippi that threatens to be severely damaged—one hopes not inundated—by the rampant commercialism which the Europeans of the 1950s called with much hostility "Americanization," and which may very well be more than we ever asked for.

Not too long ago a Northern literary critic called me "the youngest of the established Deep Southern writers who lived in the South of pre-suburbia." That is quite an intoxicating phrase. True or not, I can assure you that when I was growing up, the closest thing Yazoo City had to suburbia was the hamlet called Little Yazoo, which consisted of a general store which never had anything you ever needed, a bootlegger in the back of a dilapidated garage, a Negro undertaker who was the richest man in town, and a precarious unpainted establishment with a sign in front saying: "Roaches, minnows, worms, and hot dogs."

My growing up then was the Mississippi many of us know and remember. Ours was a lazy town, stretched out on its hills and its flat places in a summer sun, lethargic and dreamy. People sat on the front porch in dreamy nights with the grass wet with dew. We were forever playing tricks on everybody. And it seemed we were always listening to older people telling stories. Al-

239

ways the stories being told! About the eccentricities of certain ancient ladies of a generation before, about the big funeral of 1927 of a military hero from an old family and how the monoplanes flew over the grave and dropped flowers, about love affairs never consummated and rivalries which sometimes never ended in bloodshed, about old gentlemen in starched high collars and tobacco stains on their whiskers.

The black people were everywhere, moving up and down the streets, the sounds of their music and laughter wafting over from the next block—the town would have been ghostly without them. On one of these nights a big passenger plane mistook the few lights of the dirt airport for Jackson, circled around Yazoo and finally came to a skidding halt in the mud. Everyone who heard the motors drove out to the airport before the plane landed, and a representative of the chamber of commerce put up a stepladder and said to each frightened passenger climbing down, "Welcome to Yazoo."

Mississippians drive everyday from suburbias to work through urban sprawls identical to any Eastern or Midwestern city. My neighbor on Long Island, Craig Claiborne of Indianola, whose writings in the *New York Times* and elsewhere have made him the country's foremost writer on food, was telling me just the other day that even the Mississippi recipes he is getting nowadays have a certain national uniformity. "Yankee recipes from Mississippi?" I asked my friend Craig. "No, but kind of Yankee-ized," Craig said. A new air of acquisitiveness envelops the whole South. The sidewalks are gradually being demolished in Oxford and at the new McDonald's near the Ole Miss campus the proprietors had put up a photograph of Mr. Faulkner near a photograph of Ronald McDonald.

Robert Penn Warren was speaking of his native southern Kentucky when he said in an interview: "I began to look for a place down there, but suddenly I saw it was a different world. The people aren't the same people. Oh, more prosperous and all that, but not the kind I had known—with a certain personal worth. So we are stuck with a new world. With certain virtues I'd be the first to grant, but perhaps some fatal defects."

Benjamin Forkner and Patrick Samway may have been speaking of Mississippi just as of the South as a whole when they wrote in their introduction to *Stories of the Modern South*: "Certainly the post-World War II South offers little to allay the fears of the 1920s and '30s. The New South of commerce, speculation, and industrial growth has become a permanent reality. Of course no one would argue that the rapid development of the South and of Mississippi in the twentieth century has been without its advantages. Southern universities have prospered. And many of the negative legacies of the past, the oppressive poverty, the vicious sharecropping system, the rural isolation and illiteracy, the crimes of segregation, are gradually disappearing. But the necessary changes have brought their modern plagues, and no Southerner, no matter how enthusiastic he may be about progress and the new wealth, would deny that the face of the land has lost something of its old character." *

My feeling for Mississippi as a physical place today is like a montage: old men in front of a country cafe in Belzoni, watching big cars speed by; the ghastly descent on the main road into Vicksburg with the rootless franchise stores, and so close to that vast battlefield where

---

* Forkner and Samway's wonderful introduction to their *Stories of the Modern South* should be required reading for us, for much the same reason that the last two hundred pages of Shelby Foote's third and concluding volume of his *Civil War* should be read by all Americans, especially our children. I do not apologize to Messrs. Forkner and Samway for agreeing with their feelings, because they are right.

thousands of boys died; a whitewashed Negro church out in the red hills with Negro children climbing a tree beside it; the bar of a Holiday Inn in Jackson at midnight, country people in town for the day juxtaposed with executives from Chicago, all getting drunk to the strains of Willie Nelson; land devastated for some new development near Port Gibson within sight of the Presbyterian hand on the church pointing to the Lord; the eternal quiet of a crossroads hamlet in the Delta.

In a class of young writers here at the university yesterday a student asked me whether in the face of all these changes Mississippi can retain those qualities of the spirit that have made it different. I told him I did not know. I went on to suggest to the young student, however, that the preservation of those qualities must derive, in the future of Mississippi, from those old impulses of the imagination which have made the literature of Mississippi so impressive. It is no accident, I said, that Mississippi produced Faulkner, and Eudora Welty, and Tennessee Williams, and Walker Percy, and Shelby Foote, and Elizabeth Spencer and the distinguished others.

These impulses of the imagination that gave us our literature were an expression of many things:

—the act of speech, of stories handed down, where a distinctive language—which still exists in Mississippi— vivid, concrete, sly, dramatic, is deeply honored

—the language of music, the rich evocation of real, sensual things, which also remains strong and vital here

—the love of a place—where individual human beings, relationships, family histories, the link with generations gone, not only mattered, but buttressed the everyday life

—the perception of a common past; a past of guilt and tragedy and suffering, but also of courage and nobility and caring

—and at the very base of all this was that rarest and most indispensable sustenance for literature: and that is memory.

The young people of Mississippi must learn to remember who they are, and where they come from. They must be encouraged to remember.

At the Delta Arts Festival in Greenwood last spring, a member of the Chamber of Commerce asked me: "What can we do to improve Mississippi's image?" I replied that we let the people of the Bronx, or Boston, or Detroit worry about Mississippi's image as much as they desired—but that Mississippians should concern themselves with their image among one another.

On looking over these words I found myself curiously disappointed in them. There was so much to be said on a subject I feel to be at the soul not just of Mississippi, but of the America of which it is a part. But after a while, I decided the hope for belonging, for belief in a people's better nature, for steadfastness against all that is hollow or crass or rootless or destructive, is as old as mankind itself and cannot be encompassed in some formula, or credo, or statement, or rationale. Wherever we live, we Americans who call ourselves Mississippians will find a way to remember.

The Ghosts
of Ole Miss

I FINALLY CAME HOME. It was not too late.
Much of being back has to do with the land, its sensual textures—one's memory reawakened by the rising
mists on January afternoons, the oscillation of bitter
winter days and the swift false springs, the jonquils
piercing through the ice, the slow-flowing rivers and the
hush of the pine hills. In a moment of despair once in
New York City, involving lost love and the Manhattan
angst, of a Sunday morning in an autumn mist with the
church bells chiming, an honored friend said: "But you
have Mississippi. It never left you."

"Certain places seem to exist mainly because someone
has written about them," Joan Didion wrote. "Kiliman-
jaro belongs to Ernest Hemingway. Oxford, Mississippi,
belongs to William Faulkner, and one hot July week in
Oxford I was moved to spend an afternoon walking the
graveyard looking for his stone, a kind of courtesy call
on the owner of the property. A place belongs forever to
whoever claims it hardest, remembers it most obsessive-
ly, wrenches it from itself, shapes it, renders it, loves it so
radically that he remakes it in his image." I enjoy moving amidst the people and places Faulkner wrote about.
It gives me a curious serenity, these things he owns. At
25, being a writer and a Mississippi boy, I believe his
aura might have intimidated me. When asked what a

Inside Sports, May, 1980.

Southern writer could do after the example of Bill Faulkner, Flannery O'Connor said: "You get off the tracks when the Dixie Special comes through." At 45, I no longer want to leap off the tracks, for I have learned I own a piece of the railroad, too.

I like the way they sell chicken and pit-barbecue and fried catfish in the little stores next to the service stations. I like the way the coeds make themselves up for their classes. I like the way strangers on the Square or the Levy's Jitney Jungle finish your sentences for you. I like the unflagging courtesy of the young, the way they say "Sir" and "Ma'am." I like the way the white and black people banter with each other, the old graying black men whiling away their time sitting on the brick wall in front of the jailhouse, some of them wearing Rebel baseball caps. I like the intertwining of old family names. I like the way people remember their dead.

The caretaker of the cemetery has become my friend. We talk about Ole Miss football. The black gravediggers sometimes join in the conversation. They say they remember the great Ole Miss teams under Johnny Vaught when Jake Gibbs was quarterback. They watch Archie Manning, another Ole Miss boy, on TV with the Saints. They recollect how Ole Miss upset Notre Dame in '77. "A lot of things go on up in here at night, I'll tell you," the caretaker says. "Oh, what these Ole Miss students do! They drink beer and copulate under the magnolias after the ballgames. I once found a naked woman here at six a.m., down by L.Q.C. Lamar's grave. The cops won't come in here at night, though." I ask why not. He answers with animation. "Because they're *scared*, that's why!"

I find strange mementos, unusual objects of obeisance or piety, or perhaps *duty*, left by enigmatic visitors on Mr. Bill's grave. Many twigs of holly were deposited there after Christmas. Once we found a full pint of

245

bourbon. An old, soggy Modern Library edition of Yeats' poems was there one day. On Valentine's there were several small chocolate Kisses for Mr. Bill, and on Mammy Caroline Barr's grave up the way in the black section. She was Dilsey.

It is a history-making moment, the Ole Miss-Grambling basketball game, and they are playing it right here in the Ole Miss Coliseum. It is the first Ole Miss basketball team to participate in a post-season tournament—the early round of the NIT. But much more than that, it is the first time an Ole Miss team has played an all-black school. That afternoon the Grambling team, black mammoths trailed by a group of their fans from Louisiana, stroll around the Square, taking in the sights. Earlier that day, an Ole Miss law professor and former football star has gone to the pep squad and told them for God's sake not to have the student dressed in the Confederate uniform there that night.

Walking toward the Coliseum with Dean Faulkner Wells, I can tell it is a sellout by the traffic. It is a night for "Pappy"; the author of *Delta Autumn* would not have missed this momentous confrontation, so rich in irony, nor for that matter will the author of *North Toward Home*. "Of course, he'd be here right with us," Dean says. "He'd absorb all of it, and he'd miss nothing."

The Grambling team is, naturally, all black, and its small cadre of supporters, about a hundred of them, are sitting en masse high behind one of the baskets. They wave shirts and pennants and yell enthusiastically: *"Who dat . . . who dat . . . who dat tryin' to beat our Gramblin' Tii-ger!"* The Ole Miss band breaks into its first *Dixie*, the Rebel flags are flying, and the student section counters the Grambling yell with its own: *"Hotty Toddy, Gosh A'mighty, who in the hell are we? Flim flam, bim bam, Ole Miss by damn!"*

246

An unexpected thing happens: Grambling looks awful, and Ole Miss takes a big lead. The black visitors can
do nothing right. They miss easy shots, they throw the
ball away time and again. The home crowd is frenetic,
the Grambling students pathetically silent; their team
appears hopelessly outclassed. "I've got a funny feeling," Dean says. "I want Grambling to win. Pappy
would too. I just *know* it. I can't help it." Things go
from bad to worse for Grambling, and at halftime,
Dixie resounding through the din, Ole Miss has a 16-
point advantage. First I go out into the crowded hallway
to talk with two Grambling supporters who have been
sitting behind their bench shouting and waving various
objects. By their size, they look like they are Grambling
football players. "Naw," one of them says. "We're lawyers. We went to Jackson State. We came here just to see
Ole Miss get *whupped*. . . . Naw, we don't care about
them flags and *Dixie* and all that. Hell, I been in Boston.
It's a lot worse in Boston. I just want to whup Ole Miss."
Then I make my way high into the stands toward the
Grambling section. A black student in a fraternity T-
shirt stands in the breezeway with his girl. "Are you
from Grambling?" I ask him. "Aw, naw, man," he replies. "I'm a *Rebel!*" In the Grambling section I take an
empty seat next to a student and ask him about the
game. "We have a spokesman," he says, and several of
the students gesture for one of their number to come
over. He is president of the senior class. He says they
drove up in a special bus from Louisiana. "None of that
bothers us, the flags and stuff. That was a long time ago.
I'm more worried about the *referees*. We know it's a
historic occasion. A local cop told us when we brought
the bus into the parking lot." I ask if the cop was black
or white. "Well," the president says, "he was a brother."

The second half begins; Dean is more morose than
ever. The All-American Stroud sinks two soft jump
shots, and the Ole Miss lead goes to twenty points with

247

sixteen minutes to play. Grambling calls time out, and the pom-pom girls, little white lilies of Southern culture, come out for their multifarious gyrations.

Then the momentum shifts. It is Ole Miss' turn to falter. They suddenly look tired, sick almost, missing shots and committing turnovers more frequently than Grambling in the first half. Grambling has Ole Miss at its own game—run and shoot, shoot and run. As the *Hotty Toddys* fade, the *Who dats?* rise. Grambling is down to ten, six, four, two, and with 1:56 to play, they take the lead, 76–74. A quick Ole Miss shot ties the score. Dean is clapping energetically. "I still can't help it," she says. "I'm for us again." With eight seconds to play, Ole Miss inbounds the ball, trying to work it to Stroud. A pass to a black Rebel guard at the key. He shoots with one second left. Ole Miss wins, 78–76.

Pandemonium. The Grambling students get up to leave for their bus. Their coach is cursing the referees. I know it's really all right now, this Mississippi white boy does, really all right with Mississippi, despite all of it, anytime the Ole Miss cheering section can yell their victory yell, at the end of this curious, fateful moment, with a touch of respect and good will: *"Hey, Gramblin' . . . Hey Gramblin' . . . we . . . just . . . beat . . . the hell . . . outa . . . you!"*

At Smitty's where I go for breakfast, the talk during the interminable coffee breaks, among the merchants of the Square, and the legions of lawyers (why do small Southern towns have so many lawyers?), and the farmers from the farthest reaches of Lafayette County is about Afghanistan, the crazed Khomeini, the hostages, the Russkies—one morning coffee toasts were exchanged to the American ice hockey boys—and the next Ole Miss game, basketball or baseball, or how Steve Sloan, the young football coach, just recruited two enormous white twins from Lynn, Massachusetts, and a black flanker from the Delta who runs the 100 in 9.6 and made straight A's in the integrated high school, and an ambidextrous black quarterback from Bruce, a few miles south on the Scoona River. At five o'clock, some of the merchants go to the back of Shine Morgan's furniture store, behind the ovens and refrigerators, for drinks and Ole Miss sports talk before winding on home. They drink, not bourbon, but vodka, so their wives won't know. This is the courthouse-square metaphor for the commuters' pause at the Madison Avenue bars I once knew around Grand Central before the rush to the trains.

The air of youth, tonic, breathless, sexual, touches the Square. It is a contagion. On the afternoon of a game there will be Alabama or LSU or Vanderbilt pennants on the Square, streamers on the out-of-state cars in alien colors, cheerleaders in the buoyant sunshine, exuberant shouts and hee-haws and wild deep Southern embraces, punctuated here and there by the hometown Rebel yell. The SAE's or KA's, celebrating early before a game, as is their wont, emerge from the Gin or the Gumbo or the Warehouse. "Hotty Toddys" reverberate off the old facades, and more Rebel yells. Mercedes-Benzes mingle on the Square with dusty pickup trucks from out in Beat Two, Snopes country. The most beautiful coeds in America drive down to shop at Neilson's or The Image; Delta cotton money is present among the sunburnt old boys in khakis and overalls. The girls come to the Square with a sense of purpose, with sunswept hair and smiling faces. In the midst of the toenail-painting on Sorority Row, a voice down the hall had proposed a traditional way to get through the afternoon: "Anybody want to go buy some shoes?" As they browse through the shops facing the courthouse, there is a languorous ardor in their selections amounting almost to foreplay. When the moment of crisis finally arrives and the purchase of Pappagallos or Capezios consummated, they negligently toss their parcels in the back seats of baby-blue Oldsmobiles and compare notes—Dresden figures of pastoral gaiety—with practiced irony, on the beaus. Their mothers would be proud of them. Who knows? One of them may be Temple Drake. There may be a Popeye lurking in a corner of the Square, eyeing her with a venom.

The town watches all this, as it has in one or another form, since 1848, with a touch of bemusement, and envy perhaps, and no little pride. The uneducated country people of Yoknapatawpha, and the counties adjacent— Union, Calhoun, Marshall, Pontotoc, Panola, Yalobusha and, of course, Lee—must view the transactions in the university classrooms with a measure of awe: people getting *educated* at the state university for what arcane purposes. The settlers first came to this county in the 1820s and the 1830s from Carolina and Virginia, cleared the land and made churches and roads and schools and had a courthouse square for themselves by the time of the Civil War—everything being in readiness for Federal General A. J. "Whiskey" Smith to burn it all down in 1864. With an affecting poignance, they named their town Oxford because they wanted to get the new state university to dignify their raw terrain, and they were happy when they got it, by a one-vote margin of a plenary committee of the state legislature. One of the early rules prohibited dueling during class hours. On a gray winter's day, the atmosphere electric for a game, one perceives how Ole Miss sports is the buttress to the local emotions. All universities should be in small towns.

The campus is only a few blocks down University Avenue. Here the town and Ole Miss seem to merge, little enclaves and outpockets and cul-de-sacs of youth and age. The campus does not have the intense, self-contained beauty of Washington and Lee, or Sewanee, or Chapel Hill, or the University of Virginia, but it almost does. There is a loveliness to it, an unhurried grace, with its gently curving drives, its shady bowers, its loops and groves and open spaces crowned with magnolias, oaks, and cedars and lush now with forsythia and dogwood and Japanese magnolias and the pear trees in the early spring; the ancient Lyceum at the crest of the hill, the new library with its inscription in the stone, "I believe that man will not merely endure . . . he will prevail," the football stadium only a stone's throw from all this and named Hemingway Stadium (after the law professor, not the writer) in Bill Faulkner's hometown. A ten-year-old son of the town, a bright and sensitive boy who lives in "The Rose for Emily House" and who has the name Goodloe Tankersley Lewis, asked his mother suddenly, why do we call it Ole Miss? This took her aback, for she is an Ole Miss girl, too. Finally she said, "It means the old things."

It is a place of authentic ghosts. Few other American campuses for me—W&L perhaps, or VMI in a different way because of the Battle of New Market, or U. Va.—envelop death and suffering and blood, and the fire and sword, as Ole Miss does. The bloodbath of Shiloh was only eighty miles away. Tupelo is closer, and Corinth, and Brice's Crossroads where Nathan Bedford Forrest's mad genius was exhibited, and Holly Springs where Earl Van Dorn made his brilliant raid on Grant. But Shiloh, just across the Tennessee line, fought in the springtime's flowering of 1862, among boys untested in battle, was the nation's first traumatic trial then—23,000 out of 100,000 dead, wounded, or missing; and they brought the wounded and dying boys down into Mississippi on trains, burying them along the railroad tracks as they died. Hundreds of boys, North and South, died in the

Ole Miss hospital and the churches and on the galleries and lawns of the campus, their corpses stacked like cordwood, buried now in unmarked graves in a wood behind the Coliseum.

There is a Confederate statue on the campus also, given to the university by the Faulkners as the one on the Square was. The University Grays, all Ole Miss boys, suffered bitter casualties in that war. One hundred and three of their number were the first wave of The Charge at Gettysburg. They reached the Federal entrenchments on Cemetery Ridge, and even the Federal artillery, fighting hand-to-hand with bayonet and saber. At Gettysburg, if you have ever been there, this spot is called "The High Water Mark of the Rebellion," perhaps the closest that doomed nation ever came to winning, and it obsesses me with many strange and brooding things that it was Ole Miss boys, average age 19, who were the apex.* In the year 1866, 45 per cent of the public funds of the State of Mississippi was allotted to the purchase of artificial limbs. It is a campus which has known defeat. On lonesome twilights in the Grove, everything silent and deserted with the students away on spring vacation, in a palpable hush I feel the pull of this uncommon past.

In 1962, three months after Faulkner's death, John Kennedy sent in 30,000 federalized troops during the riots over the admission of the first black student, James Meredith. Two people were killed in the polite actions which followed. One of the memorable photographs of that tragic time, only eighteen years ago, is of United States airborne troops, rifles in hand, sitting in the football stadium and watching the Rebels run through their drills. They changed the next home game, against the University of Houston, from Oxford to Jackson because of the trouble. Squirrel Griffing threw four touchdown

---

* None of the one hundred and three survived.

252

passes in the first half. Ross Barnett stood on the fifty-yard line and, placing his Stetson on his heart as the band played Dixie, spoke of the fortitude of the Sovereign State of Mississippi. Forty thousand people cheered. "It reminded me of the Nazi youth rallies," an Ole Miss person said years later. "Mississippi had hit rock bottom. The only place we could go was up."

As with all places which have suffered profoundly, Ole Miss is imbued with distinction and civility. And as with the proud and unfathomable state which has nurtured it, and well over a century ago brought its university to a town named *Oxford*, once the terrible albatross of race was removed, once the flagrant brutalities were conquered, once the public cruelty and the cruelty of public discourse were confronted and at long last challenged, then Ole Miss could go on being what it always was, which it is today: the most complicated, histrionic, colorful, crazy, and warmly kind state university in America.

Last fall, I came to Oxford for the Ole Miss-Georgia football weekend. I drove up from Yazoo City through the Delta and got here just in time; the Ole Miss-Georgia football game began in the Gin Saloon off the Square on a Thursday afteroon and ended, more or less begrudgingly, in the bar of the Memphis airport on a Sunday night. Ole Miss plays two or three football games in Oxford every season, but since the stadium only holds 40,000, the other home games are in the larger stadium in Jackson 150 miles south.

The Georgia fans began populating the Square by Friday afternoon, their celebrative impulses muted somewhat by their ignoble three-game losing streak. The splendid atmosphere was further desecrated by several Georgia cars with horns that played *The Battle Hymn of the Republic*, which is the melody of their fight song, recently adopted. On the Square one of our number, as we were en route to the fourth party of the day out on the campus, shouted at the Georgia revelers: Why not go all out and play *Marching Through Georgia*?, an admonition received with violent New South hostility. Will someone please put Sherman in Georgia again and give him a box of matches? a comrade suggested. There is a catfish place in the country hamlet of Taylor. After the seventh party of the day, it was to this faubourg that we repaired. In the grocery store, thirteen Ole Miss partisans and one Yankee, with small Rebel flags propped up in jelly glasses around the tables, ate catfish and drank champagne, and many toasts were exchanged. An affectionate emotion seized the evening, having to do with knowing people other people knew, and other Mississippi towns we knew, and relatives long dead we knew of. Graphic descriptions of the physical doom of the Georgia Bulldogs on the morrow were set forth in a colorful idiom.

It is no doubt a cliché, yet true, that Southern football is a religion, emanating direly from its bedeviled landscape and the burden of its past. They once drew 28,000 to their *intra-squad* game at the end of spring practice. There are trappings of piety in the midst of the most celebrative modes. The day of the game arrived, crisp and matchless; a fresh wind had sprung up from the Gulf. On the highways into town, the cars were bumper-to-bumper by eleven a.m. In the Ole Miss Grove, under the trees just now turning to autumnal hues, the tailgating began the night before the kickoff; the traditional Ivy League tailgating, which I have known, is an anemic *ersatz*. Far out in the distance, the Ole Miss band was playing *Dixie*, and its magic strains sounded from dozens of radios, mingling now and again with the infernal *Battle Hymn of the Republic*. A gray horse named Traveller II was led by a student dressed in a Confederate colonel's uniform through the immense throng. One group of Delta planter people, as is their habitude, ate and drank from a long table immaculately draped in the best linen, with place settings of china and silver. Someone played cassettes of honored Rebel games from the past, and then Lee's Farewell to the Army of Northern Virginia. "Here's to the Tri-Delts of Ole Miss," an aging lady garbed in the red-and-blue shouted handsomely from next to a Cadillac. Two men came to our Winnebago, sipping from a pint of Jack Daniel's. They sat motionlessly on the grass. "Whoever you are," one of them said, "we're on the same side. To hell with them Atlanta Yankees." Small boys with Rebel jerseys played merciless tackle, and angelic Mississippi Lolitas formed in cheerleading clusters and shouted: "Ole Miss, by damn!" Half an hour before the kickoff, a strange calm descended. "I've got butterflies in my stomach," a man from Vicksburg said. Others seemed in silent prayer. An orgasmic moment was coming in the lovely little stadium up the way.

In the packed stadium, with many standing on a slight rise dotted with magnolias just behind one of the end zones, Ole Miss moved to a swift fourteen-point lead. The rival bands continued to taunt one another with *Dixie* and *The Battle Hymn of the Republic*. Sometimes, when both were especially exasperated, they played the two at the same time. After a fifteen-yard pass on a third-and-twenty which got Ole Miss near midfield, the white quarterback embraced his black flanker in front of the Johnny Reb bench. Black and white Ole Miss players exchanged soul-slaps after the second touchdown. Forty thousand people, less the Georgians, stood in unison and gave the Rebel yell. Georgia's next *Battle Hymn* seemed a gesture in pathos. It would have saddened John Brown.

Then, enigmatically, Georgia struck for a quick touchdown in a dread autumn's silence fed only by the intrepid shouts of the badly outnumbered visitors and their ironic fight song. At the half the score stood 14–7, with the premonition of further Georgia momentum in the second half. Yet there was a brief rejuvenation at halftime. The Ole Miss band, majorettes, cheerleaders, and pom-pom girls, the latter in numbers sufficient to have overrun Grant at Old Cold Harbor, strutted onto the Astroturf to honor America. As the band played *Yankee Doodle*, *God Bless America* and *My Country 'Tis of Thee*, the pom-pom girls twirled dozens of American flags, and the public address announcer spoke of America and its virtues: its democracy, its unity, its courage, its kindness, its love of all citizens regardless of race, creed and religion. Totalitarian communism was criticized. Moving into a replica of the United States, the band played a rousing *America the Beautiful*, slowing down with its final lustrous strains. There was a dramatic pause on the field. The Ole Miss band broke into a *Dixie* that might have been heard in Bolivar, Tennessee. A Confederate flag thirty yards long was unfurled at midfield. Hundreds of smaller Rebel flags waved majestically in the stands. At that moment the white and black Rebels roared through the entranceway for the second half.

All for nothing. Georgia rallied and scored the decisive touchdown with 8:44 to play, 24–21. A last, desperate Ole Miss series produced four incomplete passes. The Grove, after the game, for the post-tailgating, was the largest wake I ever attended.

Here is a catalogue of things:
There are some 700 black students at Ole Miss. The pretty black coeds in abundance on the campus add to the Ole Miss tradition. Almost half the football team is black, and more than half the basketball team. The

baseball team is all white, which, with notable exceptions, is more or less true in the Southeastern Conferance. My neighbor across the street from me on Faculty Row is Cleveland Donald, a native of Mississippi who was the second black student here after James Meredith. He did his undergraduate degree here and then got a Ph.D. in history from Cornell. "I came back to Ole Miss because I'm a Mississippian," he says, "and I wanted to come home." He is the director of the Black Studies program. His freshman and sophomore class is large and all of his students are from Mississippi. It saddens him that most of them will leave the state when they get their degrees: no economic opportunity, he says. The classroom is a sea of black faces. Not one white student is enrolled. The questions about writing are generally good, and eager. All these young people are products of the massively integrated Mississippi public school system, an event which took place a decade ago. Ben Williams of my native Yazoo City and later a defensive lineman with the Buffalo Bills was one of the first outstanding black athletes from that new system. So was Walter Payton of the Chicago Bears and Columbia, Mississippi. In a recent photograph of my old hometown football team, I counted sixteen white boys and sixteen black. They are still called the Yazoo Indians.

What do the Ole Miss blacks think of the symbols in the athletic setting: the Confederate flags, Colonel Rebel, *Dixie*, even the name "Ole Miss"? Lately there has been an outpouring of letters to the state's newspapers criticizing these symbols and calling Ole Miss a "racist" school. I have kept an eye cocked to such things and have found little or no basis for them. The fraternities and sororities, of course, are white, with a handful of black Greek organizations, and there seems to be a minimum of "social" mingling—for there is a very long way

257

to go here—but there exists a courtesy between the races that the North might do well to emulate. Ironically, it is the athletes who seem in the first wave of the new integrated Mississippi society. They live and eat and travel and practice and play together, and I have witnessed a genuine comradeship among them in the off-hours. A year ago Ole Miss brought in a remarkable group of young black athletes from Mississippi towns. After a time, in fact, my writer's hunch was that the letters to the papers were nothing if not a purposeful campaign on the part of certain athletic competitors to embarrass Ole Miss in the recruiting wars.

The question lingers about these symbols of the past. After several healthy forays into the Jack Daniels, an Ole Miss graduate from down in Holmes County said to me one night of a basketball game, "They took away our public schools. Now they want to take away our Colonel Rebel." There was a tone to this, not of anger, but of an almost resigned sorrow. In modern-day America, there is too much fashionable tampering with authentic tradition. At the peril which such contentions evoke, I argue that this juggling with expressions of the past is reminiscent of the way the communists are eternally rewriting history, obliterating symbols with each new guard. Finally, one could make a strong case that *Dixie* and the flag and the names "Ole Miss" and "Rebels," deriving from old suffering and apartness and the urge to remember, are expressions of a mutual communal heritage, white and black, springing from the very land itself and its awesome strengths and shortcomings. As a historian friend of mine once remarked, "There's nothing wrong with the Confederate flag. The Civil War was fought over more than slavery."

In 1971 the color barrier was broken in football at Ole Miss with the signing of Ben Williams and James Reed of Meridian. In his senior year the students elected Ben

258

Williams "Colonel Rebel" and inducted him into the Ole Miss Hall of Fame. When he is not playing with Buffalo now, he is an officer in a bank in Jackson. He said:

I came to Ole Miss because it was a challenge to me, and I liked a challenge. Also, I was recruited by Coach Junie Hovious, and I admired him a lot. He helped me make up my mind, plus I felt like I could make a contribution at Ole Miss. As far as what had gone on before—in terms of race—my attitude was that I couldn't change history. All that had already happened before at Ole Miss. If I couldn't deal with that, I shouldn't have come. I have no complaints about the way I was treated at Ole Miss. Nobody ever called me a nigger or anything else, and it wasn't just because I was bigger than most people. My aim was to get an education and play football, and I accomplished that.

Buford McGee, an outstanding black halfback brought in by Steve Sloan last year, said he came here because he wanted to get a good education and because it was close to home. "I never thought about the Rebel flag or *Dixie* as anything but school spirit. I don't think it was ever meant to embarrass blacks or anybody. Until the writers brought it up, I hadn't thought about it, one way or the other. It's the way students have always shown their support at Ole Miss."

Ole Miss basketball was once a pariah, the mediocre Rebel teams playing to lackadaisical crowds of 1,500, many of whom were lonesome students who came to the games to do their homework. But all that changed sharply with the arrival of Warner Alford, the athletic director, one of the best Southerners I know, who brought in a Bobby Knight protégé named Bob Weltlich as coach. This season, playing to capacity crowds of 9,000, and led by the SEC's second leading all-time

259

scorer John Stroud (no one will ever surpass Pete Maravich) Ole Miss won more games than it had in 42 years, and carried both LSU and Kentucky down to the last seconds at home. The games in the Coliseum became smaller, tauter versions of the home football games. The country people have taken to coming in with their wives and sons and daughters, mixing there with the fancy Delta folk, flasks in hand, who have driven two or three hours though interminable miles of dead cotton stalks to see for themselves an Ole Miss team which finally became competitive. The socializing, as in the Grove before a football game, was a thing to behold, and the flamboyance of the flag-waving crowd, and the spectacle on the floor. Alabama showed up with one white on its traveling squad, Florida with three, Mississippi State with four. LSU did not play a single white, and Auburn was not far behind. Often I would spot my son David, moving about in the stands or along the floor with his Nikons and Canons, going a little berserk with the photographic challenge.

We played an elaborate trick on Gloria Jones, widow of my friend the novelist James Jones and an editor now with Doubleday, who came down in February to talk with my students. I love Gloria as a sister, and have forever been impressed by her verve for life, which is undergirded by her uncanny intuition. Driving down a street with me, she would suddenly point and shout, "That's a Snopes house!", and she was right every time. One morning I returned from my writing class to find Gloria in an arm chair reading aloud to my dog Pete, who was sitting enthralled at her feet, from Faulkner's *The Bear*. She had been reading from the section about the hunting dog Lion, and she was saying to Pete: "You're better than Lion, Pete. You can *whup* him!"

On the day of the Ole-Miss Alabama game, several of my friends and I told Gloria that I had been appointed the Ole Miss basketball coach. In truth, I had been invited by Warner Alford to sit on the bench with the players and coaches, an invitation I accepted because I like that courtside perspective. Many telephone calls came to Gloria that afternoon, while I was away at class, ostensibly from players and others in the athletic department, asking for my diagrams of plays and my intrepid zone defenses. The novelist John Knowles, who was also visiting here, equally impressed her with my grave new responsibilities. Never much for sports with the exception of the horses, where she further employs her witch-like hunches on trips to the tracks with Danny Lavezzo of P. J. Clarke's or the actor Martin Gabel to come home enriched—she has been known to confuse baseball with ice hockey—she took the news of my position as head basketball coach in stride.

On the bench that night, I wore an Ole Miss windbreaker and carried a clipboard. Gloria and Knowles were sitting several rows behind. Ole Miss took an early lead over Alabama, which might as well have been called the Black Crimson Tide, and tenaciously maintained it. With my clipboard, I held several mock conferences with the Ole Miss substitutes. The margin tightened late in the first half. "A minute and twenty seconds to go and Willie's four points ahead," Knowles reported he told Gloria. "God, you've got a good memory," she replied. "How do you know all that?" "Look at the scoreboard, darling," Knowles said. At halftime, as I went into the dressing room to give my pep talk, various plants in the crowd came over to tell her I was doing a swell job for a rookie. "Is this the last inning?" Gloria asked Knowles near the end. Ole Miss won decisively, and at the party afterwards, others congratulated me within her hearing. A few days later, when she was back in New York, she met the novelist Winston Groom at Elaine's. "How's Morris doing down there?"

he asked, for Groom was soon coming to lecture also. "Frankly I'm a little worried," she replied. "They're keeping him too damned busy. He's not only teaching literature classes, they've also got him coaching the Ole Miss basketball team."

As part of the Ole Miss sports and literary scene this winter, George Plimpton came down to speak to my classes. Plimpton has never been above a hoax either. As an undergraduate at Harvard, he once concealed himself in some trees and joined the Boston Marathon just behind the leader, 100 yards from the finish, beating that tired Korean by several feet. He is one of the most unusual of contemporary Americans, and one of the most charming, and he possesses an emphatic lineage. I think he was ready for anything.

An overflow audience came to hear The Plimp, at which was read a quite legitimate letter from the Governor, which I feel bears quoting:

Dear Mr. Plimpton:

"*. . . You are an honored guest today at our State University. Your literary and editorial genius is notable. Your athletic talent has encouraged you to play quarterback, throw baseballs, drive racing cars, block against champions, and slam cymbals together in the symphony orchestra. Your comradeship with our Southern writers in New York City, where you so graciously keep them out of trouble, has helped bring the "Grand Ole Union" back together again.*

As Governor of Mississippi, I herewith extend a pardon to your great-grandfather, Adelbert P. Ames, the Republican Reconstructionist Governor of our beloved State, and present a document of safe conduct through the ghosts of old enemy lines. I pledge that you shall remain free and unmolested in the Sovereign State of Mississippi for 12 hours, beginning at 9:45 a.m. today,

February 26, 1980, ending at 9:45 p.m. on that day,
when I understand that your plane departs north from
Memphis. I cannot, however, speak for the Governor of
Tennessee on this matter.
With all best wishes from the people of Mississippi, I
am

Sincerely yours,
William F. Winter
Governor

Plimpton was so relieved by this pardon of at least
one of his great-grandfathers, as well as by his temporary safe conduct, that he gave a classic, virtuoso perfor-
mance.

That evening there was a dinner for Plimpton in "The
Rose for Emily House"; a gracious glass-topped table
was bedecked with candles in that ancient manse.

All of a sudden during the dinner for Plimpton, there
was a savage knock on the front door, and a tall, burly
Oxford cop entered the dining room, his .38 revolver in
view, his walkie-talkie blaring staccato. "Which is the
Yankee George Plimpton?" he demanded. "On authority of the Governor of Mississippi and Mayor Leslie of
Oxford, it is my duty to warn you that it is now eight
p.m., and you have exactly one hour and 45 minutes
before the good will of this sovereign state vanishes. I'm
ordered to escort you to the city limits." The Plimp,
after his initial surprise, turned to the group and said
wistfully, "Well, I guess I better be going." The officer
unceremoniously whisked Plimpton to a limousine with
a Confederate flag on its fender. Siren blazing, the police
car led the way to the town line. Stopping there, the cop
got out and intruded his head through the limousine
window. "Never let the sun shine on your posterior in
Miss'ippi after 9:45 p.m.," he warned, and was gone.
On the way to the Memphis airport, The Plimp said:
"What would my great-grandpappy think?"

263

My best friends here are Dean Faulkner Wells and her husband Larry Wells. Dean, like her uncle and her father before her, goes to all the Ole Miss games, and like them she ardently supports the Rebels in football, basketball or baseball. Once, at a football game in Jackson, she was so angered by an Auburn man in front of her who refused to stand for *The Star-Spangled Banner* that she hit him over the head with her Confederate flag. As a teenager, she burst into her uncle's workroom as he was typing. "Pappy," she said, "I've got great news. An Ole Miss girl just won Miss America." Her uncle looked up at her and replied, softly: "Well, Missy, at long last somebody's put Mississippi on the map." Every November 10, which was the day her father was killed, Mr. Bill would go alone to the St. Peter's cemetery and spend hours at his brother's grave. On one November 10, in 1950, he returned home from his solitary visit when someone in New York telephoned his wife Estelle that he had won the Nobel prize.

Despite his size, Dean's father was a superb athlete, just as is his thirteen-year-old grandson, his daughter Dean's boy Jon by a previous marriage, known to us as "Jaybird," an indefatigable spirit who wanders the town and the campus playing ball by day or night and keeping everyone posted on the Rebel statistics and who, for the life of me, is really Chick Mallison in *Intruder in the Dust*, either Chick or Tom Sawyer. Dean Faulkner played second base for Ole Miss and was noted for his deft fielding but weak hitting. There is a story about him in the Ole Miss-LSU game of 1931 that is still told in the town, at Smitty's and Shine Morgan's Furniture Store. Dean and Bill's father Murry owned the most impressive car in Oxford, a Buick sedan convertible, and during the Depression when neither the Faulkners nor anyone else had any money, he prided himself on his car. This elder Faulkner was standing behind the backstop at the Ole

Miss baseball field when his son Dean came to bat in the bottom of the ninth inning, bases loaded, one out and the Rebels trailing LSU by three runs. His father emerged from around the backstop and caught up with his son. "Drive them in," he said, "and the Buick's yours." To the general astonishment, his light-hitting son proceeded to hit a fastball far over the left-fielder, and as he rounded third, there was his father, standing on the plate with the keys to the Buick in his hand. From that day on, while the father walked, Dean was seen on the streets of the town and the backroads of Yoknapatawpha, driving little white and black children all around.

One solitary midnight, I found myself alone in the Square. A cold wind was whipping in from Kansas by way of Memphis and the upper Delta; spring would have to tarry a few days. I felt the ghosts of Ole Miss football games on golden, vanished afternoons when my father brought me here as a child: of Junie Hovious and Merle Hapes and the first college game I ever saw in 1940; of Charlie "The Roach" Conerly's heroic fifty-yard passes and Barney Poole's sliding catches, of Farley Salmon running the Notre Dame Box and Oscar "Buck" Buchanan, our Yazoo High School coach, making his tackles from linebacker. I felt the ghost of an Ole Miss girl I once loved, many years ago. I felt the ghosts too of Major De Spain and Uncle Ike McCaslin and Gavin Stevens and Lucas Beauchamp and John Sartoris and Buck Hipps and Quentin Compson and Emily Grierson and Candace Compson and Joe Christmas and Flem Snopes and Temple Drake and Dilsey and the dog Lion. Lord, Mr. Bill, I wish I had known you!

In a rush in that moment I knew, too, that all these ghosts, conjured up in the preternatural desolation of the Square, were all for me, just because I had come home. It was not too late.